# THE WISE MINORITY

# THE WISE

## by Leon Friedman

# MINORITY

The Dial Press  New York 1971

*Library of Congress Catalog Card Number: 77–92733*

PRINTED IN THE UNITED STATES OF AMERICA

FIRST PRINTING

# Acknowledgments

I am indebted to Fred and Nancy Rosen, David Zimmerman and Zita Steinberg, and Michael Ferber for their help in piecing together many of the events described in these pages; also to Alan Levine, Marvin Karpatkin, and Gordon Lapides for making available to me many of their files and papers on the Resistance. My special thanks must go to Miriam Rosen for her sharp pencil and her sharper conscience; and to Karen Kennerly, a patient editor and a helpful critic.

Laws: We know what they are and what they are worth. They are spider webs for the rich and mighty, steel chains for the poor and weak, fishing nets in the hands of government.

—*Proudhon*

Liberty is not the mere absence of restraint, it is not a spontaneous product of majority rule, it is not achieved merely by lifting under-privileged classes to power, nor is it the inevitable by-product of technological expansion. It is achieved only by a rule of law.

—*Supreme Court Justice Robert H. Jackson*

# Contents

# An Argument for Draft Resistance and Civil Disobedience

# Introduction

We are a nation of lawbreakers; more particularly, we are a nation of *conscientious* lawbreakers. From the Boston Tea Party to the latest campus disorders, in virtually every period in our history, some sizable group has felt aggrieved by the laws, has refused to obey them, and has loudly proclaimed its justification for doing so. Indeed, such violators insist that disobedience serves a positive social function—they act not for their own personal gain, but to bring about some greater good for society. There is hardly a reform movement in the history of the United States that did not feel it necessary or desirable to violate established laws as part of its campaign for justice.

Of course, democratic theory demands that every citizen obey the law. It makes no exception for selfless disobedience. Some years ago, Professor Louis Lusky of the Columbia Law School spoke of "the pivotal compact of the open society, the terms of which are: ungrudging acceptance of the present law in return for effective access to the processes of orderly change." [1] President John F. Kennedy said in a nationwide address in 1962:

Our nation is founded on the principle that observance of the law is the eternal safeguard of liberty and defiance of the law is the surest road to tyranny. . . . Americans are free . . . to disagree with the law, but not to disobey it. For in a government of laws and not of men, no man, however prominent or powerful, and no mob, however unruly or boisterous, is entitled to defy a court of law.[2]

These words were directed at the Southern reactionaries who defied court orders against segregation. The liberal allies of the civil rights movement endorsed that position wholeheartedly. Yet seven years later, draft resisters, student rebels, and black militants openly defy the law with the warm support of those who castigated George Wallace for standing in the doorway of the University of Alabama. And the previous Southern defiers of the legal system are now the most zealous defenders of law and order on the campuses and in the ghettos.

While we celebrate the great rebels in history—Jesus, Martin Luther, the Pilgrims, George Washington—we are unwilling to give contemporary disobeyers the same leeway. We assert the moral basis of our laws, but are unwilling to excuse disobedience that is grounded on a higher morality. We insist that riot, disorder, and disobedience cannot be rewarded, yet we consistently listen to the grievances behind such disturbances and implement appropriate reforms.

This book will try to suggest under what circumstances defiance of the law can be viewed as legitimate. If we take seriously the tenets of equality and freedom, of democracy and economic security, and of conscience and morality, when can we "legitimately" disobey the law? What social or political purpose does disobedience serve? What are the limits or dangers of conscientious defiance of the state?

The recent National Commission on the Causes and Prevention of Violence saw a crucial distinction between acts of violence (whether legitimate, legal, or other) and peaceful methods of protest (whether illegal or not). The study on these pages views the American experience through a different perspective; it asks why Americans have conscientiously and rationally defied the law—violently or peacefully—to advance an articulated political or social program. The line between the two approaches is often difficult to draw—were the consumer-type riots in Negro ghettos in the 1960's conscientious or not? Were they for personal gain, in that looting often took place, or part of a social movement to improve the economic conditions of the Northern blacks? I am not concerned with reactionary violence, such as that perpetrated by the Ku Klux Klan in the past one hundred years or by other vigilante groups throughout our history. My central focus is on illegal protest as a tactic in political or economic reform movements in America.

Nor is this book primarily concerned with "civil disobedience," however defined. The open, nonviolent, conscientious, symbolic, "courteous and cheerful" acts of illegality usually associated with civil disobedience are only part of the history described here. The mountainous literature on civil disobedience in recent years (the Index to Legal Periodicals alone lists one hundred articles since 1965) has unfortunately emphasized the necessity of peaceful violations—violations which can fit neatly into the existing political and legal structure with a minimum of stress. But much of the literature on the subject ignores the history of conscientious disobedience— violent or nonviolent—in American history. What in fact has happened when individuals or groups have gone beyond the limits suggested? How has the majority reacted?

An amateur historian who examines earlier periods of stress in America is likely to be astonished at the similarity of response to reform agitation and conscientious lawbreaking throughout our history. The same arguments were used against the Abolitionists of the 1850's as are directed against the draft resisters at the present time. Accusations of treason and anarchy heard now when black militants riot were voiced in the early days of the labor movement. It is as if the same script has been used for every episode of change in American life.

One reason for this pattern is the curious tension between consensus and conflict in our history. For many years, "consensus" theories of the American experience have been in fashion. America was seen as having escaped the Old World upheavals—the clash between feudalism and liberalism, between capitalism and socialism, between royalism and democracy. We have had only one political idea to guide us—an outgrowth of the English Liberal tradition of John Locke which was transplanted here and grew without serious opposition from older or newer ideas. The American way of life— a peculiar blend of irrational nationalism and enlightened individualism—has been our only philosophy. In the most brilliant presentation of this thesis, in *The Liberal Tradition in America,* Louis Hartz writes:

One of the central characterists of an nonfeudal society is that it lacks a genuine revolutionary tradition, the tradition which in Europe has been linked with the Puritan and French revolutions: that it is "born equal," as Tocqueville said. And this being the case, it lacks also a tradition of reaction. . . . a society which begins with Locke, stays with Locke, by virtue of an absolute and irrational attachment it develops for him . . .

It has within it, as it were, a kind of self-completing mechanism, which insures the universality of the liberal idea . . .[3]

However, a group of younger historians, including Staughton Lynd, Barton Bernstein, Jesse Lemisch, and Eugene Genovese, have recently pointed out that America has had fully as much oppression and injustice as any European country. Although ideological unanimity existed, economic and political conflicts have been a recurrent part of our history. Negroes, the lower economic classes, workers, tenant farmers, and disenfranchised women have had to fight establishment enemies who controlled not only the nation's legal and political machinery, but its only ideology as well.

Thus the absence of a contending philosophical tradition left the oppressed classes in a frustrating dilemma. Unlike European socialists, they could not justify resistance to the established order by relying on a new ideological structure; for the political establishment could claim with justification that *they* were the legitimate heirs of revolutionary leaders. Those who would try a shortcut and disobey the "majority will" were looked on as traitors to the American tradition. George Kennan has recently written:

If you accept a democratic system, this means that you are prepared to put up with those of its workings, legislative or administrative, with which you do not agree as well as those that meet with your concurrence. This willingness to accept, in principle, the workings of a system based on the will of the majority, even when you yourself are in the minority, is simply the essence of democracy. Without it, there could be no system of representative self-government at all.[4]

But the rhetoric of the Establishment contains many fallacies. "Democracy," "majority will," and "law" are not equivalent concepts. The current law may be the reflection of a bygone majority, maintained through political inertia and the interests of a smaller and more powerful group that benefits from its preservation. A law, though fair on its face, may be applied in a way that unfairly discriminates against a dominated group. Is resistance to that application to be considered treason? Violation of the law may define its scope in a way that may educate the majority and lead to its annulment.

Conscientious disobedience can be seen as an affirmation of the principles of the American experiment and the rule of law. Virtually every proponent of resistance to the state in our history has appealed to our own revolutionary tradition to justify disobedience. The premise that consent is the only basis for legal obligation, that government is subject to check by a higher law, and that man's conscience can transcend the state's demands are explicit notions in the American ideology. The testing of these principles under the pressure of conscientious disobedience can revitalize them in each generation. These ideas have retained their vigor because of the new definitions given them through challenges to the system, often brought about by aggrieved lawbreakers. If we are to have only one American ideology, its implementation needs frequent verification and redefinition.

Furthermore, the conscientious lawbreakers claim their own actions are more consistent with the moral principles that form the basis for American law. Thus, they reaffirm not a specific enactment, but the foundations of a legal order which must be in phase with the ethical stance of the people.

Most important, disobedience to the law can be the strongest lubricant of the democratic process. Its educative role in defining grievances and injustices in American society has been crucial in every period of our history. From the Whiskey Rebellion through the Abolitionist period to the civil rights movement, it has shown America how hollow its promises could be and how contradictory the application of its basic principles. The study that follows attempts to analyze the problem of disobedience through a series of case histories in which opposition to law played that educative role.

Not every reform movement required such tactics. The spread of universal male suffrage in America was generally accomplished with a minimum of disturbance (unlike the situation in England and other European countries), although an armed revolt was necessary in one state to liberalize its voting laws.[5] The imposition of government controls over business, the income tax amendment, and the New Deal reforms were brought about peacefully, and many of the recent civil rights victories in the South came to pass through nonviolent political protest, though some form of "illegality" played a part in even these situations.

Our pride in such sophisticated, peaceful reforms has resulted in a curious amnesia regarding our violent history. The public reacts to our contemporary disobeyers—draft resisters and student rebels— as if they were dangerous violators not only of the law but also of our entire political tradition. In fact, they are following some of our finest torchbearers.

# Part One

# THE HISTORY

# 1

# The Intellectual Foundation

In late 1790, James Wilson, recently appointed an Associate Justice of the United States Supreme Court, delivered a series of lectures on law at the College of Philadelphia. President Washington and Vice-President Adams came to hear the distinguished lawyer delineate the principles of law that would govern the young republic.

In best eighteenth-century style, Wilson began his examination of government with a discourse on man himself. Following the neo-Lockean ideas of the English Dissenters, he expressed an optimism about the human animal that not even Jefferson could share.

What is the efficient cause of moral obligation?—I give . . . this answer —the will of God. This is the Supreme law. His just and full right of imposing laws, and our duty in obeying them, are the sources of our moral obligations. If I am asked—why do you obey the will of God? I answer—because it is my duty to do so. If I am asked again—how do you know this to be your duty? I answer again—because I am told so by my moral sense or conscience.[1]

In the ideal society, municipal law—the rules by which a state or nation is governed—will coincide with the law of nature. In those circumstances, man will consent to the imposition of laws upon him, since they are based on the commonly recognized moral law. "All human laws should be founded on the consent of those who obey them," [2] Wilson continued.

Of course, Wilson recognized that "the people" never acted unanimously, and therefore the "consent of the people" must necessarily be the consent of the majority. But this did not trouble him. "That the majority, by any vote, should bind not only themselves, but also those who dissent from that vote, seems, at first, to be inconsistent with the well-known rules—that all men are naturally equal; and that all men are naturally free." But the minority are "bound by their consent originally given to the establishment of the society for the purposes which it was intended to accomplish." [3] If the minority felt aggrieved by the acts of the government, Wilson saw at least one alternative: "They have a right to retire, to sell their lands, and to carry off their effects." [4]

Wilson, however, did not think that "the people," acting through their majority in the legislature, would oppress any smaller group in society. Mistakes or honest differences in opinion could always occur, but deliberate evil by a democratically chosen government toward its constituents seemed too remote to consider. In addition, even mistakes could be rectified by other organs of the government.

Instead of being uncontrollable, the legislative authority is placed, as it ought to be, under just and strict control. The effects of its extravagances may be prevented, sometimes by the executive, sometimes by the judicial authority of the government, sometimes even by a private citizen. . . . Whoever would be obliged to obey a constitutional law, is justified in refusing to obey an unconstitutional act of the legislature—and . . . when a question, even of this delicate nature, occurs, every one who is called to act has a right to judge; he must, it is true, abide by the consequences of a wrong judgment.[5]

Wilson did not expand this last point; however, since consent is the basis of all legal obligation, and man's conscience would lead him to observe the law, even a single individual's disapproval of a law must be given consideration by the government. Perhaps the law *is* unconstitutional, or at the least, unwise. When it is applied against the citizenry, their reaction may reveal unfairness which the government or the majority has not yet realized. But the practical problem of running a government which necessarily would have less than unanimous support finally required the minority to acquiesce. Here Wilson had to justify minority obedience by the fiction of the original social compact. Or, he suggested, an unsatisfied few might emigrate. But even if one man disapproved of a law, Wilson would still give him the "right to judge." If he was wrong he must pay the consequences, but his "right" to act was unquestioned.

That a single man might protest an unjust law was a popular concept years before the Revolution. Isaac Backus, a Massachusetts Baptist, wrote in 1768:

we are not to obey and follow . . . in an implicit and customary way, but each one must consider and follow others no further than they see that the end of their conversation is Jesus Christ the same yesterday, and today, and forever more . . .[6]

The revolutionary ideas of the colonies that led them to break from England were not restricted to defiance of the English Parliament. "Any legislature, wherever located or however composed, deserved only the obedience it could command by the justice and wisdom of its proceedings. Representative or not, local or not, any agency of the government could be defied."[7]

After the Revolution, these sentiments were still in the political atmosphere. They drew strength from three interrelated themes which, springing from John Locke's social compact theory, formed the basis not only of Wilson's thought, but of that of most of his contemporaries: consent as the basis of legal obligation, deference to individual conscience, and the existence of a higher law superior to the law-making authority.

In Jefferson's words from the Declaration of Independence, "to secure these rights, governments are instituted among men, deriving their just powers from the consent of the governed . . ." When the overwhelming majority of the colonists favored dissolution of the ties with England, no one questioned this proposition. But the difficult question of minority disapproval of a specific law passed by a republican legislature was not examined in detail. The dilemma faced by Jefferson and Madison in opposing the Alien and Sedition Acts in 1798 was to show how perplexing this question could be. Although Wilson (and Locke before him) used the myth of the social compact to attack absolutism, the notion of consent as the only basis for political control had revolutionary implications against majority rule as well.

Martin Luther's concept of the priesthood of the individual helped bring the idea of deference to individual conscience into the European political mainstream, and it was the dictates of conscience that drove the English dissenting sects to America.[8] The Founding Fathers had no difficulty transferring this notion into freedom of worship for all religions. The Virginia Declaration of Rights of 1776 stated: "all

men are equally entitled to the free exercise of religion, according to
the dictates of conscience . . ." But few thinkers of the time
worried about the possibility of conscience dictating disobedience to
the secular law of the majority. And no one considered what would
happen if the claims of conscience were based on humanitarian
rather than religious grounds.

While the concept of a higher law superior to the law-making authority can be traced to Cicero's "right reason, harmonious with
nature, diffused among all, constant, eternal . . . ," [9] a more immediate source for the colonists was Lord Edward Coke's 1610 decision in
*Dr. Bonham's Case*. The Lord Chief Justice there stated that acts
of Parliament against "common right and reason" are void. The long
existence of Magna Charta and the development of the common law
gave Coke a strong lever against the Stuart kings' attempt to impose
arbitrary rule. Fifteen years before the Revolution, in the Writs of
Assistance case of 1761, James Otis went back to Coke and declared
that "should an act of Parliament be against any of God's natural
laws, which are immutably true, their declaration would be contrary
to eternal truth, equity and justice, and consequently void." [10] Otis'
argument, Coke's original decision, and Locke's writings pointed to
certain ideals which were superior to municipal laws and limited
those enactments in accordance with the law of nature.

Aside from these ideological notions, the Founding Fathers had
certain pragmatic reasons for not accepting the word of the majority
as the sole basis for legal obligation. In the first place, Wilson's liber-
tarian ideas brought only shudders from Federalists like Alexander
Hamilton and John Adams, who equated democracy with the clamor
for paper money and debtor relief laws, that is, attacks upon property.
To think that the majority would not despoil property holders was, in
Adams' view, "either to babble like a new-born infant, or to deceive
like an unprincipled impostor." [11] In the Philadelphia Convention,
James Madison maintained:

Landholders ought to have a share in the government to support their
invaluable interests, and to balance and check the other classes in society.
They ought to be so constituted as to protect the minority of the opulent
against the majority.[12]

More important, the early leaders were always worried that the
not-so-silent majority, the small farmers who made up 90 percent of
the population, might revolt. Not only was their property in danger,
but their lives and civil liberties depended on controlling the masses
of yeomen.[13] Madison felt that representative government could
diffuse the passions of the dangerous majority, since the wide

geographic expanse and the multiplicity of groups in the United States made it less likely that a majority would coalesce to tyrannize a minority. Writing to Jefferson about the new Constitution, Madison explained:

If then there must be different interests and parties in society; and a majority when united by a common interest or passion cannot be restrained from oppressing the minority, what remedy can be found in a republican government, where the majority must ultimately decide, but that of giving such an extent to its sphere, that no common interest or passion will be likely to unite a majority of the whole number in an unjust pursuit.[14]

The agitation for a bill of rights in many of the ratifying states in 1787–1788 was partly based on an unwillingness to give the majority free rein. Most of the state constitutions contained declarations of rights to protect the citizens against arbitrary government action by upholding the right to habeas corpus, trial by jury, and freedom of the press and religion. Led by George Mason and Richard Henry Lee of Virginia, the Anti-Federalists insisted on such safeguards in the national Constitution. Although the defenders of the Constitution said they were not necessary, the Federalists finally accepted the need for controls over Congressional action in the field of personal rights. The Bill of Rights protected not only the religious beliefs of all citizens, but the political and civil rights of minority groups.

Thus, the founding principles of the nation contained certain untidy offshoots, certain paradoxical implications that could justify resistance to the new government's laws by the smallest minority, indeed even by a single man. While the main thrust of the theories of Locke, Jefferson, Madison, and Wilson pointed toward majority rule and minority acquiescence, deliberate roadblocks were put in the way of complete majoritism (in the form of a Bill of Rights) and intellectual ammunition existed for individual resistance when the occasion demanded.

One of the first tests of the importance of conscience and individual rights arose in the government's treatment of the Quakers. During the Revolution, most of the states allowed members of the Society of Friends to avoid military service (except in emergencies of severe manpower shortage or invasion) by finding a substitute or paying a statutory militia fine. The Society, however, felt that such a compromise constituted indirect support of war and was thus unacceptable. The patience of the Continental Congress leaders wore thin at times, particularly in dealing with the Philadelphia Quakers, who refused to take the new test oath to the Continental cause or pay special wartime taxes.* The Quakers were often accused of Loyalist leanings, and in 1777 seventeen of their leading members were arrested for supposedly treasonable relations with the enemy. Although the Revolutionaries released them in April 1778, the Friends harbored a distrust of the new government for a long time.

Smaller peace sects, such as the Amish, Mennonites, Brethren, and Shakers, also asserted their right to be exempt from military service and militia fines. Individuals not connected with any particular religious sect nevertheless were allowed to refuse military service on grounds of conscience; there are on record eight instances of isolated conscientious objection.[16] They include a Connecticut cobbler, Joseph Healey, who walked thirty miles to the state capital to convince colonial Governor Jonathan Trumbull of his sincerity. Jesse Lee of North Carolina, who later became Chaplain of Congress, explained to his militia colonel that, "I could not kill a man with a good conscience," but he did drive the regiment's baggage wagon.

Even after the war, the Quakers were not prepared to compromise their principles. Some states accepted the force of their argument and exempted them from all military obligations. The Friends also gained support for their position from various leaders of the government, including James Madison. When Madison introduced the Bill of Rights before the first Congress, one of his proposed amendments dealing with the right to bear arms in the state militia (this became the Second Amendment) contained the following language: ". . . but no person religiously scrupulous shall be compelled to bear arms." The debate that followed in the House in August 1789 and again in December 1790 anticipated many of the arguments that have surrounded the conscientious objection controversy throughout our history.

Like many Southern congressmen today, Elbridge Gerry of Massachusetts wanted to restrict the exemption "to persons belonging to a religious sect scrupulous of bearing arms." [17] William L. Smith of South Carolina insisted on including provisions which compelled conscientious objectors to pay militia fines or provide substitutes, a demand not unlike our present requirement of alternate service. The overriding doubt, then as now, was the problem of sincerity.

Who are to know [orated James Jackson] what persons were really conscientiously scrupulous? There is no tribunal erected to make them

---

* If they refused to pay a militia fine or the special taxes, their goods or property were seized by the authorities and sold, with the proceeds applied to the amounts due. Hundreds of Quakers suffered through these proceedings. Many others without sufficient property to pay the fines or taxes went to jail.[15]

swear to their scruples. If the principle were adopted . . . very few
would be found, if their own word was to be taken, not conscientiously
scrupulous.[18]

The House, however, finally decided to keep Madison's controversial
language. His clause was retained by a vote of 24–22. When the
Bill of Rights was sent to the Senate for approval in September 1789,
the conscientious objector clause was eliminated.[19] No report of the
Senate debate has been preserved. Presumably they removed the
clause for the reason suggested by Representative Egbert Benson
of New York, namely that since it affected members of the state
militias, each state should decide in the first instance who should be
exempt and on what grounds.[20]

The question of conscientious objection arose again in December
1790 during the debate on the uniform militia bill. General Henry
Knox, the first Secretary of War, had introduced a plan for enrolling
the entire citizenry of the country in a uniform militia, subject to
various exemptions, including "exemptions of religious sects." It was
proposed that anyone claiming an exemption would have to pay
an equivalent fine. Representative Aedanus Burke of South Carolina
objected to this condition:

This . . . was called the land of liberty. In it, we boasted, that no one
suffered on account of his conscientious scruples and yet we are going to
make a respectable class of citizens pay for a right to a free exercise of
their religious principles; it was contrary to the Constitution . . .[21]

James Jackson of Georgia took his predictable stand:

If the principle be adopted of requiring no compensation from the exempted, it will lay the axe to the root of the militia, and . . . the bill
might as well be postponed altogether.[22]

James Madison, as usual, supported the broadest possible exemption for conscientious objectors.

It is the glory of our country . . . that a more sacred regard to the
rights of mankind is preserved than has heretofore been known. The
Quakers merit some attention on this delicate point, liberty of conscience.
When they had it in their power to establish their religion by law they
did not.[23]

Roger Sherman seconded Madison's proposal and suggested that some
method be adopted to equalize any indemnity paid for military exemption, such as excusing the militia from a poll tax.

But under pressure from the cynics and doubters, Madison finally
moved to exempt all conscientious objectors from militia duty,

contingent upon payment of a fine—although he maintained that he personally preferred gratuitous exemption. Benjamin Bourne of Rhode Island then pointed out that some states (New Hampshire, Massachusetts, Rhode Island, and Connecticut) already exempted Quakers from military service as well as the equivalent fine.[24] Madison's proposal, he objected, would hurt rather than help this group. So for a second time, Congress voted to leave the matter to the individual states.

The debates in 1789 and 1790—so remarkably contemporary in tone—demonstrate that Congress recognized the necessity of giving conscientious objectors the exemption their consciences demanded. The Founders were prepared to make good on at least that much of their rhetoric. They failed to enact any specific provision because the initial formation of the militia belonged to the states, which in most cases were lenient in this area. But the debates show a strong recognition of the legitimacy of claims of conscience.

Important developments with respect to the "higher law" also took place in the first years of the nation. The new political leaders could not allow the law of nature to hover over the government, subject to interpretation by each citizen. To stabilize the situation, two steps had to be taken. It was necessary, first of all, to make higher law less elusive by establishing workable definitions for it. Secondly, the task of interpretation could not be left to the citizens at large; it had to be assigned to some branch of the government itself.

The second issue was easily and eagerly taken up by the judiciary —they would become the guardians of the higher law. The notion of a judge as final arbiter in the political system was not unknown at the time (the idea of higher law had been given currency by Lord Coke), but it had not developed to any great extent in the colonies. Judicial review of laws passed by popular legislatures contradicted the essential spirit of the Declaration of Independence. Three state court judges in North Carolina had been upbraided by the State Legislature in 1787, the year of the Philadelphia Convention, for asserting their right to declare laws unconstitutional.[25]

Within two years, the pendulum swung the other way. When Madison introduced the Bill of Rights into Congress in 1789, he implicitly supported the principle of judicial review, announcing that "independent tribunals of justice will consider themselves in a peculiar manner the guardians of those rights" contained in the first ten amendments and would keep the government from infringing upon the "Blessings of Liberty."

Once again, the aim was primarily to give the courts power to protect the property of the rich, although Madison and a few others anticipated the crucial protective role the courts would take in the area of civil liberties.

The guidelines for implementing judicial review came under discussion in the case of *Calder* v. *Bull,* decided by the Supreme Court in 1798. Justice Samuel Chase argued for broad, indefinite principles which would give the courts the widest scope for reviewing all laws:

There are certain *vital* principles in our *free Republican governments* which will determine and overrule an *apparent and flagrant* abuse of legislative power; as to authorize *manifest injustice by positive law;* or to take away that security for *personal liberty* or *private property,* for the protection thereof the government was established. An act of the Legislature (for I cannot call it a law) contrary to the *great first principles* of the *social compact* cannot be considered a *rightful exercise* of *legislative* authority.[26]

Justice James Iredell was unwilling to interpret the power so broadly. To him, the test was whether the Constitution permitted the exercise of the legislative power challenged: "If any act of Congress or of the Legislature of a state, violates these constitutional provisions, it is unquestionably void." However, if a law is passed within the scope of the constitutional power of the legislature, "the Court cannot pronounce it to be void, merely because it is in their judgment, contrary to the principles of natural justice."

Iredell's position prevailed after the appointment of John Marshall to the Court and the subsequent decision in *Marbury* v. *Madison.* The Constitution and only the Constitution was established as the ultimate test of a law's validity. But the vague contours of "due process," "equal protection," and "privileges and immunities" of citizenship resurrected some element of the "natural justice" idea advanced by Chase. Since the courts, through their power of judicial review, would regularly enforce its basic principles, natural law would become a vital part of the governmental processes. "Invested with statutory form and implemented by judicial review," wrote Edward Corwin in the 1930's, "higher law, as with renewed youth entered upon one of the great periods of its history, and juristically, the most fruitful one since the days of Justinian." [27]

But higher law would never be only the instrument of the courts. It would have an equally fruitful role as the people's ultimate check on government.

# 2

# The Whiskey Rebellion and the Alien and Sedition Acts

The two earliest attacks on the proposition that all laws must be obeyed were the Whiskey Rebellion in 1794–1795, and the opposition to the Alien and Sedition Acts from 1798 to 1800. The first episode grew out of Alexander Hamilton's excise tax, which was approved by Congress in 1791. Hamilton hoped to raise $800,000 a year by placing a duty on all liquors, both imported and domestic. This revenue would pay for the federal assumption of state Revolutionary War debts. On its face the rate was not oppressive, but the farmers of the Monongahela River area in western Pennsylvania, who produced close to 25 percent of the total alcohol distilled in the country, depended on whiskey for their economic survival. Transportation charges for lumber and grains were so high that the only feasible method of marketing the area's products was by distilling the grains into whiskey, which could then be shipped economically to most of the eastern states. This whiskey served as barter for the staples of the farmer's life.

The farmers complained loudly but peacefully immediately after the passage of the law. In 1792, Albert Gallatin, a brilliant Genevan who became one of the leaders of the Democratic-Republican party, drafted a petition explaining the farmers' opposition. The excise was "unequal in its operation and immoral in its effects." It was "dangerous to liberty because of the wide powers given to the enforcing officers." Further, "our peculiar situation renders this duty still more unequal and oppressive to us. Distant from a permanent market and separate from the eastern coast by mountains which render the communication difficult and almost impracticable, we have no means of bringing the produce of our lands to sale either in grain or in meal." In addition the farmers had little specie to pay the excise. "Our commerce is not, as on the eastern coast, carried on so much by absolute sale as by barter." They claimed that they had "punctually and cheerfully paid former taxes on our estates and possessions because they were proportioned to our real wealth." [1]

Congress refused to repeal the law. Under the excise statute, inspectors and collectors were appointed for each county in Pennsylvania. They immediately became the objects of harassment by the farmers. In 1791, a few excise officials were tarred and feathered, and the farmers burned down the house of one William Faulkner because it was used as the headquarters of General John Neville, the excise inspector for Washington County. Neville had been a highly popular leader in the region, but his overwhelming desire for federal office seduced him into the role of chief oppressor of his own constituents.

When the farmers refused to pay, the government did little to enforce the excise through 1792 and 1793. But the whiskey protest was becoming intertwined with the Democratic-Republican opposition to the Federalist party and its policy toward France. Early in 1793, France declared itself a republic and commenced war against England. Citizen Edmond Genêt, the new French minister to America, arrived in Charleston soon afterward and made his famous slow journey northward, greeted by enthusiastic crowds, banquets, bonfires, and liberty poles in the pro-French regions of the South. About the same time, Democratic Societies sprang up from Maine to Georgia to support the French against the hated English and to check the federal government's tyrannical pretensions and class favoritism. According to the societies, the aristocratic bias of the Federalist government manifested itself in the high salaries paid to federal officials, their condescending treatment of the small farmer, and the extravagance of federal spending. Conniving speculators from Eastern cities had bought up state bonds for pennies from the hard-pressed farmers. Now, with the assumption of state debts at full value, these men lived high at the expense of others' labor.

The Federalists saw the societies as Jacobin nests, plotting to overthrow the government. President Washington later called them "the most diabolical attempt to destroy the best fabric of human government and happiness . . ." and claimed they were "instituted primarily to sow the seeds of jealousy and distrust among the people." [2]

Inevitably the Democratic Societies became strong in western Pennsylvania. Hamilton cleverly played the eighteenth-century version of provocation politics in hopes of showing the need for a large federal standing army. In June 1794, he supported a bill allowing the state courts (who were more sympathetic to the farmers) to hear violations against the excise bill if a federal court was more than fifty miles distant from the place of the offense. The western farmers —who otherwise were forced to travel the long distance to the federal court in Philadelphia and who resented the hostility of the federal judges—had pressed for this concession. But Hamilton undermined their apparent victory by seeing to it that seventy-five processes were served under the old law (the new law not being retroactive) against distillers who had not paid their taxes in prior years. [3]

A federal marshal, accompanied by General John Neville, attempted to serve William Miller, a local farmer who refused to accept the summons. Neville's presence only aggravated the situation. "I felt my blood boil at seeing Genl. Neville along to pilot the officer to my very door," said Miller. About forty men, many armed, went to capture the marshal at Bower Hill, Neville's home. The General conveniently had with him a small armed band who drove them off. The next day, about five hundred armed farmers again attacked Bower Hill, which was by that time reinforced with regular troops. But the overwhelming number of the attackers forced the army men to surrender. The rebels then set a torch to the mansion. [4]

In succeeding days, the Pittsburgh-Philadelphia mail was stolen by the insurgents; the militia for the entire western section of the state—about five thousand men—was called to duty by the rebels. They decided to march on Pittsburgh with a demand that certain pro-excise and pro-government leaders be driven from the town or it would be burned to the ground. About three thousand militiamen marched to Braddock's Field, near Pittsburgh, on August 1, 1794. The rebels saw their action as more than just a protest against the excise. Before the march one man said, "It is not the excise law only, that must go down; your district and associate judges must go down; your high offices and salaries." [5] The government, with its new judges and its treasury officials eclipsing the familiar state machinery, was looked on as a potential tyrant.

After a day of consultation between the Pittsburgh militia and the men from Washington County, the leaders marched the men through the city to demand the expulsion of the proscribed enemies. Word was sent to the army garrison in the town that no violence was intended, and the marching men stayed far from the post. The farmers perpetrated some petty mischief and went back to their homes.

Meanwhile, key members of the federal government met on August 2, 1794, to discuss the Bower Hill episode and the militia uprising. Secretary of State Edmund Randolph, Attorney General William Bradford, Secretary of War Henry Knox, President Washington, and of course, Hamilton, met with Governor Mifflin of Pennsylvania and other state officials, including Chief Justice Thomas McKean. Mifflin, Randolph, and McKean recommended moderation and control by regular police forces of the state. Otherwise even greater resistance would occur. But Hamilton and Washington, supported by Bradford and Knox, insisted that the military must handle the rioters. They agreed to send out commissioners to negotiate with the farmers, but indicated that they had little faith in any peaceful solution.

The commissioners met with representatives of the farmers, including Albert Gallatin, in Pittsburgh on August 21, 1794. Besides the excise, the farmers complained of "decisions in the state courts which discountenanced improvement titles, and gave preference to paper titles." They claimed they were "harassed by militia duty," and the government had been "remiss in asserting the claim to navigation of the Mississippi," which was vital to the farmers' commerce. They were embittered by the appointment of General Neville as inspector of the survey, "whose former popularity had made his acceptance of the post particularly offensive." [6] After some negotiation, the commissioners promised to look into the other complaints and agreed to award a full pardon for past criminal acts to anyone who pledged to submit to the laws, pay outstanding taxes, and support the civil authorities. The farmers' representatives went back to their constituents with the government's proposals. Elections were held to decide whether to submit.

On September 10, 1794, at Uniontown in Fayette County, Albert Gallatin prepared a resolution—which sounds remarkably contemporary—in support of submission and against any further violent opposition to the government: "Resistance by force is lawful only when no legal and constitutional remedy is within the reach of the people, and when the evils arising from the oppression are excessive, when they far surpass those that must ensue from the resistance.

"You had your full share of representatives in the Legislature which enacted the law we complain of . . . . Every mode of redress

which can exist under a republican form of government is still open
to you. Violence and resistance on your part would be the attempt
of a minority to overrule, and in fact, to oppress the majority. . . ."
Gallatin urged the farmers to sign the pledge: "By such an explicit
declaration, you will adopt the best possible means to obtain a repeal
of the law, for previous submission is essentially necessary, that our
friends and the friends of our principles throughout the nation may
act in concert with us." [7] The vote in Fayette was 560 to 161 for
submission. However, in Allegheny and Washington Counties, the
most hostile areas, the offer was overwhelmingly rejected.

The Commissioners reported to Washington on September 24,
1794, that a considerable majority of the region would submit, but
"the authority of the laws would not be universally and perfectly restored without military coercion." The federal government continued its efforts to gather a militia but the states had difficulty raising
the required number of men. Finally in early October sufficient
troops were recruited for the long trek into Pennsylvania. Washington
himself commanded the main force although reports from all sources
indicated the rebellion was at an end and troops were unnecessary.
But Hamilton, still in control, could not let the curtain go down so
early on his military drama. He moved into Pittsburgh with the army
in early November, conducted a full-scale investigation into the rebellion, then aided in the judicial trials that followed.

Instead of vigorous repression, however, the federal officials proclaimed a general pardon for all but the most well-known leaders.
Seventeen were marched back to Philadelphia for trial, entering the
city like captured barbarians in a "mockery of a Roman triumph."
They stayed in jail for approximately six months until their trials for
treason took place. Most of them were acquitted. The few that were
found guilty were promptly pardoned by Washington.[8]

Why the government followed such a lenient course is still unclear.
The authorities may have foreseen the difficulty of finding willing
witnesses from the rebelling areas to testify. The sheer size of the
rebellion made legal proceedings impractical: the idea of throwing
thousands of Pennsylvania citizens into jails for opposing what they
saw as an unjust law could not have appealed to the administration.
The nation was still too close to the Revolution to consider a farmer's
protest against the government, even with a rifle, as treason.

The political repercussions of the insurrection continued for many
years. Washington considered the matter not only the most serious
affront to his administration, but an attack on the very foundations
of the Republic. In private letters he was quick to blame the Democratic Societies for the outburst.[9] The President's astonishing view of

the democratic process was that no permanent group could be formed to oppose the government's policies:

Can anything be more absurd, more arrogant, or more pernicious to the peace of society than . . . for a self-created *permanent* body (for no one denies the right of the people to meet occasionally to petition for, or remonstrate against, any act of the legislature) to declare that *this act* is unconstitutional, and *that act* pregnant with mischiefs, and that all who vote contrary to their dogmas, are actuated by selfish motives or under foreign influence, nay are traitors to their country . . .[9]

Washington's annual address to Congress, delivered in November 1794, was almost totally devoted to the subject of the insurrection, and he made a specific sneering reference to the "self-created societies." But the Republicans, led by Madison and William Giles of Virginia, struck back immediately, asking whether the Cincinnati Society—the aristocratic, military organization that supported the Federalists—should not also be censured. Joseph McDowell of North Carolina exclaimed: "Your wanton laws, begotten in darkness, first raised the insurrection." The reference to the excise was picked up by Robert Rutherford of Virginia: "Let the people then speak out. Why not let them speak out? What accusation is there for all this alarm among the stockholders? The paper holders have got a small alarm about their stock on account of the war, and in their fright imagine that the continent is ready for an insurrection." [10]

The vote on various resolutions about the Democratic Societies was extremely close, but the controversy in Congress about Washington's speech took the sting from the insurrection itself. The peaceful outcome of the rebellion and the President's clumsy attack on the democratic process gave the Republicans the opportunity to come to the aid of the western farmers without appearing to advocate violent resistance to the laws. Madison wrote to James Monroe after the Congressional debate:

If the insurrection had not been crushed in the manner it was I have no doubt that a formidable attempt would have been made to establish the principle that a standing army was necessary for *enforcing the laws.* When I first came to the city about the middle of October, this was the fashionable language . . . I hope we are over that danger for the present. You will readily understand the business detailed in the newspapers, relating to the denunciation of the "self-created Societies." The introduction of it by the President was perhaps the greatest error of his political life . . . The game was to connect the Democratic Societies with the odium of the insurrection—to connect the Republicans in Cong[res]s with those societies—to put the P[resident] ostensibly at the head of the other party, in opposition to both . . .[11]

Jefferson wrote to Madison in late December 1794 in the same vein:

It is wonderful indeed, that the President should have permitted himself to be the organ of such an attack on the freedom of discussion, the freedom of writing, printing and publishing . . . The excise law is an infernal one. The first error was to admit it by the Constitution; the second to act on that admission; the third and last will be, to make it the instrument of dismembering the Union, and setting it all afloat to choose what part of it we will adhere to . . . their detestation of the excise law is universal, and has now associated to it a detestation of the government . . .[12]

The most significant result of the insurrection was a further polarization in American politics, between the Federalists and the Republicans, the pro-French and pro-English elements, between the agrarian and the mercantile interests. Whatever the origins of the affair, its peaceful solution permitted the problem to become quickly assimilated into the political mainstream. As Gallatin pointed out in his Uniontown resolution, submission to the law was necessary "that our friends and friends of our principles . . . may act in concert with us." While the Republicans did not defend armed resistance to the law, they saw the community of interest between the Pennsylvanians and the small farmers who constituted their chief support. It was no accident that Gallatin was appointed Jefferson's Secretary of the Treasury in 1801 and stayed in that position until 1814, through most of Madison's term. In that post, he pursued a financial policy that would benefit the small farmers hardest hit by Hamilton's program. One of the first measures of the Jefferson Administration was repeal of the whiskey excise in 1802.

Whether the farmers would have achieved this victory if they had proceeded only along the path of peaceful political action is an open question. Gallatin's 1792 petition to the House was ignored, and only minor modifications in the excise laws were made before 1794. Finally, the class bias inherent in the law became unbearable to the Pennsylvania farmers. While subsequent submission was necessary to work out any political solution, the definition of the farmers' grievance and the measure of its extent was revealed by the insurrection. Eugene Rostow has recently written: "Our instinct after an outburst of violence has always been to seek a wise and generous solution through law for the conflict which gave rise to the violence." [13] While we insist that riots and violence should not be rewarded, "wise and generous solutions" to class conflicts have rarely taken place without some such spur to the political machinery. Such an outburst opens the eyes of the government and the people to the grievance that produced it. Violence or disobedience can provide an impetus for settling social and political disputes—and is so accepted by the rest of the nation. The people have realized that anarchy is not imminent when the first stone is thrown or the first shot fired by an aggrieved minority.

Within three years after the Whiskey Rebellion, the government was faced with a new challenge to its laws. By the summer of 1798, relations with France had deteriorated to the point that war looked imminent. In order to maintain the national security, Congress passed a series of four laws, three restricting the rights of aliens and the fourth, the Sedition Law, protecting the government against adverse criticism. This last punished any conspiracy to impede the operation of federal law and the utterance of any "false, scandalous and malicious" statement against the President, either house of Congress, or the government. Seditious libel could be punished in all the states under the common law, but a few months earlier, Justice Samuel Chase declared that federal courts lacked jurisdiction over common law crimes and could only try cases involving conduct made criminal by a specific federal law.[14] The Sedition Act, said many Federalists, merely put the federal government on the same footing as the states, giving it the power to punish conspiratorial and seditious statements made against its authority. Indeed, the federal law was much more lenient than state rules on the subject. In the states, the only issue for the jury was whether the statements were made. The judge would then conclude whether the offense had been committed. The truth or falsity of the defendant's statement was irrelevant if the requisite evil intent could be shown. The federal law, in contrast, permitted truth as a defense and allowed the jury to decide if the writings were defamatory or seditious.

Whatever the justification, the purpose of the new law was clear: it aimed at silencing certain vociferous critics of the anti-French policy of the Adams Administration. Since 1795, the French had been attacking American merchant ships on the high seas and had grossly insulted American authority by its request for bribes in the XYZ affair.* Nevertheless, the Democratic-Republicans led by Jefferson continued to support the French.

* Soon after his inauguration in March 1797, Adams sent a mission consisting of Elbridge Gerry and John Marshall to France to see what accommodation could be reached with the new Directory. Joining the American minister, C. C. Pinckney, in Paris in October, they attempted to make contact with the French minister of foreign relations, the chameleonic Duc de Talleyrand. Informal agents for the Directory not only insisted on a forced loan from the United States to France as a condition of peace talks, but demanded

Foremost among the government's critics were the large and popular Republican newspapers such as the Philadelphia *Aurora* and the Boston *Independent Chronicle,* as well as a number of individual Republican congressmen. A month before the Sedition Law was passed on July 14, 1798, a common law indictment had been returned against Benjamin Franklin Bache, grandson of his famous namesake and editor of the Philadelphia *Aurora,* the strongest Anti-Federalist newspaper in the country. The *Aurora* not only criticized the repressive measures taken by the government, but also published secret letters obtained from France which showed that Talleyrand had become more conciliatory and was willing to discuss all unresolved problems between the two countries. Economic pressure on the paper (Federalist sympathizers withdrew all their advertising) and two physical assaults on the editor by government supporters failed to stop Bache. On June 26, 1798, he was arrested. His lawyers insisted that under Justice Chase's ruling in the *Worrall* case, no common law indictment was possible. But Judge Richard Peters ordered him held until the circuit court met in the autumn. Before any further legal proceedings were held, Bache died in a yellow fever epidemic.

After the passage of the Sedition Law, the government did not have to rely on a questionable common law indictment against its critics. The first victim of the Act was the "spitting Lyon" from Vermont, Congressman Matthew Lyon. As one of the few Republican Representatives from New England, he was a ready target for the Federalists. In January 1798, Roger Griswold made some insulting remarks about Lyon's military exploits in the War (he had been cashiered by General Gates for withdrawing his men from the Canadian border but was later reinstated). Lyon answered the accusation by spitting in Griswold's face. The Federalists called him a "wild Irishman" and an "extraordinary beast." Before the passage of the Sedition Law, he wrote a letter to the *Vermont Journal* claiming that he saw "every consideration of the public welfare swallowed up [by the executive branch] in a continual grasp for power, in an unbounded thirst for continual pomp, foolish adulation, and selfish avarice." [15] Lyon also published anti-administration articles in his own newsletter, *The Scourge of Aristocracy and Repository of Important Political Truths.* Urged on by Supreme Court Justice William

---

an immediate bribe of $250,000 for receiving the American delegation at all. After Pinckney's famous reply ("No, no; not a sixpence!"), the Americans spent months in Paris trying to make other arrangements before finally reporting to Adams in March of 1798 that the mission was a failure. Adams passed the dispatches on to Congress, deleting the names of the go-betweens who had demanded bribes and referring to them as X, Y, and Z.

Paterson of New Jersey, who was acting as circuit court judge for Vermont, a grand jury in Rutland indicted Lyon for his letter to the *Vermont Journal* and the articles in the *Scourge*. The only issue at the trial, as far as Paterson was concerned, was whether the language Lyon used "could have been uttered with any other intent than that of making odious or contemptible the President and the government, and bringing them both into disrepute." The jury found Lyon guilty after one hour of deliberation. Paterson lectured Lyon on the day of the sentencing: "as a member of the federal legislature, you must be well acquainted with the mischiefs which flow from an unlicensed abuse of government . . ." As an example to others, Lyon was sentenced to four months in jail and a fine of $1,000.

Lyon then became the first congressman to conduct a political campaign from jail. Running for re-election in November 1798, he barely missed winning an absolute majority in the first balloting for his seat, and in the December runoff, he polled six hundred more votes than all the other candidates combined. Republican leaders easily raised the thousand-dollar fine and Lyon was released on February 9, 1799. His trip to Philadelphia turned into a triumphant march as sympathizers greeted him along the way with liberty poles, flags, toasts, and patriotic doggerel.

Massachusetts was the locale of the most severe sentencing under the Sedition Law.[16] David Brown, an intinerant laborer living in Dedham, spoke out in his home town against the government's attempt to "destroy the laboring part of the community." Rather than acting like public servants, they were showing the "enthusiastic ravings of wild men . . . determined to carry their own measures by the point of a bayonet," he said. Soon after the speech, a liberty pole was erected in Dedham with these words attached: "No Stamp Act, No Sedition, No Alien Bills, No Land Tax; downfall to the tyrants of America, peace and retirement to the President, Long Live the Vice-President [Jefferson] and the Minority; May moral virtue be the basis of civil government." The pole was cut down by a group of Federalists, and Brown was arrested as the instigator of the libelous action. The *Chronicle* commented that the British had cut down liberty poles and were called tyrants for doing so. In 1798, "the American Federal Government did the same; but they were not tyrants for doing it, because the Sedition Law forbids our calling them so." [17] Brown was tried before Justice Samuel Chase, who sentenced him to eighteen months and fined him $480. Since Brown was penniless and could not pay the fine, he remained in jail for six months beyond the expiration of the sentence until Jefferson pardoned him.

The administration's fight against the *Aurora* did not cease with

the death of Bache. William Duane assumed the editorship in November 1798 and continued the newspaper's crusade against the
Adams Administration. Violently anti-British—Duane had been deported from India for publishing articles in his Calcutta newspaper
critical of the East India Company—the new editor accused high
officials in the government of following British orders in its anti-
French activities. Eight hundred thousand dollars of British money
had been spent, wrote Duane, in influencing American policy.
Duane singled out Secretary of State Timothy Pickering—the Administration's most vigorous enforcer of the Sedition Act—as a
British agent. Pickering wasted no time in sending Duane's offensive
article to the federal attorney in Philadelphia, William Rawle. When
Duane was brought before the circuit court, he offered in his defense
a letter by President Adams which also complained of British influence in the government. The embarrassment of having such a letter
brought to public attention led the prosecutor to agree to a postponement and then to drop the indictment altogether.

On February 18, 1800, the *Aurora* published a secret report on
an electoral count bill introduced into Congress by Senator James
Ross of Pennsylvania. The proposed law provided for a Grand Committee, composed of six congressmen, six senators, and the Chief
Justice of the United States, to decide which presidential electoral
vote to count if two conflicting returns were submitted. To Duane
and the Republican senators who leaked the matter to him, it seemed
like an obvious Federalist attempt to manipulate the election of 1800.
For what other reason, wrote Duane in an *Aurora* editorial, should
a law be passed dealing with conflicting election returns. Rather than
indict him under the Sedition Law, the Federalists decided to have
the Senate investigate the breach of secrecy. The Senate issued a
summons commanding Duane to appear before it in March of 1800.
When they insisted on limiting his right to counsel, Duane's lawyer,
Thomas Cooper, withdrew from the case, attacking both the Sedition
Law and the administration's policy. Duane refused to appear before
the Senate and went into hiding until Jefferson's victory.

Since Duane had escaped their clutches, the Federalists went after
Cooper, his attorney, for his intemperate attack upon the Senate and
for a handbill he had written in criticism of President Adams. Cooper's
trial took place in April of 1800 before Samuel Chase (with Pickering sitting on the bench with him as an observer) and three other
cabinet members in attendance. Chase revealed his bias by charging
the jury that "if a man attempts to destroy the confidence of the
people in their officers . . . he effectually saps the foundation of the

government." The jury convicted Cooper, and Chase sentenced him to six months in jail.

The last important trial under the Sedition Act was that of James T. Callendar, also presided over by Justice Chase. Callendar, a Scot, had fled England in 1792 because the authorities there had charged him with seditious criticism of the government. He then joined Bache and Duane on the Philadelphia *Aurora*. Escaping from the capital when the Sedition Law first went into effect, he secured a job on the Richmond *Examiner* and continued his attacks on the government, and on Adams in particular. When Federalists discovered an abusive pamphlet Callendar had written, called *The Prospect Before Us,* they attempted to suppress its sale. Chase brought it to the attention of a Richmond grand jury in May of 1800. The state attorney-general, Philip Nicholas, defended the editor, and many distinguished citizens, including ex-Senator John Taylor of Caroline, raised money on his behalf. Chase conducted the trial in such a biased, heavy-handed way—making sure that only Federalists sat on the jury, not allowing John Taylor to testify, and making long prejudicial remarks to the jury—that the attorneys withdrew. (Chase's behavior became the basis for his later impeachment by Congress after Jefferson's victory in the election of 1800). Callendar was sentenced to serve nine months in jail and remained in prison for the full term, until the Sedition Law expired.*

The Jeffersonians found themselves in a dilemma: Congress had passed the Sedition Law by a clear majority; the President had signed it, and every Supreme Court Justice had given it his blessing in the course of his circuit court duties. Thus under best republican principles, Jefferson and Madison were compelled to accept the legitimacy of the law even though they might work through political channels for its repeal.[18] Soon after the passage of the Alien and Sedition Acts, Jefferson drafted a series of resolutions claiming that the laws were invalid. The resolutions were passed on to William Cary Nicholas of North Carolina under great secrecy—it would hardly do for the Vice-President of the United States to be known as the drafter of such revolutionary Anti-Federal documents, declaring his own Congressional laws invalid. Nicholas sent them to John Breckinridge of Kentucky who introduced them into his state legislature in November of 1798. As originally drafted by Jefferson, the Kentucky Resolutions

* There were other indictments and trials under the Sedition Law and various actions by state courts in support of Federalist policy. More detailed information can be found in James Morton Smith, *Freedom's Fetters* and John C. Miller, *Crisis in Freedom.*

asked that the states declare the laws null, void, and of no force or effect. Further, the resolutions urged the states to take all measures for providing that these laws should not "be exercised within their respective territories." * [19]

Jefferson's theory, as explained in the resolutions, was that the Constitution had been ratified by the various states as a compact and that each state, not the federal government, "was the exclusive or final judge of the powers delegated" to the central authorities. Since the Alien and Sedition Laws went far beyond the powers delegated to the federal government, it was up to the states to declare them invalid. On November 10, 1798, after only a brief debate, the Kentucky legislature passed a modified form of the resolutions noting that, "no power over the freedom of religion, freedom of speech or freedom of the press being delegated to the United States by the Constitution, nor prohibited by it to the States, all lawful powers respecting the same did of right remain, and were reserved to the States, or to the people." Thus the Sedition Act, "which does not abridge the freedom of the press, is not law, but is altogether void and of no effect." The governor of the state was requested to communicate with other states in order to obtain similar pronouncements that all such laws seize "the rights of the States" who should "concur in declaring these acts void and of no force." [21]

Madison, who had been consulted in secrecy by Jefferson in the drafting of the Kentucky resolves, prepared a similar, but more moderate, document for Virginia. The power claimed by Congress, according to the Virginia document, "more than any other, ought to produce universal alarm, because it is levelled against the right of freely examining public characters and measures, and of free communication among the people thereon, which has ever been justly deemed the only effectual guardian of every other right." The Virginia legislature passed the resolutions by a large majority and also urged the other states of the union to draft similar remonstrances.[22]

* Throughout his career Jefferson made many statements, now well known, about the right of the people to revolt. In 1787 he wrote to William Smith, "God forbid we should ever be twenty years without such a revolt [as Shays' Rebellion] . . . what country can preserve its liberties, if its leaders are not warned from time to time that the people preserve the spirit of resistance? . . . The tree of liberty must be refreshed from time to time with the blood of patriots and tyrants. It is its natural manure." To Madison he wrote in the same year, "I hold it that a little rebellion now and then is a good thing . . . an observation of this truth should render honest republican governments so mild in their punishment of rebellions, as not to discourage them too much." In 1808, while he was President, Jefferson wrote to Dr. James Brown: "Should we have ever gained our Revolution if we had bound our hands by manacles of the law, not only in the beginning, but in any part of the revolutionary conflict?" [20]

Yet none of the other states, mostly under Federalist control, followed Jefferson's suggestions. Delaware, Rhode Island, Massachusetts, New York, Connecticut, New Hampshire, and Vermont adopted resolutions condemning the idea that the states could nullify federal laws. Most of them claimed that the power to pass on federal legislation resided only in the most Federalist branch of the government—the Supreme Court.* A typical resolution came from Rhode Island—a state which was initially so averse to joining a federal union that it refused to send delegates to Philadelphia in 1787 and agreed to ratify the Constitution only because the government threatened to treat it as a foreign nation. In February 1799, the legislature resolved:

in the opinion of this legislature, the second section of the third article of the Constitution . . . vests in the Federal courts, exclusively, and the Supreme Court of the United States ultimately, the authority of deciding on the constitutionality of any act or law of the Congress of the United States.[23]

In the South, the Republicans did somewhat better. Georgia and South Carolina were sympathetic, but their legislatures did nothing in support of the Kentucky and Virginia resolves. In December 1798, the North Carolina legislature resolved that the repressive laws were unconstitutional, but they did not go as far as their neighbors to the north and west in urging resistance or asserting ultimate state control of federal legislation.

Nevertheless, the claim of Madison and Jefferson that the Alien and Sedition Laws violated the First Amendment seems incontrovertible.[24] In 1800, Madison prepared a comprehensive *Report on the Virginia Resolution* (known as the *Report of 1800*) which asserted once again that the Sedition Act was a violation of the First Amendment. He justified his position by citing the basic requirements of representative government:

The right of electing the members of the government constitutes . . . the essence of a free and responsible government. The value and efficacy of this right depends on the knowledge of the comparative merits and demerits of the candidates for public trust, and on the equal freedom, consequently, of examining and discussing these merits and demerits of the candidates respectively.[25]

If the Sedition Act were allowed to stand, the people could not be free, since

---

* With all the speculation about the source of John Marshall's assertion of judicial review in *Marbury* v. *Madison,* historians have strangely overlooked the resolutions of the Northern states answering Kentucky and Virginia and boldly thrusting that power on the Court.

they will be compelled to make their election between competitors whose pretensions they are not permitted by the act equally to examine, to discuss, and to ascertain. And from both these situations will not those in power derive an undue advantage for continuing themselves in it, which, by impairing the right of election, endangers the blessings of the government founded on it? [26]

But if Madison and Jefferson had legal logic on their side and were vindicated by the people (in the 1800 election), they were still suggesting disobedience to a law passed by the majority of Congress and sanctioned by all the justices of the highest court. Madison's more restrained Virginia resolutions perhaps fit within the contours of legitimate political dissent. But what can be said of Jefferson's proposals to Kentucky, which declared the Sedition Law void and urged the states to block enforcement of the legislation within their borders? Despite his attachment to democracy—or more likely *because* of it —Jefferson was unwilling to bow before every legislative enactment, no matter how ill-advised or dangerous it might be, particularly if the law threatened the integrity of the democratic process. The various Republican editors and congressmen who knew they violated the law by continuing their sharp criticisms of the government went even further in defying the authorities.

Madison explained the rationale behind such conscientious disobedience thirty years later, when the South Carolina nullifiers were refusing to obey a federal tariff. He wrote in 1835:

Should [all political resorts] fail, and the power usurped be sustained in its oppressive exercise on a minority by a majority, the final course to be pursued by a minority must be a subject of calculation, in which the degree of oppression, the means of resistance, the consequences of its failure, and consequences of its success must be the elements . . .
Should the constituted authorities of the State unite in usurping oppressive powers; should the constituent body fail to arrest the progress of evil thro' the elective process according to the forms of the Constitution; and should the authority which is above that of the Constitution, the majority of the people, inflexibly support the oppression inflicted on the minority, nothing would remain for the minority, but to rally to its reserved rights (for every citizen has his reserved rights, as exemplified in Declarations prefixed to most of the State constitutions), and to decide between acquiescence & resistance, according to the calculation above stated . . .[27]

On the strength of Madison's criteria, opposition to the Alien and Sedition Laws was clearly justified. The degree of oppression reached the highest order, affecting the rights of all the citizens to hear the truth about the government and its policies. Resistance was peaceful throughout, disobedience consisting only in the effort to transmit information or opinions about federal officials and their actions. Failure to resist would have meant a continuation of the repressive measures of the Federalist Party. By refusing to obey, the Republicans ensured that channels of dissent and debate about government policy remained open.

Thus, even in the first ten years of the nation's history, the Republican Party leaders and supporters systematically refused to obey laws threatening the proper functioning of the democratic process, just as the Pennsylvania farmers showed how oppressed they felt by class legislation and how far they were prepared to resist it. Their actions proved James Wilson's proposition that the extravagances of government could be opposed and prevented even by a single private citizen who had an unquestionable "right to judge" the fairness and wisdom of any law. The judgments made by Matthew Lyon, James Callendar, and Thomas Cooper—lawbreakers all—were vindicated immediately by their contemporaries and overwhelmingly by history.

# 3

# The Abolitionists

For a period of twenty years, from the early 1840's to 1860, a substantial and influential segment of the population regularly violated the established laws of the nation. During this time a number of clergymen, editors, lawyers, teachers, and the bulk of the nation's literary and artistic establishment refused to obey the Fugitive Slave Acts and state laws in support of them. These acts, passed by Congress in 1793 and 1850, compelled all citizens to help in capturing and returning runaway slaves and punished those who interfered with their rendition. Although the legislation was unmistakably sanctioned by the Constitution and upheld numerous times by the unanimous vote of the Supreme Court, there were state and federal officials at all levels of the government who sided with those who refused to obey the law, and a larger group of sympathizers, which included United States congressmen and senators, defended and encouraged their lawlessness.

Not all, of course. Most government officials warned that such behavior would lead to anarchy. Daniel Webster, Secretary of State in

1851, became so disturbed about the growing resistance to federal law that he warned in a speech at Syracuse, New York:

We hear of persons assembling in Massachusetts and New York who set themselves over the Constitution—above the law—and above the decisions of the highest tribunals . . . I tell you if men get together and declare a law of Congress shall not be executed in any case and assemble in numbers to prevent the execution of such a law—they are traitors and are guilty of treason.[1]

But such words only pushed the Abolitionists to more open opposition. The resistance spread so far into the structure of government that the lawbreakers were rarely if ever punished. More important, their conscientious opposition to law was the single most vital force in bringing down the institution of slavery.

The Abolitionist crusade had its beginnings in January 1831, when William Lloyd Garrison founded *The Liberator* in Boston. Two years later, *The Emancipator* was launched in New York, primarily as an organ of the American Anti-Slavery Society. Hundreds and then thousands of concerned citizens began to wake up to the horrors of slavery as numerous tracts came off the presses of the growing Abolitionist movement.[2]

When in the election year of 1836 the Abolitionists began to bombard Congress with petitions to abolish slavery, Southerners responded with a sweeping attempt at suppression.[3] John C. Calhoun claimed that the petitions came "in vast numbers from soured and agitated communities," and Representative Henry Laurens Pinckney of South Carolina introduced his famous "gag rule" which called for the automatic tabling of all petitions to Congress relating to slavery or its abolition. Even though John Quincy Adams protested that the resolution was "a direct violation of the Constitution of the United States, the rules of this House, and the rights of my constituents," the gag rule was approved by a large vote and remained in force until 1844.[4]

On the local level, the Southern States moved quickly and efficiently to suppress any discussion of abolition. While there had been some Southern antislavery newspapers in the 1820's, the combined impact of Nat Turner's revolt in 1831 and Garrison's call for immediate abolition in the same year wiped out any possibility of free debate in the press. Judge William Gaston of the North Carolina Supreme Court was one of the last Southern public figures who could or would openly criticize slavery in the South. Three years later, in 1835, Governor McDuffie of South Carolina proposed a law punishing abolitionist editors by death without benefit of clergy. Concurrently, the death penalty was imposed in Georgia for printing or circulating any literature tending to incite slave insurrections. Louisiana and both the Carolinas immediately followed suit. In 1836, Virginia legislation forbade any member of an Abolition society to enter the state, and in 1849 a law was passed making it a crime to say "owners have no right of property in slaves." [5]

Many Southern congressmen and other government officials freely threatened death to Abolitionists coming south, including fellow legislators John P. Hale, Joshua Giddings, and Owen Lovejoy. Georgia offered a $5,000 reward to anyone who could kidnap Garrison and bring him to the South; a Virginia newspaper offered $5,000 for Giddings' head and $50,000 for William Seward's.

The mob took up where repressive laws left off. Vigilante groups under the guise of "committees of public safety" were formed in virtually every community to deal with supposed agitators. These committees checked the mail from the North and kept tabs on all travelers coming into their communities. Tar-and-feathering was mild punishment for a suspected Abolitionist found in the Deep South. Whippings were common—one Lane Seminary student was given twenty lashes in Nashville because he wrapped Bibles he was selling in pages from *The Emancipator*. John Cornutt, a farmer of Grayson County, Virginia, publicly defended a local minister who preached an antislavery sermon. Local citizens retaliated by first tar-and-feathering, then whipping him; he brought legal charges against the attackers, who in turn broke up the court proceedings convened to hear the case. When a newly formed vigilante committee demanded that Cornutt give them assurance of his support of slavery or leave the county, he backed down.

The ultimate sanction was murder. Elijah Lovejoy, an anti-Catholic fanatic who saw slavery as a Papist creation, was shot to death by a mob attacking his newspaper office in November 1837. Garrison claimed that in the thirty years before the Civil War at least three hundred persons—many white—were lynched in the South because they were suspected of antislavery views. Russel Nye considers this figure "not too high."

The Abolitionists' problems with the federal government stemmed from the fact that Article IV of the Constitution unquestionably sanctioned and protected slavery:

No person held to Service or Labor in one State under the Laws thereof, escaping into another, shall, in Consequence of any Law or Regulation therein, be discharged from such Service or Labor, but shall be delivered up on the Claim of the Party to whom such Service or Labor may be due.

Southern delegates to the Philadelphia Constitutional Convention in 1787 had won this concession in return for agreeing to a ban on the slave trade after 1808. The first Fugitive Slave Law was passed in 1793, allowing the recapture and arrest in free territory of escaped slaves. The owner's word that the slave was his would often satisfy the court; anyone harboring a fugitive or interfering with a slaveowner was subject to a fine of $500.

The Law was rarely contested for a period of fifty years. In the 1830's some Northern states attempted to limit the Law's effectiveness with "personal liberty laws." These countermeasures guaranteed runaway slaves certain essential rights—the right to free counsel and trial by jury, extradition only by official warrant. Thus in 1837, when a slave chaser named Edward Prigg dragged a slave out of Pennsylvania and back to Maryland without a warrant, he was arrested for kidnapping. But five years later the case reached the Supreme Court, and the Fugitive Slave Law was unanimously upheld as a valid exercise of Congressional power which could not be restricted by state law. Individual states could oppose slavery only insofar as they could refuse assistance in the federal return of fugitives.[6]

A more direct challenge to the 1793 federal law came in the case of *Jones* v. *Van Zandt,* an action for the $500 civil penalty against those accused of aiding fugitives. John Van Zandt, a notorious member of the Underground Railway (perhaps a model for John Van Trompe in *Uncle Tom's Cabin*) was caught with nine fugitives in his wagon near Cincinnati. At his trial in the circuit court, John McLean —the Supreme Court Justice most sympathetic to the antislavery cause who later dissented in the Dred Scott decision—rejected the argument of Van Zandt's attorneys that "No court is bound to enforce an unjust law."

I was not prepared to hear, in a Court of Justice, the broad ground assumed, as was assumed in this case before the jury, that a man, in the exercise of what he conceives to be a conscientious duty, may violate the laws of the land. That no human laws can justly restrain the acts of men, who are impelled by a sense of duty to God and their fellow creatures. We are not here to deal with abstractions. We can not theorize upon the principles of our government, or of slavery. The law is our only guide. . . . If convictions, honest convictions they may be, of what is right or wrong, are to be substituted as a rule of action in disregard of the law, we shall soon be without law and without protection.[7]

In 1847 the full bench of the Supreme Court upheld McLean's decision against Van Zandt.[8]

The silent majority of the nation probably agreed with Justice

McLean and the Supreme Court in 1847. Although more and more Northern citizens were willing to vote for an antislavery position,[9] very few were prepared to disobey the laws protecting the institution.

As early as 1840, however, the handful of militant Abolitionists who openly defied the government had organized what became known as the Underground Railway. So many legends have grown up around the institution, and so much romance and adventure are associated with its heroes, that it becomes difficult to weed out the true accomplishments from the folklore. The legendary railway was a centralized network reaching deep into the South, with its agents snatching blacks away from cruel masters and efficiently transporting them to Canada, eluding villainous slave catchers and evil sheriffs every inch of the way. In fact, the most difficult work of organizing an escape was accomplished by the Southern blacks themselves, who could count on assistance from separate sympathetic groups once they reached the North.

A few whites did play important roles in engineering escapes. Jonathan Walker, a sea captain operating in Florida waters, transported many slaves to the Bahamas. He was eventually apprehended and sentenced to seven months in jail, and the Florida authorities branded the letters "SS"—for "slave stealer"—on his hand. Lewis Paine was imprisoned six years in Georgia for a botched attempt to transport one slave north. John Fairfield, a native Virginian, worked for a dozen years to bring blacks out of slavery. Always heavily armed, he never hesitated to shoot his way out of trouble but he was finally caught and hanged in Tennessee in 1856.

Once the blacks crossed the Mason-Dixon line, Quakers in Pennsylvania and Indiana, the academic communities in the Western Reserve of Ohio, and the clerics in Boston provided them with food, shelter, and transportation. Thomas Garrett, a Quaker from Delaware who served as a model for Simeon Halliday in *Uncle Tom's Cabin* is reputed to have aided 2,700 fugitive slaves to escape. He relied on the large population of Friends in Chester County, Pennsylvania, who transported fugitives to Philadelphia and other northern junctures from where they made their way across the Canadian border. Levi Coffin, from Newport, Indiana, earned a reputation as the "President of the Underground Railway." He arranged for a series of depots that would shelter, clothe, and feed slaves escaping from Kentucky and points south to make the long journey to Canada and freedom. For a period of over twenty years, Coffin claimed to have helped about one hundred fugitives per year. In Michigan, the Detroit vigilance committee ferried groups of fugitives across the Windsor River. A fleet of small boats worked out of Erie, New York, and Ashtabula,

Fairport Harbor, Lorain, and Sandusky, Ohio, to carry slaves across Lake Erie and land them on the Canadian shore.*

With the passage of the 1850 Fugitive Slave Law, militant opposition to slavery grew into an open national movement. Congress passed the new law as part of Henry Clay's grand compromise on slavery. California was admitted to the Union as a free state and the slave trade was abolished in the District of Columbia. No mention was made of slavery in the territorial organization of New Mexico and Utah. In return for these concessions to the North, the South insisted upon a more efficient procedure for returning runaway slaves. Like the legislation of 1793, the new fugitive act allowed owners or their agents to seize runaway slaves without any legal process. A United States Commissioner—a lower judicial officer than a judge—was to hear the case "in a summary manner." Written proof that the fugitive did belong to the alleged owner was now necessary (an advance over the 1793 law), but an affidavit of ownership would suffice. More important, "in no trial or hearing under this act shall the testimony of such alleged fugitive be admitted in evidence." The $500 civil penalty for aiding a fugitive was increased to a $1,000 fine and a six-month jail sentence. The Commissioner himself stood to gain an extra financial reward for ordering the slave to the South: if he returned the slave he received a $10.00 fee, but if he released the captive, he was paid only half that sum. Finally, and most galling to the Abolitionists, "all good citizens" were required "to aid in prompt execution of this law," and officers could "summon bystanders to their aid."

The law showed how far the federal government had humbled itself to the "Slave Power." Abolitionists attacked the procedural absurdities of the new act, particularly the provisions requiring Northern citizens to aid in apprehending blacks and preventing runaways from testifying in their own behalf. They immediately retorted that they would not obey the law. Joshua Giddings spoke defiantly in the House: "Let no man tell you that there is no higher law than this fugitive slave bill. We feel there is a law of right, of justice, of freedom, implanted in the breasts of every intelligent human being, that bids him look with scorn upon this libel on all that is called the law." [11]

Ministers and clerics in large urban centers were the chief instiga-

---

* No one knows exactly how many fugitives actually escaped from slavery. The 1850 census reported only one thousand runaway slaves in that year, a figure which corresponded to the best estimates from other sources. Over a period of thirty years the total number possibly reached sixty thousand.[10]

tors among the militants. Their sermons not only reached their own parishioners, but through reprinting in hundreds of newspapers and pamphlets, were read by tens of thousands throughout the North. Their endorsement of conscientious disobedience provided the Abolitionist crusade with its strongest moral and intellectual ammunition.

Soon after the passage of the 1850 fugitive law, Lyman Beecher, an influential Presbyterian minister and one of the founders of Lane Seminary, delivered a sermon on "The Duty of Disobedience to Wicked Laws." Quoting not only from the Bible but from Blackstone and other legal scholars, Beecher preached that "No human laws are of any validity if contrary to the law of nature." He asked what a Christian should do in the face of the requirements of federal law and evoked the image of a black woman with her child coming to a warm house on a wintry night to ask for food and shelter. "What does the law require of you? What must you do to obey this law? . . . You must shut your door in her face, or you must take her captive, and shut her up until the hounds of officers can come up. This is obedience; and if you do not do this you are a law-breaker. If you give her a crust of bread you break the law. If you give her a shawl, a cloak; if you let her warm herself by your fire an hour, you break the law."

Beecher examined the arguments against disobedience:

"I know it is wrong, abstractly considered," you say; "but the law says so, and I must do it till the law is altered. True, it seems to me wrong, but what right have I to set up my judgment against the law? True, it seems to me that this law conflicts with the golden rule, on which hang all the Law and the prophets, and nullifies all principles of honor and humanity, but what right have I to follow my own private impressions of right against the laws of the land? What right have I to say I will obey the laws of the land just so far as they coincide with my ideas of right, but when they do not, I will break them? If everybody should do so, would it not put an end to all law, and disorganize society? No, no; I must try to get this law repealed, but in the meanwhile I must keep it, even if it command me to violate every principle of the Decalogue."

But he had an answer to this claim:

Here is the stereotyped argument for all such cases made and provided, which has been used by civil and religious despotism in all ages. First pass a law that compels men to violate conscience, and then drive them to keep it by conscience. The worst of it is that these profligate preachers of integrity cheat their hearers by a fallacy, a falsehood so slyly slipped in, as to escape detection. They misrepresent the whole position of conscientious men. They represent us as if we claimed the right to violate any law that might happen not to suit our convenience, or our notions of propriety. They say that our claim of the right to violate *one* law, which we consider wrong, is a warrant for the violation of *all* laws, right or wrong. Now, this is a false conclusion. It represents us as confounding the distinction between laws which are simply *injurious* or inexpedient, and those which are positively sinful.

I may disapprove a law, I may think it unwise, injudicious, . . . and yet it may not require me to *do anything* positively wrong. I may submit to such a law, innocently, because I wrong nobody. But here is a law which commands me to *sin* positively and without apology. It commands me, when fully obeyed, to deny Christ, to renounce and abjure Christ's law, to trample under foot Christ's Spirit, and to remand Christ's flesh and blood into cruel bondage.

A law which does me some injury is one thing. A law which makes me do wrong is another. The first I may submit to while seeking its repeal. To the latter I must not give place by subjection, no, not for an hour. I must resist unto blood, striving against sin, i.e., to the patient shedding of my own blood. Hence, to disobey such a law does not disorganize society. It does not unsettle law.

The men that refuse obedience to such laws are the sure, the only defenders of law. If they will shed their own blood rather than sin by keeping a wicked law, they will by the same principle shed their blood rather than break a law which is righteous. In short, such men are the only true law-abiding men.[12]

Theodore Parker, the powerful Boston minister, developed a similar idea, with history as his support: "if disobedience to the established law be the highest virtue, then the Patriots and Pilgrims of New England, the Reformers of the Church, the glorious company of the Apostles, the goodly fellowship of the prophets, and the noble array of martyrs, nay Jesus himself, were only criminals and traitors." [13]

To the domino theory of law—that if one law is disobeyed, every other one will also fall—Parker replied: "Who is it that oppose the fugitive slave law? Men that have always been on the side of law and order and do not violate the statutes of man for their own advantage. This disobedience to the fugitive slave law is one of the strongest guarantees for the observance of any just law. You cannot trust a people who will keep a law *because it is law,* nor need we distrust a people that will keep a law when it is just." * [14]

* Judge Charles Wyzanski of Massachusetts expressed the same idea in 1969 in his opinion in *United States* v. *Sisson,* a case upholding the principle of selective conscientious objection:

When the state through its laws seeks to override reasonable moral commitments it makes a dangerously uncharacteristic choice. The law grows from the deposits of morality. Law and morality are, in turn, debtors and creditors of each other. The law cannot be adequately en-

The experience of the nation after the 1850 Fugitive Slave Law gave strong support to this stance. A week after the 1850 law was passed, James Hamlet, a hard-working Methodist from New York and no doubt a free man, was seized and sent to Maryland under the new procedures. A group of wealthy merchants immediately purchased him from his supposed owners and set him free. A year later came the famous "Jerry Rescue" in Syracuse, New York. William Henry ("Jerry"), an "intelligent, athletic mulatto" who escaped from Missouri, had settled in Syracuse.[15] Possessed of "some mechanical ability," he worked as an apprentice in a cooper's shop. At noon on October 1, 1851, three federal marshals came to his shop and arrested him on a bogus theft charge. He was handcuffed and dragged to the United States Commissioner's offices. The Liberal Party was holding a meeting in the city at the time; members of the local vigilance committee and the visiting Abolitionists came quickly to Commissioner Joseph F. Sabine's office to hear the case against Jerry. Greatly outnumbering the marshals, the Abolitionists threw Jerry down the stairs and rolled him onto the street. He ran, his hands still shackled, with a great mob following, half trying to capture him, half trying to help him escape. Three policemen caught up with him and took him back to jail. The federal marshal, Henry W. Allen, and the local sheriff, William Gardner, tried to gather whatever men were available to guard Jerry, but hundreds of vigilance committee members came to the police station that night with clubs, axes, and iron rods. They broke in the front door with a battering ram as the deputies and marshals jumped out of the windows. Jerry was taken to the home of sympathizers and from there escaped to Canada.

A few weeks later Supreme Court Justice Samuel Nelson charged a federal grand jury to issue indictments under the 1850 law against the rescuers. He described the case as calling for "grave and serious inquiry on the part of the public authorities." The acts of Jerry's helpers struck at the very foundation of a government of laws and substituted "brute force and anarchy. . . . No government is worth preserving that does not or cannot enforce obedience to its laws." [16]

The grand jury quickly returned indictments against eight individuals. In November, five more rescuers were charged, including Enoch

---

forced by the court alone, or by courts supported merely by the police and the military.

The true secret of legal might lies in the habits of conscientious men disciplining themselves to obey the law they respect without the necessity of judicial and administrative orders.

When the law treats a reasonable, conscientious act as a crime it subverts its own power. It invites civil disobedience. It impairs the very habits which nourish and preserve the law.

Reed, a prominent Negro citizen of Syracuse. The indictments were challenged before District Court Judge Alfred Conkling, who approved them wholeheartedly: "Regardless of their civil and social duties, they have broken the public peace, set the law at open defiance, and with deadly weapons assaulted and wounded its officers while executing its mandates. In thus insulting the majesty of the law, did they expect to escape its vengeance?" Conkling said that those who cannot in conscience obey the Fugitive Slave Law "may seek a residence in some other country, if he can find one where he thinks he would suffer less from misrule." [17] The trial of Enoch Reed began in Albany in January 1852, and dragged into 1853. Additional trials of the other defendants were held in Albany in 1853. Only Reed was found guilty, and he died while his appeal was pending. Every one of the juries that heard the other cases either acquitted the defendants or failed to reach a verdict.

In Massachusetts, antislavery feeling was even more widespread than in New York. Ellen and William Craft—originally from Georgia and protégés of Theodore Parker—were hunted by their owner's agents in late 1850. Parker called a meeting of the Boston Vigilance Committee—Dr. Samuel Gridley Howe, famous for his work with the blind and the deaf, Dr. Henry Bowditch, the great public health innovator, Ellis Gray Loring, an outstanding Boston lawyer, Samuel May, Wendell Phillips, Charles Ellis, another lawyer, and the two leading Negro Abolitionists of the time, Lewis Hayden and Frederick Douglass. The Crafts were immediately hidden with sympathetic families. Sixty members of the committee then went and warned the slave catchers of violence if they tried to capture the Crafts. Knight, one of the agents, had accused the two blacks of theft—they were wearing their owner's clothes when they escaped, he said—and Loring promptly had Knight and his henchman arrested for slander and later for smoking in the streets, profane swearing and cursing, reckless driving, and failure to pay bridge tolls. As the two men walked on the Boston streets after their release on bail, crowds followed them shouting, "Slave-hunters, slave-hunters, there go the slave-hunters." They left for Georgia without their quarry.

The immediate and frenzied release of blacks from attempts at reenslavement was described with fresh amazement by Richard Henry Dana, the attorney for "Shadrach": [18]

I returned to my office, & was planning out with a friend, the probable next proceedings, when we heard a shout from the court house, continued into a yell of triumph, & in an instant after, down the steps came two huge negroes, bearing the prisoner between them, with his clothes half torn off, & so stupefied by the sudden rescue and the violence of his

dragging off that he sat almost down & I thought had fainted; but the
men seised [sic] him, & being powerful fellows, hurried him through the
Square into Court st., where he found the use of feet, & they went off
toward Cambridge, like a black squall, the crowd driving along with
them & cheering as they went. It was all done in an instant, too quick to
be believed, & so successful was it that not only was no negro arrested,
but no attempt was made at pursuit.[19] [Journal entry, February 15, 1851]

The federal government could not tolerate so serious an affront to
its authority. President Millard Fillmore held a Cabinet meeting about
the episode, declared a state of emergency in Massachusetts, and
readied troops for possible use. The local federal attorney, George
Lunt, pressed charges against a group of the rescuers: James Scott,
Lewis Hayden, Robert Morris, a Negro lawyer, George Davis, and
Elizur Wright, a conservative Abolitionist, for aiding and abetting in
Shadrach's escape. Dana defended both Davis and Wright successfully, the jury voting to acquit them after two retrials. In the course
of Robert Morris' trial, his lawyer told the jury that they should
judge the law as well as the facts, and that if any of them conscientiously believed that the Fugitive Slave Law was unconstitutional, they
should disregard any instructions by the judge to the contrary. Justice
Benjamin Curtis, presiding, immediately issued a long opinion upholding the court's sole, long-established power to say what the law is.
Toward the end of the opinion he noted:

A strong appeal has been made to the court, by one of the defendant's
counsel, upon the ground that the exercise of this power by juries is
important to the preservation of the rights and liberties of the citizen.
If I thought so, I should pause long before I denied its existence. But a
good deal of reflection has convinced me that the argument drawn from
this quarter is really the other way . . . To enforce popular laws is easy.
But when an unpopular cause is a just cause, when a law, unpopular in
some locality, is to be enforced there, then comes the strain upon the
administration of justice: and few unprejudiced men would hesitate as
to where that strain would be most firmly borne.[20]

Nevertheless, exercising its unquestioned power to pass on the facts,
the jury acquitted Morris. Another jury could not reach a verdict
on Hayden, and the charges against him were finally dropped.

The next fugitive case in Boston found the federal government
prepared. Thomas Sims, a young black man from Georgia, was arrested on April 3, 1852, taken to the Boston Court House, and
guarded by dozens of policemen. Dana used all his wits trying to get
the Massachusetts court to issue a writ of habeas corpus to order his
release. When that failed, he thought up the idea of having a Massa-

chusetts criminal charge brought against Sims—assault against the sheriff who arrested him—in the hopes that this charge would prevail over the federal summons under which Sims was held. But the federal marshal refused to surrender the fugitive. To insure security in the Court House, a large chain was drawn across the entrance, although the state courts also met in the building. The sight of Chief Justice Lemuel Shaw crawling under the chain to get to his court disgusted many of the Boston establishment. Dana wrote in his journal: "Our Temple of Justice is a slave pen! Our officers are slave hunters, & the voice of the old law of the state is hushed & awed into silence before this fearful Slave power who has got such entire control of the Union." [21] Theodore Parker attacked George T. Curtis, the United States Commissioner hearing the case, with all his thunder and lightning. "He called the roll of the monsters of history to find for him a fit companion." [22] But it was useless. Sims was found to be a fugitive slave and spirited off under heavy guard in the middle of the night. Federal troops took him to a ship in Boston harbor which sailed to Savannah, Georgia. Once he landed there, Sims was publicly whipped and returned to captivity.

The last important fugitive slave case in Boston took place in May 1854, and showed without a doubt how far antislavery sentiment outweighed middle-class respect for the law. The episode again involved Theodore Parker and Richard Henry Dana in the principal roles. Anthony Burns of Virginia, the slave of a Colonel Charles Suttle, was seized in Boston on May 24. Dana came to Commissioner Edward G. Loring's court room to defend Burns, and obtained a delay to prepare his case. The night before the scheduled hearing, Parker addressed a great crowd at Faneuil Hall, the "Cradle of Liberty" in downtown Boston. "Fellow subjects of Virginia," he began, and the crowd shouted, "No, No, take that back."

"I will take it back," said Parker, "when you show me that it is not so . . . I have heard hurrahs and cheers for liberty many times: I have not seen a great many deeds done for liberty. I ask you, are we to have deeds as well as words? . . . Gentlemen, I love peace, but there is a means and there is an end. Liberty is the end, and sometimes peace is not the means to it. Now I want to ask you, what are you going to do?" [23] But here Parker hesitated, and called for a meeting at the court house the next day. However a shout from the crowd rallied a march that night "to the court house." A disorganized group moved toward the center of the city having no clear purpose in mind. With Rev. Thomas Wentworth Higginson in the lead, the more militant broke into the court house, but they were not supported by sufficient members. Higginson described the action:

Mingling with the crowd, I ran against [Martin] Stowall, who had been looking for the axes, stored at a friend's office in Court Square. He whispered, "Some of our men are bringing a beam up to the upper stairway." Instantly he and I ran round and grasped the beam: I finding myself at the head, with a stout Negro opposite me. The real attack had begun. . . . Taking the joist up the stairs, we hammered away at the southwest door of the Court-House. It could not have been many minutes before it began to give way . . . There was room for but one to pass in. I glanced instinctively at my black ally. He did not even look at me, but sprang in first, I following . . . We found ourselves inside face to face with six or eight policemen, who laid about them with their clubs, driving us to the wall and hammering away at our heads . . . to my surprise it was not half so bad as I had expected.* [24]

The soldiers on guard had no difficulty protecting Burns, but a stray shot killed a proslavery sympathizer standing guard. President Pierce telegraphed that order had to be maintained, and the next day an artillery company and hundreds of Marines from Charleston came to guard the court house.

On Saturday, May 27, 1854, the court room was filled with what Dana called "hireling soldiers of the Standing Army of the U.S. nearly all of whom are foreigners." [25] Three lines of police and two lines of soldiers guarded the building against any repetition of the Shadrach rescue. Inside the court room was the marshal's "guard" which Dana described as a "gang of about 120 men and lowest villains in the community, keepers of brothels, bullies, blacklegs, convicts, firelighters &c. . . ."

Dana argued to the court that the identification of Burns was inadequate and that Colonel Suttle had not proven his title to him. Loring was to announce his decision on Friday, June 2, 1854, and in anticipation, Mayor Jerome Smith ordered the entire military force of Boston to stand guard. Although the proof of Burns' identification was weak, he had confessed his identity to Colonel Suttle on the night of the arrest, and Loring decided this was sufficient to establish that he was Suttle's slave. Burns was ordered handed over to his master with some three thousand police and soldiers guarding his line of march to a waiting ship bound for Virginia. The flags in Boston were at half mast. Loring was burned in effigy all over Massachusetts, fired from Harvard, and eventually removed as a Massachusetts Judge

* Dana said about Higginson's participation: "The leader of this mob, I am surprised to learn, in secrecy, was Rev. T. W. Higginson of Worcester. I knew his ardor and courage, but I hardly expected a married man, a clergyman, and a man of education to lead the mob." Higginson later became the commanding officer of the first Negro regiment of the Union Army and wrote a famous book about his experiences, *Army Life in a Black Regiment*.

of Probate because of his decision. It had cost the federal government $100,000 to return Burns. A group of wealthy Bostonians immediately collected enough money to purchase Burns; he was freed, and became a minister in Canada.

An important court action grew out of the Burns affair. Justice Benjamin Curtis instructed a Boston grand jury that those obstructing execution of the Fugitive Slave Law were guilty of a federal offense. Not only those who were present when the offense was committed, but those who "though absent . . . did procure, counsel, command or abet others to commit the offenses, are indictable as principals." [26] The first grand jury did nothing, but a second one, which included William Greenough, Justice Curtis' brother-in-law, returned indictments against Theodore Parker, Wendell Phillips, Rev. Higginson, and others.

The government's theory was that those who had spoken at Faneuil Hall on May 26, 1854, and later went to the court house had counseled and encouraged opposition to the 1850 act, thereby obstructing the marshal from serving processes under the law. Parker used the opportunity for some of his most bitter sermons against slavery. "All who at Faneuil Hall stirred up the minds of the people in opposition to the fugitive slave bill, all who shouted, who clapped their hands at the words or the countenance of their favorites or who expressed 'approbation' by a whisper of 'assent' are 'guilty of a misdemeanor.' Well, there were fifteen thousand persons 'assembled in the highway' of the city of Boston on that day opposed to kidnapping . . ." [27]

The trial was a disappointment, however. The lawyers raised certain technical objections to the indictment, and the judge dismissed the case. The government did not try for another indictment. "You have crawled out of a very small hole this time, Mr. Parker," said Benjamin Hallett, the United States Attorney. "I will make a larger hole next time," Parker replied. [28]

The reaction of the Boston professional community to the Burns affair showed the change in atmosphere since the early 1850's. Not only did antislavery delegations consisting of ministers, lawyers, and teachers come from all over the state, but even conservative lawyers and merchants were outraged. Dana wrote in his journal: "the most remarkable exhibition is from the Whigs, . . . the Compromise men of 1850. Men who wd. not speak to me in 1850 & 51, & who were enrolling themselves as special policemen in the Sims affair, stop me in the street and talk treason." Amos A. Lawrence, a leading merchant, offered to pay for a prominent Whig counsel to aid Dana in defending Burns. "He said he was authorized to do this by a number of active 1850 men, who were determined it shd. be known that it was not the Free Soilers only who were in favor of the liberation of the Slaves, but the conservative, compromise men. . . . The case is precisely the same as that of Sims. But then, we were all traitors and malignants, now we are heroes and patriots." [29]

The Burns rendition, coupled with the opening guns of the Kansas-Nebraska dispute, had an immediate effect on Massachusetts politics. John B. Alley, a leading Abolitionist in the state, wrote to Charles Sumner: "Never since I have engaged in the anti-slavery cause have I seen occasion for rejoicing as now . . . The chains that have bound people to their old organizations have been snapped asunder." [30] Within six weeks a call went out for a convention to form a new antislavery party. The Free Soil leaders and a few antislavery Whigs and Democrats came together in Concord and in Boston in the summer of 1854. They took the name "Republican," following the lead of a Michigan antislavery convention. Two of the leaders of the new Massachusetts organization were Henry Wilson and John A. Andrew. By 1855, Wilson was elected U.S. Senator, and the new party was the second strongest in the state. By 1858, it made a clean sweep of the state elections. The party became so radicalized that in 1859 Andrew gave John Brown twenty-four dollars which he used for his raid on Harper's Ferry, and after the fiasco, Andrew staunchly defended Brown: "Whether the enterprise of John Brown and his assistants was wise or foolish, right or wrong; I only know that, whether the enterprise itself was one or the other, John Brown himself is right." [31] Andrew became the Republican candidate for governor in 1860 and easily won the election.

The turnabout in Massachusetts grew directly out of the fugitive slave cases in the early 1850's. If Shadrach, Sims, and Anthony Burns had been quietly returned to the South, or if they had been allowed to stay on as free men, Massachusetts politics probably would have remained the same. It was only after the blacks defied the laws which consigned them to slavery, after the Northern activists put their own bodies on the line, and after both were prosecuted for their actions, that the state's political inertia was overcome. To talk about the injustice of a law was one thing; it was quite another to see people suffer for disobeying it. The fact that Parker, Higginson, and their allies were willing to risk their own liberties to protest the evils of slavery, and that they were followed by militants in other states, unquestionably made the strongest impact upon the majority. Their changing attitude toward the "peculiar institution" was soon transformed into political action which led in turn to an electoral victory for the Republicans.

The situation in other states was similar. Ohio had always been the most important avenue for slaves escaping from the South. Lying across the Ohio River from Kentucky, it was the most direct route to Canada, and many fugitives found its residents willing to give assistance. The first Ohio case under the 1850 law involved a runaway named Louis who had been captured in Cincinnati in 1851. Rutherford B. Hayes, then a young lawyer, defended Louis. Levi Coffin described the excitement of the courtroom rescue:

Louis was crowded, and to gain more room, slipped his chair back a little way. Neither his master nor the marshal noticed the movement, as they were intently listening to the judge, and he slipped in his chair again, until he was back of them. I was standing close behind and saw every movement. Next he rose quietly to his feet and took a step backward. Some Abolitionists friendly to his cause, gave him an encouraging touch on his foot, and he stepped further back. Then a good hat was placed on his head by some one behind, and he quickly and cautiously made his way around the south end of the room, into the crowd of colored people on the west side, and, through it, toward the door.[32]

A minister and his wife eventually smuggled Louis to Canada.

The most significant Ohio case took place in 1858. Two slave-hunters came to Oberlin, Ohio, to recapture a slave known as Little John Price.* By a ruse, the Kentucky slavehunters seized Price in September and took him to a railroad station at Wellington, Ohio, from where they hoped to drag him South. But some Oberlin students had seen the kidnapping—the story spread. Hundreds of students, teachers, ministers, and free Negroes from the area came in force to free Price. When a crowd of Abolitionists poured into the small railroad town, the slavehunters and a U.S. marshal, Jacob Lowe, hid in a wood frame house near the railroad station. But the rescuers soon located them, climbed into the house, and forcefully removed Price. He escaped and was not retaken.

On December 8, 1858, thirty-seven of the Oberlin-Wellington rescuers were indicted by a federal grand jury in Cleveland for aiding and abetting the escape of a slave. The authorities decided to try only two men, Simeon Bushnell and Charles H. Langston, a Negro; the other defendants agreed to abide by the decision in those cases.

* Oberlin College had been a center of Abolitionism since 1835. In that year Theodore Weld and other students at Lane Seminary in Cincinnati debated the issue of slavery so vigorously that they offended the trustees and were asked to leave Lane. Many of the "Lane Rebels" enrolled in Oberlin, founded by Rev. John J. Shippherd, a strong antislavery man. Asa Mahan became President, and the faculty included many strong Abolitionists.

Bushnell was tried in April 1859 and found guilty. Langston was tried a month later, with the same result. At the time of his sentencing, Langston defiantly told the court:

I stand here to say that I will do all I can, for any man thus seized and held, though the inevitable penalty of six months imprisonment and one thousand dollars fine for each offence hangs over me. . . . We have a common humanity. You would do so; your manhood would require it; and no matter what the laws might be, you would honor yourself for doing it; your friends would honor you for doing it; your children through all generations would honor you for doing it; and every good and honest man would say, you had done *right!* [33]

The reaction against the convictions of Bushnell and Langston showed how widespread was the opposition to the law by 1859. Republican party organizations throughout the state passed resolutions condemning the law.[34] Local newspapers even recommended a resort to force. The Portage County *Democrat* wrote on May 11, 1859:

Let no cheek pale then, at the prospect in the not distant future, of a revolution *not bloodless!* The time has not yet come, but the dough-faced servility, and conservative timidity, and corrupt, cringing sycophancy of the times are fast hastening the day. Let the day come and God speed the right. RESISTANCE TO TYRANTS IS OBEDIENCE TO GOD! [35]

In the summer of 1859, Bushnell's lawyers applied for a writ of habeas corpus from the Ohio Supreme Court. Although the Ohio Attorney General C. P. Wolcott argued that the 1787 Northwest Ordinance forbade slavery in the area in question, the Ohio Court upheld Bushnell's conviction by a three to two vote. (Abolitionist strength had increased so much in Ohio in the next year that the voters retired one of the judges who sided with the majority.) Meanwhile a Lorain County grand jury indicated the federal marshal, Jacob Lowe, and the three slavehunters who captured Price, claiming that they had unlawfully kidnapped the young man. Since Price had escaped, there was no way of proving he had really been a slave, and Lowe faced many years in prison on the kidnapping charge. President Buchanan's Administration treated the affair quite seriously, and the President sent his Attorney General, Jeremiah Black, to arrange some solution. Black, A. G. Riddle (Bushnell's lawyer), and C. P. Wolcott reached a settlement under which all criminal charges against Lowe and his group would be dropped and the federal government agreed to dismiss the cases against the Oberlin-Wellington people.

In November 1859, William Dennison was elected governor of

Ohio on a platform pledging to block any further rendition of slaves from his state. "If I cannot prevent it in any other way, as commander-in-chief of the militia of the State I will employ the bayonet —so help me God." [36]

In Pennsylvania, the same sequence of events took place, beginning with scattered attempts at resistance during the 1840's. Three men from Cumberland County aided twelve escaped slaves from Maryland and were sued by the owner for damages. The three men were defended by Thaddeus Stevens, and when the jury could not agree on a verdict, the case was dropped.[37]

In 1851, the famous Christiana riots took place. A group of slaves led by Samuel Thompson ran away from Maryland into Pennsylvania. The owner, Edward Gorsuch, went after them and located Thompson in Christiana, Lancaster County. Accompanied by a U.S. marshal, the slaveowner, his sons, and his nephew went to the house of William Parker, who was a free Negro leader in the county. The marshal boldly entered the building but was chased out by the massive Parker, who came at him with a harpoon and an ax. Parker's wife, meanwhile, rounded up about fifty blacks to protect the runaways. Gorsuch ordered his slaves to return and went up to Parker's house to persuade them to surrender. He was met at the front door by Thompson, who was armed and refused to move. As Gorsuch signaled his men to assist him, Thompson struck him over the head with his gun, and a shot was fired from the house, killing the slaveowner. More shots wounded Gorsuch's sons and nephew and drove the marshal and his posse away from the house.[38] In the meantime, two local Quakers, Castner Hanway and Elijah Lewis, came up to Parker's house to watch what was happening. Although they did not participate in the melee, they refused to move or assist the marshal when he ordered them to do so.

The slaves escaped, and the government prosecuted everyone they held responsible for the shoot-out. Some Quaker sympathizers who were not even present during the incident, and thirty-five black Abolitionists from the county were indicted, not for murder or assault, but for treason. The government claimed that the indicted Negroes and Quakers had banded together to protect fugitive slaves in Lancaster County. Hanway came to Parker's house, the prosecutor said, by prearranged design, thus proving he was part of a wide conspiracy to block execution of federal law. Such concerted opposition to the federal government was treasonable.

Thaddeus Stevens appeared as counsel for the defense, joined by John M. Read, later a Pennsylvania Supreme Court judge. They argued that whatever Hanway and his friends may have done to resist the Fugitive Slave Law, it could not be considered treason. The jury agreed and acquitted them.

In 1853, four U.S. deputy marshals from Luzerne County were arrested by Pennsylvania authorities and charged with assault after they had shot a runaway slave, William Thomas. Justice Robert Grier of the United States Supreme Court ordered them freed since they were U.S. officers acting in the performance of their duties. Thereafter a grand jury in Luzerne returned an indictment against the four, charging them with assault and intent to kill. They again asked for the federal court to interfere, but the federal district judge permitted the state case to be heard.[39]

In the elections of November 1858, Republicans won everywhere, including Pennsylvania. Another fugitive slave case arose in April 1859, and in response to the agitation, the new Republican legislature, then in session, passed even more sweeping personal liberty laws than the Supreme Court had outlawed in the *Prigg* case.

The most serious conflict between the state and federal governments took place in Wisconsin. Newspaper editor S. M. Booth was arrested by the federal authorities for helping a runaway slave. The Wisconsin Supreme Court granted a habeas corpus writ on the ground that the 1850 Fugitive Slave Law was unconstitutional, but the federal marshal would not release him. After Booth was convicted of violating the federal law, the state Supreme Court again ordered him released, claiming the federal court had no jurisdiction to try him. The Wisconsin authorities were so openly defiant of the federal courts that the state court would not even allow a certified copy of the record in the case to be sent to the United States Attorney General to be used for further appeal.

By the time the case got to Washington in January 1859, the Supreme Court had concluded, via the *Dred Scott* case, that Negroes could never become citizens of the United States and that Congress could not ban slavery from any of the territories. The antislavery forces in the country heaped such abuse on the Court that its prestige in the North as a viable arm of the government disappeared. Chief Justice Roger Taney's opinion upholding the fugitive law was rejected by the Wisconsin legislature. It resolved that the Supreme Court's decision was "an arbitrary act of power, unauthorized by the Constitution, and virtually superseding the benefit of the writ of habeas corpus."

When the United States Attorney sought to file the Supreme Court's mandate in the Wisconsin court, the clerk refused to accept it. A federal marshal nevertheless arrested Booth in March 1860. His supporters broke into the jail in August to rescue him, but he was recaptured in October. He was finally released by President Buchanan just before the Civil War began.[40]

The activists who stepped outside the system were often encouraged to do so by their own elected representatives.[41] William Seward had begun the decade with his famous "higher law" speech. On March 11, 1850, during the debate on the compromise proposals, Seward attacked any extension of slavery in the new territories and any strengthening of the Fugitive Slave Law. As legislators, he told his fellow Senators:

We hold no arbitrary authority over anything, whether acquired lawfully or seized by usurpation. The Constitution regulates our stewardship; the Constitution devotes the domain to union, to justice, to defence, to welfare, and to liberty.

But there is a higher law than the Constitution, which regulates our authority over the domain, and devotes it to the same noble purposes. The territory is a part, no inconsiderable part, of the common heritage of mankind, bestowed upon them by the Creator of the universe. We are his stewards, and must so discharge our trust as to secure in the highest attainable degree their happiness.[42]

Owen Lovejoy in the House was even more defiant of the law.

I tell you that I have no more hesitation in helping a fugitive slave than I have in snatching a lamb from the jaws of a wolf, or disengaging an infant from the talons of an eagle . . .[43]

Joshua Giddings told his fellow congressmen:

The spirit which threw the tea into Boston Harbor will set your infamous law at defiance. The spirit which overthrew the power of the British crown will submit to no force that shall constrain them to comply with the odious provisions of this enactment.[44]

Many law enforcement officers and members of the judiciary—that last bastion of law and order—responded in the same way. Judge Theophilus Harrington of Vermont said that the only evidence of slave ownership he would accept was a bill of sale from God Almighty. Benjamin Wade, an Ohio judge in 1850, publicly declared he would never enforce the fugitive law. The two Ohio Supreme Court judges who voted to release Bushnell in the Oberlin-Wellington affair and the entire bench of the Wisconsin court in the Booth case were openly challenging federal law. The sheriffs who arrested U.S. marshals for assault and slaveowners for kidnapping, the judges who tried them, and the juries who convicted them, were all doing the same. Disobedience and defiance of an unquestionably valid federal law occurred in every Northern state, in every arm of the government, at every level, indeed in the very Congress that passed the act.

John Brown brought the question of conscientious disobedience to an explosive head. In December 1858, he attacked Fort Scott in Missouri to liberate a Kansas prisoner captured after a skirmish between free state and pro-slavery elements.[45] In the course of freeing the prisoner and eleven slaves, one of the defenders of the Fort was killed; the federal government put a price on Brown's head. Undaunted by the government and acclaimed by the people, Brown traveled in triumph through Iowa, Illinois, Ohio, Michigan, New York, and Massachusetts. He soon planned a more dramatic armed confrontation, an attack on Harper's Ferry, Virginia, where he hoped to seize the federal arsenal and give the signal for a slave uprising throughout the South.

The plan failed miserably. Ten of Brown's men were killed after the attack on October 15, 1859, five were captured, and Brown held out for less than thirty-six hours.[46] Within two weeks he was tried for fomenting insurrection, sentenced to death within three weeks, and short of two months after his raid, was hanged. Even (or particularly) under sentence of death Brown showed magnificent courage and moral grandeur, and he held the center of the national stage for weeks. On the day of his hanging, bells tolled throughout the North, memorial meetings were held in thousands of churches, and newspapers compared Brown with the great martyrs of history. Charles Eliot Norton wrote to an English friend: "I have seen nothing like it . . . The heart of the people was fairly reached, and an impression has been made upon it which will be permanent and produce results long hence . . . [Brown's raid and execution] have done more to confirm the opposition to slavery at the North . . . than anything which has ever happened before." [47]

The Republican Party did not endorse Brown's raid any more than they sanctioned wholesale disobedience of the Fugitive Slave Law. Lincoln said in his last debate with Douglas during the Illinois senatorial election in 1858 that he "constantly admitted . . . the legal right of the Southern people to reclaim their fugitives." [48] Nonetheless, the party rode to political victory on the antislavery sentiment catalyzed by John Brown.

The Northern response to the Fugitive Slave Law showed how powerful conscientious disobedience could be as a political tactic and an instrument of reform. At some point in the 1850's, a political plurality in the North arrived at the conclusion that there was something terribly wrong in dragging intelligent blacks like Anthony Burns and Little John Price back to slavery in the South. And contact with these men made the abstract horrors of that institution painfully concrete.

Thus the actions of Lewis Hayden, Theodore Parker, and the Jerry rescuers set in motion a process in which disobedience revealed the evils of the system more vividly than any amount of active political protest could have accomplished.

This point is often lost by critics who complain of the injustice of punishing the state's most conscientious citizens. Henry David Thoreau, who himself refused to pay his Massachusetts poll tax as a protest against the Mexican War, fudged the problem in his essay on *Civil Disobedience*:

Unjust laws exist: shall we be content to obey them, or shall we endeavor to amend them, and obey them until we have succeeded, or shall we transgress them at once? Men generally, under such government as this, think that they ought to wait until they have persuaded the majority to alter them. They think that, if they should resist, the remedy would be worse than the evil. But it is the fault of the government itself that the remedy *is* worse than the evil. *It* makes it worse. Why is it not more apt to anticipate and provide for reform? Why does it not cherish its wise minority? Why does it cry and resist before it is hurt? Why does it not encourage its citizens to be on the alert to point out its faults and *do* better than it would have them? Why does it always crucify Christ, and excommunicate Copernicus and Luther, and pronounce Washington and Franklin rebels? [49]

In short, government, by treating disobedience as treason instead of as a plea for reform, discourages its citizens from pointing out the government's faults through resistance to unjust laws. It "cries and resists" and severely punishes its critics who overstep legal bounds. If greater leniency were shown the "wise minority" who disobeyed a law for conscientious reasons, a government would be more readily alerted to its shortcomings.

But it is precisely because the government "cries and resists" and makes "the remedy . . . worse than the evil" that the body politic is spurred to action. Although many of the resisters were not chiefly concerned with the political implications of their actions and claimed they only followed their consciences in helping the slaves, it is always difficult to separate politics from personal morality. "The wise minority" articulated their sense of outrage at the legal order. Many others felt it less clearly, but finally were made fully aware of the evil through enforcement of the unjust laws which were directly challenged by the activists.

Thus Thoreau overlooked the final paradox in civil disobedience. The more lenient attitude toward conscientious lawbreakers which he recommended on grounds of morality would deprive them of their chief political weapon, namely the shock to the public conscience which only prosecution would be likely to produce. The fact that the disobedient act is public, nonviolent, and conscientious increases its capacity to shock and therefore to bring about a change in the law complained about. However the rescuers of Little John Price or Anthony Burns did use force without seriously diminishing their purpose. Nor was it necessary for the disobedient to readily accept punishment for the crime. Every conceivable defense was raised by Dana, Chase, and other lawyers whenever any of their clients were caught by the fugitive law. If there were some small legal doubt of the validity of the statute, it would also tend to increase the shock value of the disobedient act—how horrible punishment would be if the law were not only immoral but possibly invalid as well.

The controversy over the Fugitive Slave Law shows that much of the debate over civil disobedience misses the point. The question is not whether an act of disobedience has all the attributes which purists require: is it open, peaceful, and conscientious; is punishment gladly and eagerly accepted? Rather, the inquiry should be whether the disobedient act, whatever it is, fulfills a First Amendment purpose. Is one of its primary motives to move the political machine in a new direction by making the public aware of the reach and force of an unjust law or policy? Is it based on the broadest common moral sense of the people? Not to challenge immoral laws, to work only by peaceful methods of democratic reform, often is not enough. Those most strongly feeling the evil of the law—the wise minority—are not prepared to wait.

No one now doubts that what the activist Abolitionists did was crucial to the organization of an antislavery majority. It did not lead to an increase in personal crime by observers saying, "Well, if Theodore Parker can disobey the Fugitive Slave Law, I will pay no attention to the Massachusetts law on larceny." Anarchy did not prevail in the North because of episodes such as the Jerry rescue: the appeal to conscience and natural law which lay at the foundation of the Abolitionists' complaint was inconsistent with indiscriminate acts of violence.

The political impact of conscientious disobedience is not always acknowledged. Judges instinctively recoil from these less familiar and controllable methods of political reform. But the complaint of the "wise minority" has always needed time to make its impression.

# 4

# Labor Revolts

Over the past one hundred years, economic conflicts have been more intense and bitter in America than in any other country in the world. The fights were harsh and long; they affected millions of workers and farmers and created deep resentments that often came close to triggering revolution. The discord stemmed, moreover, from the very conditions that brought about our phenomenal economic success during the nineteenth century: a laissez-faire ideology that encouraged breakneck competition; enormous virgin territory and bountiful natural resources that invited exploitation; an entrepreneurial class that was second to none in ability, ruthlessness, and ambition; and above all, a governmental system that could be used by those on top of the economic ladder to advance their own interests.

In no other country was government so completely opposed to the laboring classes and nowhere else were so many legal rules established to stop them from improving their way of life or from increasing their share of the economic pie. The law was so blatantly wielded as a class weapon that workers and farmers felt they had to step outside the legal system merely to preserve their economic existence. They knew that the police and the courts were not neutral keepers of the public peace, but an arm of the oppressors. At the same time they tried to make political alliances to wrest away capitalist control of the state's police power. Thus throughout the nineteenth century, "illegal" activities by workers and farmers were a reaction to the government's partiality in economic disputes and became an essential instrument of political reform.

### A. EARLY UNION ACTIVITY

From the beginning, handy legal concepts and unsympathetic judges undermined all attempts to form labor unions. First efforts to suppress the labor movement took place around the turn of the nineteenth century. The government relied on the doctrine of "conspiracy" which has been the state's chief weapon against organized opposition from Federalist times to the 1968 Spock case in Boston and the 1969 Chicago Seven trial.

Journeymen shoemakers in Philadelphia "turned out" on strike in 1805 to demand that their masters restore wage cuts in the manufacture of boots for the export market.[1] (They received 25 cents more for domestic goods.) When the strike continued for some weeks, the Pennsylvania authorities arrested eight of the leaders, charging them with criminal conspiracy; the men went back to work at the lower rates. The arrests were based on tenuous English precedents and the general common law doctrine that "all confederacies whatsoever, wrongfully to prejudice a third person, are highly criminal at common law."[2] In England, the doctrine had occasionally been applied against entrepreneurs to prevent unfair competition, but now, in America, the stricture was used not against the capitalists but against the workers.

The Philadelphia Cordwainers Case, as it was called, became a cause célèbre of the day, bringing to light difficult problems of law, economics, and politics. Should the vague contours of the English common law, which gave judges wide discretionary powers, be incorporated into the American legal system? (A bill to supersede all the rules of the common law was introduced into the Pennsylvania legislature while the case was pending and lost by twelve votes.) Would a workers' combination boost the city's economy or hinder its growth? Should the Republicans fight the partisan Federalist judges who were using the common law against their interests even though Jefferson himself had called the urban workingmen "the panderers of vice and the instruments by which the liberties of a country are generally overthrown"?

The Republican Party's effort to block "Federalization" of the courts finally required that they support the shoemakers. As a result, Caesar Rodney, one year later Attorney General in Jefferson's Cabinet, defended the workers. He insisted in court that if the journeymen were treated fairly, experienced artisans would come from throughout the world to work in American shops; prosecution could only drive away skilled workers and increase the price of goods. Besides, it was subversive of American freedoms to prosecute men for trying to better their condition. But the conservative Republican judge, recorder Moses Levy, countered Rodney with the predictable claim that a combination of workers would interfere with the "natural" regulation of wages. Artificial increases, inconsistent with the law of supply and demand, would boost the prices and destroy trade in the city. Applying this laissez-faire logic, he told the jury that the law must condemn any organized activity on the part of the workers to better their lot. The jury found the strike leaders "guilty of a combination to raise their wages." Since the authorities were interested only in establishing a precedent, they asked for a mild sentence, and the defendants were fined eight dollars.[3]

The precedent was an important one. Subsequent criminal conspiracy cases were heard in Baltimore and New York in 1809 and in Pittsburgh in 1815.[4] Hatters, tailors, and spinners were prosecuted for picketing or striking in the 1820's. "The . . . conspiracy cases proved disastrous to many of the nation's early labor organizations . . . . The cases, in effect, destroyed the efficacy of the early labor organizations by strangling their activities."[5] New York State strengthened the questionable common law conspiracy doctrine and added an extra weapon to the fight against unionization by enacting a written statute in 1829 making it a crime to commit an act "injurious .'. . to trade or commerce."[6] After twenty tailors were found guilty of violating the law by picketing, the judge, John Edwards, proffered a statement of monumental hypocrisy. "Every American knows . . . that he has no better friend than the laws and that he needs no artificial combination for his protection. They [artificial combinations] are of foreign origin and I am led to believe mainly upheld by—Foreigners."[7]

After thirty years of suppression, labor's right to organize and strike was declared legal in 1842. A group of journeymen bootmakers had joined together in Boston in the 1830's. One of their fellow workers, Jeremiah Horne, refused to follow union rules and after a long dispute was fined seven dollars. Rather than pay, Horne complained to the district attorney in 1840 that the Bootmakers Society was illegal, relying on the earlier Cordwainers cases. Robert

Rantoul, Jr., in the midst of a fight to codify and reform the common law, defended the union. In his argument to the jury and trial court, he stressed that the state was trying to punish the workers by applying the restrictive rules of the English common law which "were part of the English tyranny from which we fled. They are repugnant to the Constitution and to the first principles of freedom." [8]

After losing in the trial court, Rantoul appealed to the Massachusetts Supreme Judicial Court, led by Chief Justice Lemuel Shaw, who later was to play such an ignoble role in the Abolitionist controversies of the 1850's. The judge declared that, to be guilty, the workers must combine to accomplish an illegal end or they must combine to accomplish a legal end by illegal means. Shaw found, first, that it was not unlawful for workers to organize to raise their wages or even to force other workers to join their society. As for the means adopted, the journeymen were individually free to work for an employer or not. "In this state of things," Shaw added, "we cannot perceive that it is criminal for men to agree together to exercise their own acknowledged rights in such a manner as best to subserve their own interests." He noted that the workingmen's activities were part of the competition that pervades all business life. ". . . It is through competition that the best interests of trade and industry are promoted." [9]

The widely disseminated *Hunt* decision became the "Magna Charta of American trade unionism." [10] The earlier Cordwainers cases from 1800 to 1815, the conspiracy cases of the 1820's, and the New York cases of the 1830's had seriously restricted union growth. But in the wake of the *Hunt* case, only a few courts would rely on a criminal conspiracy charge against labor organization.

The fact that union organizing and collective bargaining was once thought of as coercive and illegal shows how subtly the interests of the dominant class become entwined with the legal process itself. The law tends to preserve a political and economic structure that benefits one group within the state. It is easy to identify an attack upon the structure as an attack upon the government and upon society itself. The unions offended the prevailing political sentiment in the early 1800's and therefore had to face restrictive laws which undermined their power. The idea that the workers might have a right to band together to pursue their own interests in a more effective way was rejected out of hand by almost all the judges of the early nineteenth century, for whom an employer's freedom of contract and right to control his property was far more important.

For fully one hundred years, the legal process was to be used by the employer class to undercut the strongest assertion of labor power. In 1926, Edwin E. Witte wrote: "The decisions of the courts today upon what conduct in the furtherance of the objects of labor unions is lawful, are not one whit more liberal than the doctrines announced in the earliest conspiracy cases." [11]

## B. LABOR VIOLENCE

While the authorities permitted labor to organize after the *Hunt* case, they soon found ways of blocking any effective use of the workers' unified strength. The new capitalist entrepreneurs after the Civil War squeezed the workers dry, and then quickly squelched labor's desperate counterresponse with the state's full police power. Skillful propaganda attributed the resulting violence to labor, and it forfeited public sympathy for its cause, allowing the employers to take even more repressive measures. The forty years after the Civil War were the blackest period in American labor history.

It began with the widespread publicity surrounding the secret society of Irish immigrants known as the Molly Maguires, an episode which convinced many that labor would engage in any type of violence to further its ends. In the 1850's, a large community of Irish settled in the anthracite coal fields of Pennsylvania. Fleeing the terrible famine in their homeland, these refugees soon found themselves confronted by other problems—religious prejudice and severe economic pressure. Supervisory personnel in the mines were generally of English or Welsh origin, Protestant, and native born. Rumors of an Irish secret society formed to protect the miners soon spread throughout the region. By the late 1860's, an average of fifteen men a year—foremen, policemen, owners or their agents—were murdered in the anthracite region, and although the authorities made not a single arrest, all the crimes were blamed on the Molly Maguires.

During the same time, the miners themselves formed a Workingmen's Benevolent Association. At first they won some concessions from the mine operators, but overproduction led to drastic wage cuts and a bitter strike in 1871. When violent incidents against mine owners and their underlings continued in 1872 and 1873, Franklin B. Gowen, head of the Philadelphia and Reading Railroad and an important shipper and mine owner, hired the Pinkerton Detective Agency to investigate and specifically to determine if there was any connection between the miners' union and the Molly Maguires.

Pinkerton sent a young detective, James McParlan, to infiltrate the Mollies. He eventually became a "bodymaster"—one of the enforcers of the organization—and sent precise accounts of their activities to Pinkerton and Gowen. Although McParlan reported that most of the active Mollies, the executioners, were not union men at

all, but saloon keepers, "idlers and roughs, more concerned with
internal squabbling than with mining," Gowen saw the chance to
blame the workers for the murders and to club "all union activity
under the guise of preserving law and order." [12] He and Pinkerton
gathered evidence over a period of years and then arranged for the
arrest of the Molly leaders.

McParlan testified in the first sensational trial in May 1876 and
in the proceedings that followed—most of them prosecuted by
Gowen himself as a special district attorney. His stories of the
avenging function of the Mollies and the wide extent of its membership for illegal purposes made headlines across the country. The
connections between the Mollies and the miners' union were very
tenuous and the defendants had practically no relation to the union
movement as a whole; but the press, encouraged by employer
groups, emphasized that the victims were always union enemies and
editorialized that labor militancy led to the murders.[13]

The Molly Maguire trials convinced many that labor would engage in any type of violence to further its ends.* This was confirmed
in the great riots of 1877. The spring of that year, various eastern
railroads announced a wage reduction for most of their employees.
On July 16, forty firemen and brakemen of the Baltimore and Ohio
spontaneously walked off their jobs in Camden Junction, Maryland.
The next day the stoppage spread to Martinsburg, West Virginia.
The state militia was called in to keep order, but the soldiers sym-
pathized with the workers and many refused to fight their fellow
townsmen. The Governor asked President Rutherford Hayes for
regular troops, who arrested the leaders and finally stopped the disturbances.

The worst center of disorder was Pittsburgh. Strikers from the
Pennsylvania Railroad closed down the local terminal. Again the
militia was brought into service, but they also joined the workers.
The Governor then sent in the Philadelphia militia who became nervous at the defiance of the crowd and fired into it, killing over twenty
men. (A grand jury later called the incident "an unauthorized, willful,
and wanton killing . . . which the inquest can call by no other name

---

* The labor movement itself accepted the Mollies as their own martyrs.
Eugene Debs wrote in *Appeal to Reason*: "It is true that their methods were
drastic, but it must be remembered that their lot was hard and *brutalizing*;
that they were the neglected children of poverty, the product of a wretched
environment . . . The men who perished upon the scaffold as felons were
labor leaders, the first martyrs to the class struggle in the United States." Louis
Adamic observed: "By killing mineowners and bosses by the dozen, by beating up hundreds of others, the Mollies unquestionably improved the working
conditions not only for themselves but for all the miners in the anthracite
regions of Pennsylvania and saved many workers' lives." [14]

but murder.")[15] The people became enraged, set fire to and destroyed $5,000,000 of railroad property, and then drove the militia out of the city. A larger military force was sent into Pittsburgh a few days later to restore calm.

Railroad workers started a walkout in Chicago and were quickly joined by workers in other trades. Led by Albert R. Parsons, a young labor agitator from Alabama, the workers pressed for an eight-hour day in a series of strikes. In late July, the strikers engaged in pitched battles on the city streets against thousands of police and militiamen. Thirty men were killed and hundreds wounded.

The Railway Strikes of 1877 and the ensuing riots in Pennsylvania, San Francisco, and St. Louis were spontaneous outbursts of the lowest economic classes who had suffered through the crash of 1873 and its aftermath. In terms of the numbers killed and property destroyed, they dwarfed the summer racial uprisings of the 1960's. Similar proletarian outbursts (including the Paris Commune of 1870–1871) were taking place in Europe at the time. Four years of terrible deprivation and an even longer period of constant opposition by the employers (who would often reduce their workers' already inadequate wages in the most casual manner), the working class' lack of effective political power, and the absence of any hope for the future brought the rage of the people to a boiling point. But most of the killings and property damage was due in fact to the overreaction of the authorities. The Pittsburgh outburst, for example, got out of hand only because the militia decided to deal with a hostile crowd by firing into it.

Moderate political opinion was offended by the violence of the times and supported many repressive measures to hamstring labor organization. Criminal conspiracy laws were strengthened, and armories were built in the centers of the larger cities to enable the militia (newly organized into the National Guard) to hold off future worker-mobs. The public accepted all the retaliatory devices that the bosses were to use in coming years—the yellow-dog contract, the black list, importation of foreign strikebreakers, and the lock-out.

The next major outburst was the Haymarket affair. In the spring of 1886, the union movement campaigned for the eight-hour day in all industries. Chicago was the center of the agitation and a bitter labor dispute with the McCormick Harvester Company added to the tension in that city. A group of McCormick strikers held a mass meeting near the plant on May 3 and were peacefully dispersing when the strikebreakers were let out of the plant. They were promptly embroiled in a fight with the strikers. In the ensuing melee, the police shot into the crowd, killing four men.[16]

August Spies, an anarchist who had been addressing the McCormick rally, prepared a fiery circular, headlined "Revenge!" advocating that the workers arm themselves and "destroy the hideous monster that seeks to destroy you." He called for a rally the next day, May 4, 1886, at Haymarket Square to protest the police action of the day before. The rally was held at night and Spies, Albert R. Parsons, and Samuel Fielden, another anarchist leader, spoke to the workers. The speakers harangued the crowd about the class struggle and the oppression of the workers, but the meeting remained peaceful. Rain started to fall, and Mayor Carter H. Harrison left the square, convinced "nothing is likely to occur to require interference." He told a police captain that he could send his men home. For unknown reasons, the captain disobeyed the orders and sent a squadron of 176 police to break up the proceedings, which were about to end in any event.[17] As the police marched to the speaker's stand, a bomb exploded, killing a sergeant and injuring over sixty men. In the exchange of gunfire that followed, ten workers were killed and over fifty injured. Seven of the police also died, probably from bullets fired by their fellow officers.

Who threw the bomb is still a mystery. It could have been an agent provocateur, a citizen with a nonlabor grievance against the police, or a madman. However, the police and the public assumed immediately that the anarchists, and therefore the labor movement, were to blame. The authorities arrested Spies, Parsons, and Fielden as well as five other anarchists who were not even present at the meeting. The fact that anarchists had theoretically advocated violence—particularly the use of bombs—against the police was sufficient to charge the leaders with the crime, a chilling foreshadow of another Chicago trial, eighty-three years later. They were tried in July 1886, quickly found guilty, and seven sentenced to be hanged. Judge Joseph E. Gary, who presided at the trial, found that the defendants "had generally by speech and print advised large classes to commit murder and had left the commission, the time, the place, and when to the individual will, whim or caprice . . . of each individual man who listened to their advice." [18] Spies, Parsons, and two others were executed in November 1887. One other defendant committed suicide and three others were freed in 1893.[19]

The reaction of the authorities to Haymarket was predictable. New antilabor laws were passed in almost every state. Prosecutors brought criminal conspiracy charges against union members and arrested the leaders for intimidation or inciting to riot when they organized strikes. The trade unions saw that political action alone could offset the antilabor legislation, and alliances were formed with

Greenbackers, Anti-Monopolists, Single-Taxers, Grangers, and members of the Farmers Alliance. This united front pressed for various kinds of labor legislation in the next decade, including laws calling for arbitration of industrial disputes and factory and mine safety, prohibiting the worst abuses of child and woman labor, and fixing maximum hours. The record of enactment was spotty, but enough of an advance was made to encourage the labor movement to greater political activity in the ensuing years.

Yet simultaneously, labor was suffering its greatest defeats in the 1890's—namely, the Homestead and Pullman strikes. The Carnegie Steel Company, with Henry Clay Frick as general manager (Andrew Carnegie was in Scotland at the time), ordered a series of wage cuts in 1892 and while the employees were preparing to strike, the company closed down the large Homestead plant in July 1892. Frick dismissed every one of the workers, union and nonunion, claiming that he would deal with them individually, not with any organization that claimed to represent them. Three hundred Pinkertons came down the Monongahela River in barges to guard the plant. But the workers discovered the plan and, armed, thousands were on hand at dawn on July 6, 1892, to repel the agents.

The Pinkertons attempted to land nevertheless. They were shot at—the detectives fired back: three agents and nine strikers were killed, and over thirty men wounded. Greatly outnumbered, the Pinkertons surrendered. In a few days, seven thousand troops were dispatched to the city and restored order.

On July 23, 1892, a Russian-born anarchist, Alexander Berkman, entered Frick's office and shot him twice, but the wounds were not fatal. As scabs poured into Homestead in the coming months, they were ambushed, beaten, and some wounded by armed strikers. Before the strike ended in total victory for the company, forty men had died and over four hundred were wounded. With his plant manned by many newly arrived immigrants and Negroes who worked for a fraction of the union wages, Carnegie increased his profits enormously in the next decade, making possible the philanthropy of his later years. The union did not recover its position in the steel industry until after World War I.[20]

Another strong union crushed by the authorities was the American Railway Union, organized by Eugene V. Debs. Employees of the Pullman Palace Car Company walked off their jobs in 1894 to protest a 22 percent cut in their wages and the firing of their union representatives. George Pullman, the paternalistic owner of the company, refused to talk to the union, and Debs called for a sympathetic boycott against the Pullman company by all railway employees throughout the country. Since Pullman cars were carried on virtually every carrier, the effect of the strike was felt nationwide. United States Attorney General Richard Olney met the crisis by having the local federal district attorneys in Chicago secure an injunction—one of the first issued in a labor dispute[21]—forbidding the union from interfering with the delivery of the mails or otherwise unlawfully restraining commerce in violation of the Sherman Anti-Trust Act. The injunction was read to a group of sriking workers on the Rock Island Railroad outside of Chicago on July 2, 1894, and when they failed to disperse, the administration had an excuse for sending in federal troops. (The records of both the Chicago police and the General Managers Association—a semi-secret group of railroad executives in Chicago that decided employer strategy during the strike—show that no serious disturbances occurred until federal troops arrived.) The state militia and five thousand federal marshals were already on hand. Still, Olney was concerned that the liberal governor of the state, John P. Altgeld, would handle the situation with restraint,[22] and the Attorney General was determined to precipitate a crisis. He succeeded. Once again, the most serious violence was brought about by the troops, who responded with bullets to the strikers' insults and brick-throwing. Before the strike was over, thirty-four men were killed. Altgeld sent the militia into the city after violent disturbances began, and within hours fourteen thousand armed troops patrolled the streets of Chicago.

In the meantime, the government brought charges against Debs for violating the injunction issued against the union. On appeal to the Supreme Court, it unanimously held that the injunction was properly issued since the government had a duty to insure that freedom of the mails and of interstate commerce be maintained. Debs had violated the injunction and therefore could be punished for contempt.[23]

Attorney General Olney congratulated himself that the *Debs* decision and the dispatch of troops were vital for the continuation of government. "We have been brought to the ragged edge of anarchy,"[24] he said. Others in the country were not so sure. The use of federal soldiers, the arrest of seven hundred union leaders, the jailing of Debs, and the heavy-handed use of the injunction to break up an economic dispute perturbed many outside the labor movement. After the hysteria receded, a presidential commission investigated the strike, castigated the Pullman company for provoking the confrontation, and excused the union from any blame in initiating the violence.

"Real responsibility for these disorders rests with the people themselves and with the Government for not adequately controlling monopolies and corporations, and for failing to reasonably protect the rights of labor and redress its wrongs." [25] The report of the commission called for the government to "fully recognize" unions "by law; to admit their necessity as labor guides and protectors, to conserve their usefulness, increase their responsibilities . . ." The commission recommended compulsory arbitration of all labor disputes concerning the railway system.

As usual, the liberal proposals of a Presidential commission were all but totally ignored.* Congress did not implement any of the proposals made by the Commission until thirty years later and its chief recommendation—for legal recognition of collective bargaining—was not enacted until 1933.

Nonetheless the Pullman strike was a turning-point in labor-management relations. The injunction allowed the authorities to put the workers outside the law as soon as they started to strike. Just when the unions had learned the lessons of organization and collective action, the courts found a means to block any effective use of their new power.

The use of the injunction in a labor dispute was a peculiarly American innovation. (In England the Court of Chancery refused to intervene in industrial conflicts after a few abortive attempts in the 1860's.) [26] The Sherman Anti-Trust Act of 1890 banned "every . . . combination . . . or conspiracy in restraint of trade or commerce among the several states, and the courts soon saw the opportunity to catch unions in the net of the new law. After the *Debs* decision, the federal courts issued injunction after injunction at the behest of management to stop even the most peaceful strikes or labor activity.

The exact number of injunctions issued against unions from 1895 to 1932 when the Norris-LaGuardia Act banned their use in the federal courts is unknown. Felix Frankfurter and Nathan Greene in their famous book on the subject found only 118 reported federal cases between 1901 and 1930, but they discovered that hundreds of unreported injunctions had been issued in the same period.

In the great majority of these cases, management was successful in enjoining union activity. Of 118 reported federal cases, the employer prevailed in over one hundred. Furthermore, the relief was

* Recently, the same fate has met the recommendations of the United States Riot Commission (headed by Governor Otto Kerner), Milton Eisenhower's Violence Commission, the Walker Report on the Chicago riots, and the Cox Report on the Columbia student uprising. As Murray Kempton has pointed out, as things get worse, our presidential reports get better.

swift. In 88 of the 118 cases a temporary injunction was issued in a matter of days after the complaint was filed; in 70 of those cases an ex parte restraining order was issued by the court and the defendant unions never even had the opportunity of being heard.[27]

Furthermore, that initial restraining order was often the final legal action in the case. "It is undeniably the fact that the preliminary injunction in the main determines and terminates the controversy in the court. The tentative truth results in making ultimate truth irrelevant." [28] In case after case the initial court order, backed up by militia regiments, destroyed whatever power the unions sought to assert against the employers.

Some courts attempted to distinguish among strikes—higher wages, shorter hours, and better working conditions were thought permissible goals. But strikes for a union shop, or other devices to strengthen an existing union were banned. Some judges found peaceful picketing objectionable. An Iowa federal court said: "There is and can be no such thing as peaceful picketing, any more than there can be chaste vulgarity, or peaceful mobbing, or lawful lynching." [29]

Injunctions would generally run against the widest range of individuals and forbid the broadest possible activity. The Debs injunction applied to certain named defendants, "all persons combining and conspiring with them and all other persons whomsoever." In another famous labor case, *Bucks Stove and Range Co.* v. *Gompers (1911)*, the defendant union was forbidden from "interfering in any manner with . . . the complainant's . . . business."

The same year that the *Gompers* case was decided by the circuit court, the Supreme Court issued a still harsher decision against labor. The Hatters Union of Danbury, Connecticut, had organized a boycott of the Loewe Company after a bitter strike against that clothing manufacturer. Loewe sued the union under the Sherman Act, claiming that it was engaging in a conspiracy in restraint of trade. Although there was no precedent for suing a union for damages under the antitrust laws, the Supreme Court upheld a judgment of $240,000 against the union.[30] The case suggested that all union activity could be interpreted as an illegal conspiracy under the antitrust laws and employers could therefore sue unions for damages and bankrupt them. By law, management could not only block the union, but break it as well.

The federal judges who heard the injunctive and damage suits against labor were for the most part totally unsympathetic to the workers. Even after Congress in the Clayton Act of 1914 had specifically provided that "no injunction . . . shall be granted by any court . . . in any case between an employer and employees," the federal courts narrowly interpreted the language and continued to enjoin all kinds of union activity. Frankfurter noted that "hostility to all picketing was too deeply engrained in the mental habits of the federal judges to yield to the language of the Clayton Act." The Supreme Court eventually held that the Clayton Act was simply "declaratory of what was the best practice always" and did not substantively change the law as previously interpreted.[31]

Furthermore, the United States Supreme Court declared unconstitutional many types of prolabor legislation by both the state and federal governments. Laws banning yellow-dog contracts or fixing maximum hours or minimum wages were found invalid in a series of decisions from 1890 to the 1930's.[32] These laws interfered with the workers' "freedom of contract" said the Supreme Court, and therefore violated the due process clause of the Fourteenth Amendment.

The courts' frequent use of the injunction and its antilabor bias in other cases confirmed the working class' view that legal justice was the privilege of management. A few judges anticipated the inevitable resentment of the workers and the violent direction it had to take. Justice Brandeis complained that the injunction was "endowing property with active militant power which would make it dominant over men." [33] The United States Commission on Industrial Relations said in 1915: "There exists among the workers an almost universal conviction that they . . . are denied justice in the enactment, adjudication and administration of law, that the very instruments of democracy are often used to oppress them and to place obstacles in the way of their movement towards economic, industrial and political freedom and justice." [34] A federal judge wrote in 1922: "Force and violence are strangers to neither party to strikes . . . the parties forget that aggression incites retaliation, and violence breeds violence. Then, too, the pickets of one are generally confronted, if not over-awed, by armed guards of the other, and by police, sheriffs, and marshals, who too often forget they are public officers with duty to protect both parties, and mistakenly assume they are partisans of one party or the other." [35]

From 1890 to 1935 when the Wagner Act guaranteeing the right to organize was passed, there was hardly a year when some violent clash did not take place. In a paper submitted to the National Violence Commission in June 1969, Philip Taft and Philip Ross detailed the extent of labor violence in this period.[36] Their findings show the following typical incidents:

| Year | Location of Dispute | Cause of Violence | Government Interference | Men Killed | Men Injured |
|------|---------------------|-------------------|------------------------|------------|-------------|
| 1890's* | Coeur d'Alene, Idaho | lowering of wages lockout by mine owners | federal troops | 6 | 20 |
| 1890's | Tennessee | use of convict labor in coal mines | state troops | | |
| 1894 | Alabama | use of Negro strikebreakers in coal mines | state militia | 6 | |
| 1895 | Brooklyn, N.Y. | use of strikebreakers | 7,500 militia | 1 | |
| 1897 | Hazelton, Pa. | sheriff firing on peaceful miners protesting high prices at company store | sheriff deputies | 18 | 40 |
| 1898 | Virden, Ill. | use of strikebreakers in miners' strike | national guard | 14 | |
| 1900's | Albany, N.Y. Pawtucket, R.I. Waterbury, Conn. San Francisco Philadelphia Columbus, Ohio | transit strikes use of strikebreakers | troops | approximately 20 | |
| 1901 | San Francisco | use of strikebreakers | local police | 5 | unknown |
| 1902 | Carbon County, Pa. | use of strikebreakers, company police | entire national guard | 14 | 58 |
| 1901– 1903 | Telluride County, Colo. | use of strikebreakers; seizing of mine by workers | state militia | 5 | unknown |

\* In 1892 the metal miners in Coeur d'Alene, Idaho, seized a mine after the owners had hired armed guards and strikebreakers in a labor dispute. A mine and a quartz mill were dynamited by the men before the Governor brought in militia and federal troops. Martial law was declared, union men were arrested and kept in stockades, and the leaders convicted of conspiracy. Nevertheless, in the coming years workers organized the Western Federation of Miners and rapidly won recognition from many owners. One notable holdout was the Bunker Hill and Sullivan Company in Coeur d'Alene. In 1899, a group of masked men seized a Northern Pacific train, drove it to Bunker Hill, and then dynamited the entire mill. Governor Frank Steunenberg immediately asked for federal troops (the Idaho National Guard was in the Philippines at the time), and again the area was placed under martial law. The state auditor, Bartlet Sinclair, replaced pro-union local officials with antilabor men and had large numbers of union members kept in makeshift stockades for months. Steunenberg was later killed by a bomb and William Haywood, the I.W.W. leader, was tried for the crime. Clarence Darrow successfully defended him.

| Year | Location of Dispute | Cause of Violence | Govern- ment Inter- ference | Men Killed | Men Injured |
|------|---------------------|-------------------|------------------------------|------------|-------------|
| 1903– 1904* | Cripple Creek, Colo. | use of state militia after peaceful strike | state militia | 42 | 112 |
| 1905 | Chicago | use of strikebreakers in teamster strike | special po- licemen | 20 | 400 |
| 1906 | Gray's Harbor, Wash. | use of strikebreakers in seamen's strike | sheriff | 2 | |
| 1909 | McKees Rock, Pa. | steelworkers strike or- ganized by I.W.W. | private guards, special deputies | 13 | |
| 1909 | Great Lakes | canceling seamen's union contract | regular po- lice | 5 | |
| 1910 | Chicago | refusal to negotiate with garment workers' union | police, pri- vate guards | 7 | |
| 1911 | Illinois | use of strikebreakers in Illinois Central Railroad strike | state militia | 13 | |
| 1912 | Ely, Nev. | use of strikebreakers in mining strike | state police | 2 | |
| 1912 | Cabin Creek, W. Va. | use of detectives, pri- vate guards in coal mining strike | state militia | 13 | |
| 1913 | Mount Hope, N.J. | shooting of steel work- ers by company guards | private guards | 5 | |
| 1913 | Ludlow, Colo. | use of armed guards in mining strike | private guards | 45 | |
| 1915– 1916 | Bayonne, N.J. | shooting of oil work- ers by company guards | sheriff | 10 | |
| 1917– 1918 | Gary, Ind. | strike against U.S. Steel | state militia | 20 | |
| 1919 | Farrell, Pa. | private guards attack steel strikers | state militia | 3 | 11 |

* In the Colorado labor wars of 1903–1904, the Governor of the state, James Peabody, declared martial law and sent troops into the mining towns where strikers fought armed company guards. Local vigilantes, organized into a Citizen's Alliance, helped the militia round up all union members, hundreds of whom were kept in jail or open bullpens without trial and then deported to Kansas. After many complaints were made about the high-handed military treatment of the workers, the commanding general of the state troops, Major Thomas McClelland, commented, "To hell with the Constitution . . . We are not following the Constitution."

| Year | Location of Dispute | Cause of Violence | Government Interference | Men Killed | |
|------|---------------------|-------------------|------------------------|-----------|---|
| 1920 | Denver, Colo. | transit strike | federal troops | 7 | 81 |
| 1920–1921 | Logan County, W. Va. | mining strike | private guards | 31 | |
| 1922 | Herrin, Ill. | mining strike | private guards | 25 | |
| 1922–1923 | 27 states | Railroad shopmen's union strike after wage cuts | special deputies | 33 | |
| 1927 | Walsenberg, Colo. | coal miners' strike; pickets killed by private guards | special constables | 6 | |
| 1929 | Marion, N.C. | textile workers' strike; pickets killed by private guards | state militia | 6 | 24 |
| 1930's | Harlan County, Ky. | coal miners' strike | deputies | 10 | |

This report to the Violence Commission concluded that violence was almost always unsuccessful as a labor tactic.

The victories gained by violent strikes are rather few, for the use of violence tends to bring about a hardening of attitudes and a weakening of the forces of peace and conciliation. A community might be sympathetic to the demands of strikers but as soon as violent confrontations took place the possibility was high that interest would shift from concern for the acceptance of union demands to the stopping of the violence.[37]

The premise behind this statement is that labor chose violence as an initial and deliberate strategy in its disputes with management, which is a gross misinterpretation of the report itself. The implication for black militants and student rebels is that they must avoid the mistakes of labor and reject violence as a political or social weapon.

Such an approach discounts the way in which labor violence arose. In the period from 1877 to 1937, the bulk of the violent deaths was the result of force being used *against,* not *by,* striking employees. Time after time the police, armed constables, or private guards would disperse peaceful pickets by shooting into crowds of unarmed workers. Such incidents took place in Hazelton, Pa. in 1897, Ipswich, Mass. in 1913, Metuchen, N.J. in 1914, and Farrell, Pa. in 1919. As late as May 30, 1937, ten unarmed pickets were killed and thirty wounded by police "protecting" the Republic Steel Corporation plant in South Chicago, Ill. A Senate Committee reported that police violence was not justified in that situation since the workers merely used abusive language and threw a few bricks in front of the plant.

The arrogance and stubbornness of capitalist leaders such as George Pullman and Charles Schwab of Bethlehem Steel, who refused even to talk to union representatives, let alone bargain in good faith with them, drove labor groups into asserting what little economic power they had through strikes, boycotts, and picketing. The owners responded by employing strikebreakers and armed guards backed by the courts and troops. At that point the workers sought to neutralize the employers' superior force in order to avoid total defeat. Necessarily this meant intimidating the scabs and Pinkertons hired by the bosses, and the confrontation would lead to violence, generally initiated by the strikebreakers. Thus labor violence was not the opening play but more often a last defensive measure by the workers.

It is difficult to believe the workers would have been more successful if they had quietly picketed while strikebreakers took over their jobs. The less militant craft unions of the A. F. of L. won many disputes because they represented smaller economic units composed of workers with special skills, not because they had public opinions on their side and did not engage in violence. Even so, the period of active employer counterattacks from 1900 to 1920 was a time of retreat for even the craft unions, whose peacefulness did not save them from wage cuts and open shop campaigns.

The second conclusion of Taft and Ross—that violence always failed to help labor—is also questionable. Union leaders eventually became aware of the publicity value of violence. Labor journalist Louis Adamic writes: "Evil labor conditions or even strikes in the United States are big news, as a rule, only after either the workers or the police or both employ violence . . . Labor leaders recognize the importance of getting their causes before the public. Often the only way they can get it is to resort to, or provoke the police to, violence." [38] Insofar as labor leaders deliberately provoked violent incidents, they concluded that publicizing their grievances could more than offset any adverse reaction to these clashes. Certainly by the 1930's, labor disorder no longer offended the majority of the country and important reforms could still be instituted after the bloody strikes of the early New Deal.

Even in the 1890's and 1900's, class solidarity followed directly from the worst clashes and most serious economic defeats of labor. Violence and official suppression can promote group self-awareness and thus increase the strength and cohesion of a dominated class. It can also encourage alliances with other dominated classes which then open the ultimate possibility of political success through democratic means. Bruce Peck has recently written about deliberate acts of disobedience:

1) They may be provocative, i.e., they may tend to disrupt the normal functioning of the state, provoking the dominant interest group into a display of coercion which cannot be reconciled with the values or ideals upon which it bases its claims that existing social, political, and economic institutions are legitimate. This disclosure of hypocrisy is intended to weaken the persuasiveness of these claims within the dominated group and among members of other interest-groups who are potential allies of the dominated group.

2) They may promote group self-awareness by exposing the manner in which it is exploited and identifying the group responsible for its exploitation. This acts, in turn, to further unify the dominated group.

3) They may forcefully articulate the demands of the dominated group to other groups and to the dominant group, demonstrating that the dominated group, having become aware of the actuality and the causes of its exploitation, refuses to remain quiescent or merely supplicative.[39]

All of these purposes were unquestionably served by labor militancy. The constant use of the police by the state on behalf of the employers taught the workers that raw force was the chief instrument of American-capitalistic government. The working class became fully aware of the extent of their oppression. The class conflicts showed the farmers and other oppressed groups the extent of business control of the economy and government, and made possible the political alliances that brought about the reforms of the Progressive Era, Wilson's New Freedom Program, and the New Deal.

It was not until the Norris-LaGuardia Act banned federal court injunctions in labor disputes and the National Industrial Recovery Act of 1933 guaranteed the right of workers to bargain collectively that violence began to wane. The Wagner Act, passed in 1935, provided even stronger institutional machinery for resolving labor disputes and put the government in the role of umpire rather than antagonist. The proposals made by the Presidential Commission in 1895 following the Pullman strike were finally adopted forty years later, after thousands of violent incidents had proved their validity.

The history of labor violence in America, "the bloodiest and most violent labor history of any industrial country in the world," [40] shows how crucial is the use of public power in any social struggle. England avoided violent industrial disputes by permitting the widest leeway to the parties so they might resolve their problems by economic power alone. Even autocratic European governments, such as Prussia, passed paternalistic laws protecting certain of labor's rights. Similarly, the ruthlessness of American industrial barons could have been tamed by the government as it was finally during the New Deal.

What produced the continuous violence of the labor struggles here was the misuse of governmental power. Unless the state, at the very least, preserves some semblance of impartiality in social conflicts, and gives reform movements some chance for maneuver, it will abdicate its claim to legitimacy, which is the best safeguard of peace and order.

# 5

# Farm Revolts

The farmers' conflicts with the Establishment were somewhat different from those of the labor unions. True, the farmers found the legal machinery of the state closely allied with their economic enemies —the large landowners, railroad entrepreneurs, and capitalist customers. And, like the laborers, they knew that force would impress upon the nation the extent of their grievances. But the farmers had much greater numbers and therefore more political power than the unions ever possessed. Once the farmers marshaled their forces, they were able to win political victories which eventually offset the economic power of big business.

One of the most widespread and bitter farm revolts took place in the early 1840's in the area surrounding the Helderberg Mountains near Albany, New York. Nearly 300,000 farmers lived on enormous estates there, tied to the land by a system of feudal tenure established in the 1600's and still in force in the 1830's. The efforts of the farmers to do away with the degrading stranglehold of a few baronial owners showed how crucial defiance of the law could be in movements of political and economic reform.[1]

The leading patroon of the area was Stephen Van Rensselaer III, who had some 100,000 tenants and a domain as large as that of many medieval kings: more than a million acres of land encompassing all of Albany and Rensselaer Counties and part of Columbia County. Van Rensselaer's tenants had all the burdens of ownership but none of the benefits. They could rent a piece of his land for a purchase price of four fat fowls and ten to fourteen bushels of winter wheat each year. The feudal requirement of service to the landlord exacted from each farmer one day's work per year, with his team, to the "seller." The tenant was responsible for paying all the taxes, but Van Rensselaer retained all mineral, water, and timber rights for himself. Use of the land was restricted to farming. The property might be sold, but the new purchaser was subject to all the conditions of the original sale, and the patroon could collect one quarter of the selling price.

Fully two million acres of land were held subject to these restrictions by families such as the Van Rensselaers, Livingstons, Verplancks, and Desbrosses. Before 1839 most of the farmers grudgingly accepted the system, especially since many of the owners were generous in overlooking rent payments in hard times. But on the death of "The Good Patroon," Stephen Van Rensselaer III, in January 1839, his holdings passed to his two sons, Stephen IV and William, who immediately pressed for payment of past-due installments from their tenants. A farmer delegation came to see Stephen IV in May 1839, calling for the substitution of money rent for produce, the grant of all natural resource rights to the tenants, the end of the quarter-sale restriction, and the forgiving of all back rents. They also insisted on some plan allowing purchase of free title to the land at a price of about two dollars an acre. Stephen flatly rejected the terms without even talking to the farmers. The leaders of the farmer delegation, Lawrence Van Deusen and Hugh Scott, called a mass meeting on July 4, 1839, where the principles of the Declaration of Independence and the example of the Boston Tea Party were vehemently discussed.

Skirmishes commenced a month later, when Stephen IV decided to evict delinquent farmers as a reply to their protest. The first deputy carrying ejectment papers was greeted by the concerted blasts of tin horns, but managed to serve his warrants without further incident. The next process server came a week later; a group of fifty farmers forced him to burn all the summonses, and then treat his assailants to drinks at the local tavern. In December, a one-hundred-man posse under Sheriff Michael Artcher was turned away from the Helderbergs by a thousand farmers wielding pitchforks and clubs. Artcher promptly called on Governor William H. Seward—later a Senator, and Secretary of State under Lincoln—for armed militia. Seward complied, but at the same time indicated his sympathies with the farmers' position and pledged to look into their grievances.

Throughout 1840, Seward and a legislative committee tried to mediate the dispute. But Stephen Van Rensselaer preferred things as they were, and in March of 1841 he instructed the new sheriff of Albany County to seize the livestock of farmers persistent in not paying back rent. Before the sheriff could hold an auction, a group of "Indians" appeared "dressed in loose pantaloons and tunics of brilliant calico, decked with fur, feathers, and tin ornaments," [2] their faces either painted, or masked with sheepskin. The "Indians" drove off the potential bidders for the cattle, and the auction had to be postponed.

The "Indian" disguise—symbol of the Boston Tea Party—became the farmers' emblem. The leaders of the movement continued to stress political organization in 1842 and 1843, but the ineffectiveness of the legislature convinced the farmers that they had to move into extra-legal avenues. Anti-rent associations sprang up in every county early in 1844. Each community organized "Indian" bands, and many farmers pledged to fight the landlords "as long as life lasts." At the start, the "Indians" restricted their use of force to forestalling the service of legal papers upon them. If a deputy refused to burn all the summonses in his possession, he was likely to be tarred and feathered, but actual armed confrontations were avoided.

The landlords, however, reacted with a call for more police protection. In the summer of 1844, they put pressure on William C. Bouck, the new Democratic governor, to call out the militia, as Seward had done four years before. Instead, Bouck rode into the Helderbergs and talked sympathetically with the farmers, promising to look into the matter again and to prevent wholesale evictions until he completed his investigation. Stephen IV, however, insisted on precipitating a crisis. Assuming that the farmers' rowdiness would eventually antagonize Bouck, Van Rensselaer sent additional deputies into Albany County to evict nonpaying farmers. They were all tarred and feathered and their papers burned. The stalemate continued.

At this point the professional men in the area joined the movement. Dr. Smith Boughton assumed leadership of the "Indians" in Columbia County. Under the name "Big Thunder," he successfully blocked many sheriffs' auctions. In the autumn of 1844, the Democrats nominated United States Senator Silas Wright as their candidate for governor in a move dictated by Martin Van Buren, still in command of the party machinery. Wright, a "Barnburner"—a member of the more radical wing of the party—had a reputation among the farmers as a progressive Jacksonian. Although he said little about the anti-rent movement during his campaign, they hoped for the best from him and helped to elect him to the governorship.

Support of the movement, however, was abruptly set back by two incidents which occurred in December 1844. General Jacob Livingston, one of the largest landowners in Schoharie County, was physically attacked by a group of "Indians" after trying to collect his rents in person. A few weeks later, Elijah Smith, a landlord's agent, was killed by a rifle shot from some "Indians" while trying to cut wood on a farmer's plot.

The press and moderate public opinion immediately urged the governor-elect to restore law and order. The churches, heavy recipients of the landlords' largesse, also insisted that the governor do something about the anarchy in the Helderbergs. Wright ordered artillery from the state militia to Albany. In early January 1845, cavalry detachments came up the Hudson from New York City to the troubled counties. Recognizing that they could not risk a fight against trained troops, the "Indians" withdrew into the hills, and after a short time the bulk of the troops returned to the city.

To meet the claims of "anarchy," a bill was quickly passed through the legislature making it a crime to appear in public armed and in disguise, or to refuse to help a law enforcement officer in discharge of his duty. The law was designed to punish the "Indians" even when they gathered to protest peacefully. The farmers saw the new law as proof that Wright had thrown his lot in with the landowners.

March 1845 saw the outbreak of new "Indian" raids. Law enforcement officials retaliated with systematic raids on anti-rent strongholds. Osman Steele, a deputy from Delaware County, gathered a vigilante force of "drunken rabble" who dragged farmers from their homes in the middle of the night, "grossly insulted" their women, and threw them into jail without charges. Nevertheless, the "Indians" were inventive enough to prevent every single eviction or forced sale in Steele's domain through the spring and early summer of 1845. Sometimes the farmers would turn out in force for any auction of their friends' cattle. They started bidding when the first cow was put up for sale, and continued to bid until the price reached several thousand dollars and darkness stopped the proceedings. Or when cattle were sold, they were stampeded away as the buyer led them out of the mountains. Occasionally the cattle were shot, and the owner reimbursed through a mutual insurance plan provided by the farmers.

Alvan Bovay, a lecturer and writer who supported the farmers, described one attempted sale in the Helderbergs:

The good old custom, which so generally obtains among the farmers
elsewhere, of blowing tin horns for dinner, is here an obsolete idea. The
delicate instrument is now only used in these parts on great occasions of
state, such as the grand entry of the sheriff of Albany, and perhaps the
same honor is paid one of his inferiors. When the august minister of the
law appears on Capitol Hill taking his course toward the setting sun, the
first farmer, as in duty bound . . . sounds his horn; straightway then,
family after family, hamlet after hamlet, and village after village, take up
the sound and throw it forward until it climbs the Helderberg, sweeps
through the valleys beyond the passes on to the borders of Schenectady,
Schoharie and Greene. For a minute every hill and vale and quiet recess
in the twenty-four-mile square resound with the delectable music of the
tin horn; then all is silent as the grave. The hammer is dropped on the
anvil, the scythe in the field, the plow in the furrow, and all is busy
preparation to honor the approach of the sheriff. Soon again a single
horn is heard—it indicates the road by which the gentleman proceeds.
He passes another farm house, and the eternal horn rings forth his
progress. . . .

The people came in great numbers; the sheriff came, but the horses,
the cows and the sheep did not come. In short, it was a sale whereat
nothing was sold. No obstruction, no indignity of any kind was offered
to the officers. They patrolled for two hours or so in search of the horses
&c. . . . which were advertised for sale, but so especially dry was it
(We have had a beautiful rain since.) that the animals had probably (?)
wandered off in quest of water or more pleasant pasturage. The fates
were adverse, the fun was spoiled, the sheriff drove away his own team
and nothing more, the crowd slowly closed up the passage after him, and
all was still.[3]

In August 1845, the law enforcement officials of Delaware County
embarked on a major test of strength with the anti-rent movement by
calling an auction of the cattle of a well-to-do but delinquent farmer,
Moses Earle. As a countermove, the "Indians" came onto Earle's land
in solid ranks and blocked potential bidders from approaching the
barn where the auction was to take place. The officers were outnumbered, and the sheriff and Peter Wright, a lawyer for the landowner,
tried to drive the cattle off the land so that they could be sold away
from the interference of Earle's friends. The "Indians" blocked the
way, but Wright drew a gun, and in the ensuing battle, Deputy Steele
was killed.

The "Indians" scattered through the countryside. Newspapers bit-
terly attacked the murdering anti-renters, and a five-hundred-man
posse tracked down the farmers who had been present at Earle's farm.
Edward O'Connor, thought to have fired the fatal shot, was arrested
along with William Brisbane, a leading anti-rent speaker, Moses

Earle, and hundreds of other "Indians." Using the Steele murder as a pretext, Silas Wright continued to support the landlords and sent three hundred troops into Delaware County to help the owners collect their rents. After the jails were full, temporary pens were built to house the captured "Indians."

Over one hundred farmers on Earle's farm at the time of Steele's death were held for trial in Delhi. In September 1845, six weeks after the killing, the first trials began before Circuit Judge Amasa J. Parker. The judge was thought to have an open mind about the anti-rent movement, but he soon disappointed the farmers, ruling that all those in disguise at Earle's farm were guilty of felony murder.

In rapid order, Edward O'Connor and John Van Steenbergh, a twenty-one-year-old farmer, were sentenced to be hanged (the sentences were later commuted). Many others, including Brisbane and Moses Earle, pleaded guilty to manslaughter to avoid a death sentence; Earle and four others were sentenced to life imprisonment; ten more received long prison terms.

In the same month, Dr. Smith Boughton was tried at Hudson in Columbia County for leading the "Indians" and interfering with the sheriffs' performance of their duties. Judge John W. Edmonds, who had once practiced as a liberal lawyer defending workers in Geneva, presided at the trial and was even more heavyhanded and partial than Judge Parker had been. John Van Buren, Martin's son and heir apparent and Attorney General of the state at the age of thirty-five, personally handled the state's case. His father, who as President had been the champion of the common man, came to the courthouse on the last day of trial to give his son his moral support in the prosecution of the down-rent leader. The state was aided by a spy in the defense camp who reported on Dr. Boughton's trial tactics. Everyone knew that the doctor was "Big Thunder," but the state resorted to perjured testimony to prove its case to the jury, and the judge himself listened secretly to the state spy's story and participated in prosecution strategy. When the jury reported they could not agree on a verdict, Edmonds insisted that they keep on trying. They finally found the doctor guilty.

Before he sentenced the doctor, Judge Edmonds lectured him on the evils of disobedience to law:

Your offense in fact is high treason, rebellion against your government, and armed insurrection. Until you came among them the tenantry of the manor was a quiet, orderly, law-observing people. . . . You have been the leader, the active instigator, the principal fomenter of all these disturbances. You have made yourself an example of disorder and violence, and you have caused many erring and misguided men to follow

it, to their ruin and the disturbance of the public peace. . . . The
sentence of the court is that you be confined to prison for the term of
your natural life.[4]

The actions of Parker and Edmonds proved to the farmers that
sweeping reforms were necessary before they could achieve justice
for their cause. Not only was it necessary to do away with the tenures,
but the administration of the laws themselves had to be changed.
A state constitutional convention had been called for June 1846 and
the farmers elected enough delegates to insist on a clause providing
for an elected judiciary who would necessarily be responsive to the
farmers rather than the landlords.*

They had also gathered their political strength for the November
1845 elections, and down-rent candidates won sweeping majorities
throughout the region, even in law-and-order communities. Despite
the presence of militia in many towns and the unfavorable reaction to
Steele's death in the summer, the public was offended by the Delhi
trials and the heavy sentences meted out to the farmers. Their long
years of agitation had made the community sensitive to the justice of
their demands.

By January 1846, the politicians recognized that their own careers
were tied to the farmers' demands. Governor Silas Wright himself
proposed that the legislature act to do away with the feudal leases:
peace had finally come to the Helderbergs and the farmers' claims
could be examined on their merits. A legislative committee headed
by Samuel J. Tilden recommended prohibitively high taxation of the
landlords' holdings and the breaking up of the large tracts upon the
deaths of the owners. The state senate refused to follow all the
recommendations of the Tilden committee, but they were forced to
go along with a heavy tax on landlords' income from long-term leases,
and they outlawed seizure and sale of a tenant's property to pay for
back rent.

By November of 1846, anti-rent sentiment became even stronger.
Silas Wright's late conversion to the cause did not save him from
defeat by Whig candidate John Young, whose anti-rent credentials
dated from the early 1840's. After his election, Young quickly pardoned the anti-rent leaders still in prison.

A number of the landlords made their peace with the farmers for
the best cash settlement they could negotiate. John A. King sold all
of his rights to 15,000 acres in Schoharie County for $25,000. Even

---

* New York State has retained an elected judiciary. However, in the 1960's,
reformers claimed that the system allowed control of judicial selection by the
party bosses, and that appointed judges would be more capable and independent. The proposal lost in the 1967 constitutional convention.

Stephen Van Rensselaer offered his lands to the farmers for one dollar an acre. Some of the landlords resisted reform, however, trying to provoke again the turmoil of the early 1840's which had alienated the state legislature from the farmers. Charles Livingston continued to harass his tenants by levying on their property for unpaid rent. When they failed to respond by force, he hired some "Indians" of his own to upset the auctions he had called for. This ruse was discovered, but he persisted in using his hired hands to intimidate the anti-rent leaders.

It was only with the election of new judges by the people that the patroon system finally came to an end. The down-renters managed to elect Whig leader Ira Harris to the Supreme Court, and he arranged for the election of Amasa Parker as a justice in order to solidify his political base. Parker had also moved with the times, and when a case came before him in 1850 challenging the legality of the quarter-sale restriction, he held it unconstitutional. Soon after, Harris ruled that Stephen Van Rensselaer's title to his lands was defective and that he could not maintain any action against the tenants who failed to live up to the terms of their leases. That decision was modified on appeal, but the legal doubt concerning the basic leases made the landlords wary of any wholesale attack against the farmers who refused to pay their rents. Increasingly, individual cash settlements between landlord and tenant confirmed the farmer as absolute owner of his plot.

Skirmishes between farmers and landowners still went on, but assumed a rather different character. A speculator named Walter Church bought all the Van Rensselaer titles, hoping to squeeze some more profit from the farmers before the tenure system was totally destroyed. He had a few brief victories when the courts upheld certain types of leases he imposed on his tenants. But the farmers refused to pay, took their fight to the legislature, and continued to battle the landlord's agents and deputies. Gradually, during the 1860's and 1870's, the number of farms under lease dwindled. As late as 1945 some of the upstate farms around Albany were still subject to feudal leases, and a few farmers trying to sell their land were shocked to discover that their property was burdened by anachronistic rent obligations that had not been paid for generations.

The real fight had, of course, been won in the 1840's. If the farmers had used only economic power and peaceful political tactics, they would have been ground to defeat by the landlords before they could have organized any kind of political counterattack. The New York dispossess laws, rooted in the English common law system that favored a landlord's right to reclaim his property in summary proceedings and levy on his tenants' goods for back rent, were made to order for repressing the down-rent movement. (The laws are still in force and now favor slumlords in urban centers who can evict non-paying tenants in a matter of days.) The movement needed some breathing time to organize itself, seek out other allies, and press for political changes to attack the system directly. As the law in the Helderbergs was not being used as a fair arbitrator of conflicting claims, but as a powerful weapon for one economic group against an incipient democratic movement, disobeying the law became necessary in order for the political machinery to assimilate the problem and make the necessary compromises. In his classic work on the subject, Henry Christman wrote:

> The most revolutionary Anti-Renter had always realized that feudalism could not be defeated on the field of battle; only the ballot could destroy that unholy alliance of wealth and government. Nevertheless, in the tenants' darkest hour, the calico army had proved its worth. The "Indians" had kept the landlords' agents and the sheriff at bay until the movement grew into a political force—until it could stand the loss of its leaders without the slightest thought of retreat. Had not the "Indians" protected the livestock and the tools of the Anti-Renters from forced sale, Anti-Rentism would have been choked off in infancy in the ravines of the Helderbergs, where it was cradled. Deprived of their means of livelihood, a few farmers would have been cuffed into submission, and dissuasion of the rest would have followed.[5]

The resistance of the farmers drew the nation's attention to the anachronistic feudal system still operating in the land of liberty. Our political rhetoric insists that men should not be rewarded for riot and disobedience. But it is rare for deep-seated resentments to be dissipated without some type of outburst. The public became fully aware of the grievances only because they were illuminated by the disorders. The economic oppression by the landlords and the basic unfairness of the system revealed by the down-rent tactics finally outweighed the public's concern about the illegal countermoves of the "Indians." Ultimately, the political process must settle these disputes and *ultimately* the laws enacted on the basis of the compromises are obeyed. But disobedience can lubricate the process and preserve the political integrity of the expropriated group until the final adjustments can be made.

The pattern of farmer lawlessness took a different form in the West, where the problem was not too much government, but not enough. In many cases, the existing legal structure was inadequate for the farmers' needs, and they had to establish rules and regulations to govern themselves.

The vast stretches of public domain land in the upper Mississippi Valley drew thousands of farmers in the 1830's. No government of any kind existed in the area; under applicable treaties, Indian tribes owned title to much of the territory, and a law of 1807 prohibited possession of any federally owned land until it had been properly surveyed and plotted. Nevertheless, farmers settled down in increasing numbers in what is now Iowa, Wisconsin, and Illinois, building homes, clearing and plowing the land, and establishing sizable communities. The settlers were not troubled by the fact that they were trespassers and could not secure legal title to their land, indeed could not claim any of the benefits of government until the requirements of the 1807 law were met.

To meet the need for some rudimentary form of government, the farmers organized land clubs, which became a substitute for public authority. The clubs had formal constitutions, periodic elections of officers, and an elaborate system for determining rights to land between disputing claimants. A limit was placed on land holdings that more or less conformed to the territory a man could reasonably cultivate—generally a man could not claim more than 320 acres. The prime purpose of the clubs was to protect a squatter's right to his land from interference by later settlers, land speculators, claim jumpers, and the government.

Violence became necessary if later squatters tried to settle on land already set aside for a club member. The members would burn the houses and barns of intruders and destroy their crops if the squatters refused to move or settle with the prior claimant. When the land was finally surveyed and auctioned by the government, the clubs made sure that no one would bid above the $1.25 government minimum price. A club representative would ordinarily be the only bidder, and land speculators and later squatters who tried to offer more were intimidated into withdrawing their bids. In a few instances, the clubs informally "tried" and convicted those who disobeyed club edicts, and carried out the sentences themselves.[6]

This pattern of squatters protecting their rights continued through the nineteenth century. The frontier wars between farmers and cattlemen, cattlemen and sheepherders, large ranchers and small landholders, all took place outside the ambit of law. Iowa land club activities were minor tiffs in comparison to the indiscriminate violence on the western plains after the Civil War. In Wyoming, a full-scale war erupted between cattle owners and sheepmen, culminating in organized raids on the herders and systematic slaughter of their sheep. In Texas, the small ranchers fought the large syndicates who tried to enclose hundreds of square miles of range lands by barbed wire.

But the most powerful enemy of squatters' rights in the nineteenth century were the new railroads. The federal government would grant them rights of way across thousands of miles of public domain land. As a bonus for laying down track, the railroads would be given title not only to land immediately contingent to the contemplated road-beds, but to millions of acres on either side, generally alternating sections on either side of the line. The railroads encouraged settlers to buy this land since farm communities on their right of way would be dependent on their line to ship produce to market, but promises to sell were frequently not honored.

The Southern Pacific Railroad, owned by the "Big Four"—Leland Stanford, Collis P. Huntington, Mark Hopkins, and Charles Crocker —was the most guilty of this practice. It circulated pamphlets through-out the country enticing farmers to settle in the San Joaquin Valley. After Herculean work to build irrigation ditches and cultivate the land, the farmers learned that the railroad planned to sell the improved land to the highest bidder for $25 to $40 per acre, rather than to the settlers at a promised price of $2.50 per acre. The land had increased in value only because of the farmers' efforts, and they were not going to let the railroads evict them from their homes while reaping the benefits of their work as well.

In 1878, the farmers of Tulare County in the San Joaquin Valley organized a settlers' league to fight the railroad which had earned the title of the "Octopus." There was some legal doubt of the Southern Pacific's claim to the land—the railroad had not taken up its patents for many years in order to avoid taxes, and its survey allegedly departed from the Congressional grants. The farmers claimed that the railroad circulars promising the land at $2.50 per acre were legally enforceable. The league therefore instituted test cases to determine the railroad's rights. The Southern Pacific won in the lower court, and the settlers appealed the case to the Supreme Court. While the cases were pending, the Southern Pacific instituted various actions of ejectment against the farmers. After members of the league drove out two new purchasers of land, the railroad sent armed posses to back up additional ejectment suits. On May 11, 1880, a group of five armed men, including a federal marshal, rode out to the farm of one Brewer (located in the Mussel Slough area of what is now Kings County) to dispossess him. The league had gathered that day in the town of Hanford to hear an address by Californian Judge David S. Terry.[7] When word of the marshal's arrival reached the meeting, fifteen armed settlers rode back to meet the party. Brewer refused to accept the writs and his friends disarmed the marshal. In response to demands that the other five surrender their weapons, one of them, Walter J. Crow, a notorious gunman, fired his shotgun into a farmer's face. Soon four farmers and two members of the marshal's party were dead.

Anti-railroad feeling ran so high that the remaining eleven farmers were only charged with resisting a federal marshal. They received brief prison terms and were hailed as heroes after their release. The railroads eventually won their lawsuits, but they did not exploit the victory to the point of driving the inhabitants off the land; they recognized the growing political power of the farmers. In most cases they avoided further friction by allowing them to continue in possession of the land for a modest annual rental fee.[8]

In the early 1900's a new farmer revolt broke out, similar to the down-rent movement but directed against a new enemy: the mammoth trusts that controlled so much of America's economic life. The tobacco growers of the "dark patch" sections of Kentucky and Tennessee—the counties in the eastern half of the states that grew a darker grade of tobacco leaf—rose up against the tobacco trust that had become the only customer for their products. In the 1890's most of the tobacco sold in the black patch section was still sold at auction to a number of independent processors. By 1900, the American Tobacco Company had bought up almost all the competition. It entered into agreements with Imperial Tobacco (a large English concern) and Regie Tobacco (a purchasing agent for other foreign companies) under which they divided up the dark patch region into separate marketing areas. The farmers were then forced to deal wtih only one buyer who set his own price for the crop. In the first effective year of the agreement, 1903, the offering price to the farmers was four cents for a pound which cost him six cents to produce. In addition, the tobacco trust had arranged for a federal tax on cured tobacco sold directly to the consumer so that it would be economically impossible to sell cured tobacco (for chewing and rolling) directly to the general public.

The farmers answered the following year with the Dark Tobacco District Planters' Protective Association. Every member pledged his crop to the Association which would set a high price for the tobacco. In the first year, the Association set eight cents per pound as the going price for the crop. The tobacco trust buyers retaliated by offering eight-and-a-half cents per pound to individual farmers if they would not join the Association. The hold-outs among the farmers— "Hill-billies" as they came to be called—became the target of Association recruitment men. Allow the Association to be defeated, warned the leaders, and the price will revert to four cents.

In the first year, the Association managed to sell the entire crop pledged to it to a German concern for an average of seven cents per pound. In 1905, they received a slightly higher price, also from foreign purchasers. But the American, Imperial, and Regie buyers still managed to purchase sufficient tobacco from nonmembers. Several of the Association leaders decided that their only chance for success lay in forcing reluctant farmers into the Association. A secret organization was formed for the purpose of taking all steps necessary to fight the trust and punish stubborn hill-billies. Members of the new group took a blood oath not to reveal its secrets or betray its members. Blindfolds were used to bring initiates to meetings, and an elaborate system of passwords (one was "silent brigade") and secret signs protected the organization against intruders. The night riders were organized into a military structure with a commanding general, colonels in charge of all the lodges in a single county, and captains heading thirty-man teams. Just as the down-renters were led by a local doctor —Smith Boughton—so the night riders were led by Dr. David Amoss from Cobb, a small town in Caldwell County, Kentucky. The colonels included elected officials from the region, including one sheriff—Sam Cash of Lyon County.[9]

Officially, the Planters' Protective Association disowned the night riders. But close ties existed nevertheless. The leaders of the silent brigade attended executive committee meetings of the Association, and there was a significant overlap of membership.

The most spectacular acts of violence performed by the night riders involved the dynamiting of tobacco warehouses owned by the tobacco trust. On December 10, 1905, a Regie Tobacco factory in Trenton, Kentucky was dynamited by a large group of masked riders. A year later, on December 2, 1906, 250 armed men rode into Princeton, Kentucky and destroyed two factories and 400,000 pounds of tobacco. In December 1907, the night riders openly invaded Hopkinsville, Kentucky and blew up two warehouses filled with non-Association tobacco.

The dynamiting, neatly spaced over a two-year period, was not so much designed to intimidate the tobacco companies, as to impress the public and the hill-billies with the strength of the farmers' organization. Far more effective in bringing the hill-billies into line were individual acts of coercion by small groups of night riders. Farmers were given every opportunity to join the Association. If they refused to cooperate and continued to sell to the tobacco trust, they would be visited at night by the silent brigade, threatened, often whipped, and some were even killed. Their plantbeds of tobacco would be raked up, or their barns burned.

Surprisingly, the state governments in Kentucky and Tennessee did what they could to help the Association. Laws were passed in both states requiring farmers to honor their pledge to sell their tobacco through the Association. Triple damages could be imposed on both the buyer and the seller if the pledges were violated. Thus farmers who reluctantly signed with the Association, changed their minds, and tried to sell individually found their escape blocked by the law.

After two years of continuous pressure and occasional terror, nine-tenths of the farmers in the black patch signed up as members of the Association. By 1908, American Tobacco was forced to deal with the farmers' group if it wanted any tobacco from the region. The price for the 1908 crop went up to almost nine cents per pound and some of the better grades sold at twenty-five cents. From 1910–1914, prices increased even more and the marketing arrangements established by the Association—cooperative warehouses, numerous salesrooms and selling agents, and the opening of direct channels to foreign purchasers—obtained yet higher incomes for the farmers.

The federal government also took up the cause of the tobacco farmers. Since the basic reason for the low farm prices was the absence of competition brought about by the merger of the major tobacco companies, the government instituted an antitrust action against American Tobacco on July 10, 1907, charging it with monopolization.* The case was tried in May 1908, the company found guilty, and the decision upheld on appeal to the Supreme Court on May 29, 1911. American Tobacco was ordered to divest itself of various of its subsidiaries, which thereafter became active competitors of the giant concern. Within a few years, the farmers of the dark patch region could sell to independent tobacco processors, such as R. J. Reynolds Co., P. Lorillard Co., and others which had formerly belonged to American Tobacco. Prices for tobacco then followed normal market pressures, rising and falling according to supply and demand.

The federal tax on cured tobacco was also repealed: the House of Representatives had passed a bill doing away with the impost in 1905, 1906, and 1907, but Senator Nelson W. Aldrich from Rhode Island

* The government prosecutor was James C. McReynolds, a native of Elkton, Kentucky, later Attorney General under Woodrow Wilson and finally a Justice of the U.S. Supreme Court from 1914–1941. McReynolds was the most reactionary of the "Four Horsemen" who consistently opposed the New Deal measures of Franklin Roosevelt.

blocked consideration of the measure in the Senate. Finally, in 1909, a repeal bill was attached to the Payne-Aldrich Tariff and was signed by President Taft on August 5, 1909.

The activities of the night riders were crucial to the improvement of the farmers' condition.[10] Of course, they had violated the law:

> In legal terms, they were criminals because they committed lawless acts. But *were* they criminals? The growers had asked for help, and had received none. There is no reason to believe that they wanted to take the law into their own hands; but if they had not done so the tobacco industry could have been completely ruined during 1906 and '07. At the turning point of such a crisis, two years is a long time! [11]

The number of night riders is difficult to estimate. James O. Nall claims about ten thousand members, and another forty thousand actively cooperated in one way or another. Association farmers totaled three times that number. Included in the silent brigade were many professional men—the doctor was the chief and many lawyers had joined, as well as judges, sheriffs, ministers, and members of the legislature. The fact that the violence was a last resort, that it was used judiciously for a specific purpose, and that the demands of the farmers for a decent return from their crops was so reasonable, created a favorable public response to the rebellion.[12]

Farmer violence never disturbed the nation as much as union militancy. It was not allied to revolutionary doctrines, such as anarchy, socialism, and communism, that tainted many of the labor groups. The farmers, after all, were only claiming a slightly larger cut of the pie, and the crisis died down as soon as their demands were filled.

We now think of farmers as the most stable and conservative group in the country, the staunchest defenders of law and order; to some extent this is true. The government's generous agriculture program of subsidies, land banks, and guaranteed prices has locked the farmers (although not the farm workers) into defense of the status quo. But the existing system of governmental largesse, so beneficial to the farmers, was itself the outgrowth of a rebellion.

When agricultural prices declined so disastrously in the late twenties and early thirties, Midwestern farmers felt desperate measures were necessary to increase the amounts they received for their products. In Iowa, where mortgage foreclosures affected the greatest number of farmers, they decided to withhold their goods from market until prices at least covered the cost of production. In August 1932, tens of thousands of farmers stopped shipping anything to market. Not only did they withhold their own wheat, corn, and hogs, but they took to the highways to stop nonparticipating farmers from selling their products. Logs were thrown in front of trucks carrying grain or milk, and rocks were hurled at sheriffs and police who tried to protect the truckdrivers. Throughout the autumn of 1932, the withholding movement spread and force was often used to block food deliveries.

By the winter of 1932–1933, the farmers decided to do something directly about foreclosures. In Madison County, Nebraska, the friends of a defaulting mortgagor blocked a sheriff's sale by intimidating outside bidders and then offering only one cent for the items auctioned. The idea of penny sales spread quickly, and again and again, a farmer's house and goods would be sold for a few dollars put up by his friends who would immediately return them to their original owner. Lawyers representing the insurance companies who owned the mortgages were physically attacked, and one judge who did not protect farmers' mortgage rights as thoroughly as they wanted, was kidnapped and almost lynched in Le Mars, Iowa.[13]

The agitation "publicized the farmer's plight and prompted political response more effectively than any ill-organized peaceful withholding movement." [14] Rather than order troops to disperse the farmers and enforce the law, the new Democratic administration moved at breakneck speed to enact a new farm reform bill. Within ten weeks of Roosevelt's inauguration, the Agricultural Adjustment bill passed, providing for payments to farmers to curtail production of certain overproduced crops. The Commodity Credit Corporation guaranteed loans to farmers who pledged their crops at a set price. Emergency legislation was passed to refinance farm mortgages and thus prevent foreclosures.

The nation as a whole was far more lenient to its lawbreakers during the desperate years of the depression. Farmer lawlessness in 1932–1933 did not keep Congress from implementing the New Deal farm reform measures, any more than the violent strikes of 1933–1936 prevented passage of the Wagner Act. The basic structure of the New Deal farm subsidies continues up to the present day, while the farmers, suffering from historic amnesia, attack students and blacks for their lawlessness.

# 6

# Test Cases and
# Minority Groups

The rhetoric of the government demands unfailing obedience to the law—to all laws, by all people, at all times. But who is to say finally what "the law" is? Everyone accepts the proposition that the courts, and ultimately the Supreme Court, have that responsibility.* Implicit in the notion that the courts are the final arbiters of the law is the right of conscientious men to disobey laws they feel in good faith are unconstitutional. How else can the issue be brought before the judges? [1] In short, a challenge to law can be made on two fronts: outside the system, through disobedience that generates popular agitation and hopefully leads to *political* change; and inside the system, through disobedience that provokes legal argument and ultimate *judicial* repeal. Thus the supremacy of our written Constitution and the crucial role of the courts in interpreting what it means necessarily anticipates a challenge to specific laws by those who feel oppressed by them.

* The Court itself has explained this: "[The] federal judiciary is supreme in the exposition of the law of the Constitution, and [this] principle has . . . been respected by the Court, and the Country as a permanent and indispensable feature of our constitutional system." *Cooper* v. *Aaron*, 358 U.S. 1, 18 (1958).

In fact, no less than eighty-six federal laws and over seven hundred state or municipal enactments have been declared unconstitutional by the United States Supreme Court. Most of them were brought under judicial scrutiny because someone, somewhere, refused to obey the semblance of law, "what has passed through the legislature, [and] which is printed where laws are printed," [2] as Professor Charles Black has described it.

Striking examples of this pattern are found among recent Supreme Court decisions protecting two minorities who refused to obey laws applied against them: the Jehovah's Witnesses during the 1930's and 1940's, and the civil rights workers in the South in the 1950's and 1960's.[3]

In the early days of the New Deal, the Jehovah's Witnesses undertook a campaign of zealous proselytizing throughout the country. They managed to offend not only most of their potential converts but almost all the public officials of the towns and cities they invaded. Not for nothing has Zechariah Chafee called them a "sect distinguished by great religious zeal and astonishing power of annoyance." [4] Their brand of liberal Protestantism views all organized religion (particularly the Catholic Church) with distrust. They are fanatic pacifists who refuse to have any dealings with the military and insist on ministerial deferments for all their members on the grounds that every adherent is a minister of the faith. In the 1930's, they chose to pass on their message in the most offensive ways possible, refusing to salute the flag, which they regarded as a "graven image," and defying outright the police regulations designed to restrict their conversion activities.

In 1936, one Alma Lovell went around the town of Griffin, Georgia, trying to sell Jehovah's Witnesses' pamphlets from door to door, to solicit contributions, and to otherwise advertise her religion. A town ordinance specifically forbade the distribution of literature without a permit, which Alma refused to apply for. She was arrested for violating the law and sentenced to fifty days in jail in lieu of paying a $50 fine.

The case was appealed to the state appellate courts and then to the United States Supreme Court. The City of Griffin argued that its ordinance was a police measure designed to prevent littering of the streets. No restriction on freedom of religion or freedom of the press was involved, they argued. The Supreme Court, through Chief Justice Charles Evans Hughes, disagreed. "The liberty of the press is not confined to newspapers and periodicals. It necessarily embraces pamphlets and leaflets. . . . We think the ordinance is invalid on its

face. Whatever the motive which induced its adoption, its character is
such that it strikes at the very foundation of the freedom of the press
by subjecting it to license and censorship." [5]

In 1940, still another important constitutional decision was handed
down through a similar challenge. Newton Cantwell and his two sons,
Jesse and Russell, went from door to door in a heavily Catholic
section of New Haven, Connecticut, playing a phonograph record
containing an offensive attack on the Catholic Church. They then
asked for contributions. The police arrested them for soliciting money
for a religious purpose without the approval of a public welfare
official, as required by a local law. Again, the Witnesses knew about
the law but paid no attention to it, and again, the Supreme Court
reversed the convictions. Justice Owen Roberts said:

In the realm of religious faith, and in that of political belief, sharp
differences arise. In both fields the tenets of one man may seem the rankest
error to his neighbor. To persuade others to his own point of view, the
pleader, as we know, at times resorts to exaggeration, to vilification of
men who have been, or are, prominent in church or state, and even to
false statement. But the people of this nation have ordained in the light
of history, that, in spite of the probability of excesses and abuses, these
liberties are, in the long view, essential to enlightened opinion and right
conduct on the part of the citizens of a democracy.[6]

The Jehovah's Witnesses suffered a temporary setback in 1940 over
the issue of the American flag. Many members of the sect had ordered
their children not to participate in the flag saluting ceremonies in
their schools. When, as a result, two children of Jehovah's Witnesses
were expelled from the Minersville, Pennsylvania grammar school,
the parents, Lillian and William Gobitis, sued to have them re-
admitted and took the case to the Supreme Court. In an eight to one
decision (only Chief Justice Harlan Fiske Stone dissented) the Court
found that the salute fostered national unity, "the basis of national
security" which was "an interest inferior to none in the hierarchy of
legal values." [7] Thus the children could be compelled to salute the
flag or suffer the penalties under state law.

The decision produced a wave of repression against the Witnesses.*

* Alpheus Mason reports: "In the wake of the Court's stamp of approval
of the compulsory flag salute, religious bigotry and fanatical, unthinking patriotism became rampant. Jehovah's Witnesses, it was said, 'don't believe in
Religion; to them Religion is a Racket of making money by selling Judge
Rutherford's volumes.' Vigilante committees took it upon themselves to enforce respect for the flag by violent means. Between June 12 and June 20,
1940, hundreds of attacks on the Witnesses were reported to the Justice Department for possible action by the FBI. At Kennebunkport, Maine, King-
dom Hall was burned. At Rockville, Maryland, within twenty miles of the

The second world war broke out a year later, and the pressures toward unity and obeisance to the State were particularly heavy. But many, if not most, of the Witnesses refused to knuckle under. The flag was still a graven image to them, regardless of what the Supreme Court might say. Although the final legal determination on this point had been made in the form of an almost unanimous Supreme Court decision, their children still refused to salute the flag and many continued to be expelled from school.

In 1942, a Witness named Walter Barnette brought suit against the West Virginia State Board of Education, which had adopted a resolution requiring flag salutes by all teachers and students in the state. A federal district court disregarded the earlier *Gobitis* decision of the Supreme Court and held the flag salute requirement unconstitutional. On appeal the Supreme Court reversed itself and Justice Robert Jackson wrote, in one of the most memorable opinions of the century:

The very purpose of a Bill of Rights was to withdraw certain subjects from the vicissitudes of political controversy, to place them beyond the reach of majorities and officials and to establish them as legal principles to be applied by the courts. One's right to life, liberty, and property, to free speech, a free press, freedom of worship and assembly, and other fundamental rights may not be submitted to vote; they depend on the outcome of no elections. . . .

National unity as an end which officials may foster by persuasion and example is not in question. The problem is whether under our Constitution compulsion as here employed is a permissible means for its achievement. . . .

Focusing on what is the final danger of repressing dissent, in words which have frightening application today, Jackson continued:

Those who begin coercive elimination of dissent soon find themselves exterminating dissenters. Compulsory unification of opinion achieves only the unanimity of the graveyard. . . .

If there is any fixed star in our constitutional constellation, it is that no official, high or petty, can prescribe what shall be orthodox in politics, nationalism, religion, or other matters of opinion or force citizens to con-

---

majestic Supreme Court building, police joined a mob attack on a Bible meeting. At Litchfield, Illinois, a crowd of a thousand townsfolk milled around sixty canvassing Witnesses, burning their tracts, overturning their cars. At Connersville, Indiana, the Witnesses' attorney was beaten and driven out of town. At Jackson, Mississippi, a veterans' organization banished the Witnesses and their trailer houses from the city. Similar incidents occurred in Texas, California, Arkansas, and Wyoming. The Department of Justice traced this wave of violence directly to the Court's decision in the first Flag Salute case." [8]

fess by word or act their faith therein. If there are any circumstances which permit an exception, they do not now occur to us.[9]

In subsequent years, the Supreme Court protected the Witnesses against a city license tax on their sales of religious literature from door to door,[10] against laws forbidding knocking on doors to give occupants handbills,[11] and preventing Witnesses from distributing their literature in a privately owned town.[12] In two cases in the early 1950's, the Court required that municipalities give Witnesses permits to hold meetings in the public parks.[13]

During the period from 1938, when the first Jehovah's Witnesses case came before the Supreme Court, until 1954, when most of the cases stopped, the group lost only four decisions.* In the twenty-odd cases won, this small, weak, and unpopular minority made fundamental changes in American law. They firmly established the right of all minorities to use the streets and public parks to deliver their messages. And they made clear that the government could not compel any overt expression of obedience or loyalty from its citizens. These precedents advanced political freedom in this country by several degrees, and such an advance was made possible by the determination of the Witnesses not to obey a law they deemed restrictive of their rights and in violation of the Constitution.[17]

There were unpopular splinter groups other than the Witnesses who refused to obey repressive laws patently designed to constrain their political, economic, or social activities. Various state syndicalism laws were applied against the Communist Party in the 1930's which forbade even the holding of peaceful meetings under Communist auspices. In 1934, the state of Oregon convicted a Party member named Dirk De Jonge for lecturing at a public meeting in Portland, on the general topic of local longshoremen strikes. The judge sentenced De Jonge to seven years in jail, but the Supreme Court reversed the conviction. It ruled: "The greater the importance of safeguarding the community from incitements to the overthrow of our institutions by force and violence, the more imperative is the need to preserve inviolate the constitutional rights of free speech, free press,

---

* In two cases, the Court decided that members had to request a permit designed to regulate the use of the public streets before they could hold a parade in the main avenue of a town.[14] In another, the Justices upheld the conviction of a Witness who used "fighting words" against a city marshall, calling him a "God damn racketeer" and a "damned fascist." [15] The Court also upheld a Massachusetts law (applied against a young Witness handing out religious literature) that forbade children to sell newspapers on the streets. The State's interest in regulating child labor, ruled the Court in a five to four decision, was more important than the right to distribute the materials.[16]

and free assembly in order to maintain the opportunity for free political discussion, to the end that government may be responsive to the will of the people . . . Therein lies the security of the Republic, the very foundation of constitutional government." [18]

The Southern states were particularly sensitive to Communist activity in their territory. When Angelo Herndon, a black Communist, came to Atlanta, Georgia in 1934 to enlist members in the Party, he was arrested under a Georgia law against inciting insurrection. (The law was passed after Nat Turner's 1831 revolt and was originally designed to prevent further slave uprisings.) The Georgia authorities did not take well to the Communist plan for "Self-Determination for the Black Belt" under which the blacks would take over the deep Southern states and rule them as a separate governmental unit. A Georgia jury sentenced Herndon to twenty years in jail. Again the Supreme Court reversed.

The power of a state to abridge freedom of speech and of assembly is the exception rather than the rule and the penalizing even of utterances of a defined character must find its justfication in a reasonable apprehension of danger to organized government. . . . Where a statute is so vague and uncertain as to make criminal an utterance or an act which may be innocently said or done with no intent to induce resort to violence . . . a conviction under such a law cannot be sustained.[19]

In one sense, the Communist Party cases came to the Supreme Court by accident. The defendants did not set out to test a particular law by ostentatiously violating it, with the specific purpose of obtaining a constitutional ruling on its validity. However, many times in our history a defendant has taken precisely that path, and has attempted in the process to get maximum political mileage out of the test case as well—the most famous being the 1873 trial of Susan B. Anthony.

The passage of the Fourteenth Amendment in 1868 gave the women's suffrage movement a new argument, for the amendment declared that all persons born in the United States were citizens and were entitled to all the privileges and immunities of citizenship. By its terms, it would seem to include women within its protection and therefore, the suffragists claimed, they should have the privilege of voting in all elections immediately, just as all male citizens did. Susan Anthony pressed this point in lectures during 1871 and 1872, and on November 1, 1872 she put theory into practice. On that date, Miss Anthony and fifteen other women appeared at the registration office of the Eighth Ward in Rochester, New York, with a copy of the Fourteenth Amendment and the New York election law. Only men were affirmatively allowed to register by the law but it did not expressly deny the vote to women, and she demanded to be enrolled. Somewhat baffled, the inspectors let themselves be persuaded to register the women. Five days later, at the actual election, the sixteen women reappeared at the polling place and were allowed to cast their votes.

By this time, the Democratic papers of Rochester had pointed out that federal law prohibited any person voting without the legal right to do so and that New York law did not give that right to women. On Thanksgiving Day, November 28, 1872, federal marshals served warrants of arrest on each of the women who had voted. Trial was set for the summer of 1873.

In the meantime, Miss Anthony used the indictments for the most effective agitation on women's suffrage that had been seen up to that time. She was the star of the women's rights convention in Washington two months later. In her opening speech she said: "I stand here under indictment for having exercised my right as a citizen to vote at the last election." Before the trial took place, she delivered not less than fifty speeches in upstate New York pressing her constitutional argument that the Fourteenth Amendment granted the suffrage to women. "I not only committed no crime, but instead simply exercised my citizen's right, guaranteed to me and all United States citizens by the National Constitution beyond the power of any State to deny." [20]

The trial took place in Canandaigua, New York in June 1873. Presiding was a newly appointed Justice of the United States Supreme Court, Ward Hunt, a protégé and tool of Senator Roscoe Conkling. The government decided to get the trial over with as quickly as possible and not to allow Miss Anthony to use it as a forum for her views. Instead of putting her on the stand, the government read a transcript of her testimony at a preliminary hearing. To counter this strategy, Miss Anthony tried to fire her lawyer and act as her own attorney, so she could speak directly to the jury. The judge refused;* indeed, Judge Hunt would not even permit the defense to put on any evidence answering the government's case. He ruled that the question of whether the Fourteenth Amendment granted women the right to vote was purely a question of law on which he alone could rule. He told the jury: "I have decided . . . that under the Fourteenth Amend-

---

* The procedure followed by Judge Hunt in 1873 was duplicated almost exactly by Judge Julius Hoffman in Chicago in 1969. He also refused to let a defendant representing a political outgroup defend himself—Bobby Seale of the Black Panthers. Like Miss Anthony, Seale could speak only after being found guilty (of contempt, in his case) and before sentencing.

ment, which Miss Anthony claims protects her, she was not protected in a right to vote. And I have decided also that her belief and the advice which she took do not protect her in the act which she committed. If I am right in this, the result must be a verdict on your part of guilty, and I therefore direct that you find a verdict of guilty." [21]

Miss Anthony's lawyer, Henry R. Selden, objected vigorously. It was unheard of for a judge to direct a guilty verdict without giving the jury a chance to consider the case. Even anti-suffragist newspapers wrote indignant editorials about the procedure. The *New York Sun* demanded that Hunt be impeached. He refused to back down and set the next day for sentencing. In accordance with the usual procedure, he asked Miss Anthony whether she had anything to say before he pronounced sentence. At that point, her first opportunity to speak at her own trial, she rose to her feet and began:

Yes, your honor, I have many things to say; for in your ordered verdict of guilty, you have trampled under foot every vital principle of our government. My natural rights, my civil rights, my political rights are all alike ignored. Robbed of the fundamental privilege of citizenship, I am degraded from the status of a citizen to that of a subject; and not only myself individually but all of my sex are, by your honor's verdict, doomed to political subjection under this so-called Republican government.

Hunt tried to stop her, but Miss Anthony continued:

Your denial of my citizen's right to vote is the denial of my right of consent as one of the governed, the denial of my right of representation as one of the taxed, the denial of my right to a trial by a jury of my peers as an offender against the law, the denial of my sacred rights to life, liberty, property.[22]

Hunt then fined her $100, a lenient sentence under the circumstances. Rather than order her imprisoned until the fine was paid (which would have allowed her to take an immediate appeal), Hunt permitted her to stay at liberty. No effort was ever made to collect the fine, and therefore Hunt's rulings were never questioned by a higher court.*

---

* President Grant eventually granted Miss Anthony a full pardon after a Senate committee questioned Justice Hunt's actions. A test case on women's suffrage did come to the Supreme Court in 1875. Virginia Minor sued a register of voters in Missouri to allow her to vote. The Supreme Court unanimously held in *Minor* v. *Happersett* that the Fourteenth Amendment did not add to the privileges and immunities of citizens. If the states did not permit female citizens to vote before the Amendment, they could not claim any additional rights after it was passed. Suffrage was never coextensive with citizenship, the Court said.

John Van Voorhis, Selden's assistant, said in later years, "There never before was a trial in the country of one-half the importance as this of Miss Anthony's. That of Andrew Johnson had no issue which could compare in value with the one here at stake. If Miss Anthony had won her case on the merits, it would have revolutionized the suffrage of the country and enfranchised every woman in the United States." [23]

Even though she lost, there were many gains for the movement. Miss Anthony prepared a full report of the trial, had it printed, and circulated thousands of copies. Women throughout the country sent in money and promises of support to suffragist organizations. More than any other single event in the suffrage drive, the trial politicized and activated women who then joined in the many state campaigns to change the election laws. The idea that the leader of the movement could be treated so shabbily by the government, found to be a criminal because she asserted the right to vote under the Fourteenth Amendment, made action imperative. The integrity, honesty, and gentleness of Miss Anthony played its part also. Her motives were so pure, her cause so obviously just, and the reaction of the government so outrageous, it was no longer possible to look upon the drive for woman's rights as something trivial and laughable—the nation's reaction up to that point.

The test case device was used during the New Deal years also. In one case, the state of Texas tried to restrict union activity by passing a law requiring any union organizer to obtain a permit from the Secretary of State before trying to solicit membership in a union. R. J. Thomas, the president of the United Auto Workers in 1943, went to a meeting in Houston to address a group of workers immediately before a National Labor Relations Board-sponsored election. Humble Oil obtained an injunction against Thomas' speaking before the workers without complying with the Texas registration requirement. Thomas spoke anyway, and in blatant disregard of the statute, directly solicited one member of the audience to join the union. He was tried and convicted for violating the law in question.

The Supreme Court reversed; Justice Wiley Rutledge found that while the state had the power to regulate labor unions, any law it passed "must not trespass upon the domains set apart for free speech." By requiring a union organizer to obtain a permit before he could talk to potential members, the law transgressed the First Amendment. "As a matter of principle a requirement of registration in order to make a public speech would seem generally incompatible with an exercise of the rights of free speech and free assembly." [24]

The civil rights workers of the 1960's used all of these techniques to the greatest advantage. They violated local laws both to test them and to mobilize political support, and the Supreme Court vindicated their acts in almost every instance. The civil rights movement, in fact, had its genesis in an act of conscientious disobedience. On December 1, 1955, a Negro seamstress, Mrs. Rosa Parks, refused to move to the back of a bus in Montgomery, Alabama and was promptly arrested under a local law requiring segregated carriers. Led by Rev. Martin Luther King, Jr., the Negroes of Montgomery organized a boycott of the buses until the policy of segregation was overthrown. A year later, the federal courts upheld their protest, declared segregated carriers illegal, and no longer permitted the city to arrest Negroes refusing to sit separately in municipal buses. Mrs. Parks' act, though "illegal" at the time she committed it, was upheld by the courts and led, in the words of Louis Lomax, to "the birth of the Negro revolt."

Multiplying Rosa Parks' action, Negro and white demonstrators disregarded a series of repressive laws designed to keep the Negro in an inferior status in the South or otherwise to hamper his political activities. In many cases, otherwise neutral or nondiscriminatory laws were applied consistently against the assertion of Negro rights. To test the laws or their application, civil rights workers had to defy the authorities in case after case and take their complaints to the only effective forum that would hear them: the federal courts and eventually the United States Supreme Court. Again and again, their position was upheld and the state laws used against them were invalidated.

The first such case took place in 1960 when a young Negro law student named Boynton refused to move from the white section of a bus terminal restaurant in Richmond and was arrested and convicted. Boynton had been traveling from Washington, D.C. to Montgomery, Alabama, and the Supreme Court held that the Interstate Commerce Act required nondiscriminatory treatment of all interstate travellers in both buses and terminals along the way.[25]

In February 1960, the first sit-ins took place in Greensboro, North Carolina. Four students at the nearby A & T College sat for hours at a Woolworth's lunch counter without being served. Thousands of others throughout the South did the same in the following months. Expanding on the new tactics, hundreds of Negro school children in Columbia, South Carolina marched to the state capitol building in March 1961 to protest segregation in general. They refused to obey the police who ordered them to move, and although the protesters were peaceful and did not obstruct any public thoroughfare, many were arrested for breach of the public peace. Again the Supreme Court reversed. Justice Stewart found that there had been no disturbance of any kind and that the law was being manipulated to suppress the First Amendment rights of the demonstrators.[26]

In Greenville, South Carolina, a group of black teenagers sat in at a "5&10" lunch counter. The manager reminded them of a local ordinance that required that all restaurants be segregated, and demanded that they leave. The blacks remained and were charged with trespass. The Supreme Court ruled, however, that the equal protection clause had been violated.[27]

Although the city of New Orleans had no statute requiring segregated restaurants, in 1961 some sit-inners refused to leave a lunch counter in a local department store and were arrested under the Louisiana Criminal Mischief Statute. The Supreme Court concluded that city officials and the police were enforcing a segregation policy through their public statements and activities; such practices amounted to state action forbidden by the equal protection clause of the Fourteenth Amendment. The convictions were reversed.[28]

The civil disobedience campaign in Birmingham, Alabama in 1963 triggered major victories for civil rights. For years "Bull" Connor (the white supremacist safety commissioner of the city) and his racist allies had so frightened the wavering white merchants who controlled the city that little advance had been made in desegregating any part of the city's life. Civil rights organizations brought various law suits in the late 1950's, with only minor success. In 1962, the Southern Christian Leadership Conference under Rev. Martin Luther King, Jr. demanded desegregation of lunch counters and other facilities in the major stores, nondiscriminatory hiring of Negroes, and the creation of a biracial committee to reduce racial tensions. But they delayed any direct action, to insure Connor's defeat in the mayoralty election of March 1963. Then, small demonstrations began at Birmingham's lunch counters. When Rev. King led larger protest marches to the city hall, Connor met them with vicious police dogs. King and his allies requested parade permits from Connor to hold marches on Good Friday and Easter Sunday, but Connor told them: "No, you will not get a permit in Birmingham, Alabama to picket. I will picket you over to the city jail." He then went into court on the Wednesday before the march was scheduled for an order enjoining SCLC from holding any weekend parades. King defied the injunction and led a Good Friday demonstration—it was more like a stroll of about sixty people through downtown Birmingham—without the required permit. He and Ralph Abernathy were promptly arrested and sent to jail for five days. While he was imprisoned, King wrote his famous "Letter from Birmingham Jail." [29]

The arrest of King for simply holding a peaceful march to protest segregation led to a significant escalation in the civil rights struggle. Larger and larger marches were held in April and early May, all without permits. The authorities retaliated by using water hoses, powerful enough to rip bark from the trees, against the demonstrators, mostly Negro teen-agers. Connor arrested thousands of protesters peacefully meeting outside local churches or trying to march to the downtown marketing area. News pictures of the demonstrators being knocked down by the stream of water hoses or set upon by the police dogs shocked the conscience of the nation, and the Birmingham campaign became a major issue for the Kennedy Administration. Continuous pressure was applied by the federal government to settle the affair, and finally on May 10, 1963 an accord was reached granting the Negroes almost every point they had demanded. The Birmingham episode spurred the President into introducing his first comprehensive civil rights legislation, which eventually became the Civil Rights Act of 1964.

These advances were achieved chiefly because of the "illegal" tactics of the civil rights organization in demonstrating and protesting without the permits required and in the face of court orders to the contrary. Eventually the United States Supreme Court held in the *Shuttlesworth* case that the Negro demonstrators could not be punished for parading without a permit since the municipal code gave the city too much discretion in granting or denying licenses.[30] But by a five to four vote, it held that King should have obeyed the court order against marching, even though the underlying law requiring a permit was unconstitutional. In the *Walker* decision the Court said: "One may sympathize with the petitioners' impatient commitment to their cause. But respect for judicial process is a small price to pay for the civilizing hand of law, which alone can give abiding meaning to constitutional freedom." [31] Many critics have attacked the distinction made by the Supreme Court in these two cases. But the final outcome of the two cases was less relevant than the political results of the direct action in Birmingham. The fact that the same action could be "legal" or "illegal," depending on whether a permit law or a court injunction was the basis for the prosecution, shows how irrelevant the law can sometimes be in the face of the strong political currents unleashed by resistance. The *Walker* case was decided in the spring of 1967 and the *Shuttlesworth* case two years later, by which time King's tactics had been overwhelmingly vindicated by history.

The public accommodations sections of the 1964 Civil Rights Act established the right of every Negro to full, nondiscriminatory services in restaurants, hotels, and other facilities throughout the country. There is absolutely no doubt that the campaign of direct violation of law begun in Greensboro in 1960 and culminating in Birmingham was the immediate cause of the legal changes made four years later. As Solicitor General Erwin Griswold commented about the "illegal" lunch counter sit-ins and freedom rides of the early 1960's, "We cannot fail to recognize the fact that it was these tactics which succeeded in putting the basic issues squarely before the courts and the public. And it was in this way that the law was clarified in the courts and that legislative changes were brought about." By focusing the nation's attention on the conditions under which Southern Negroes were forced to live and showing how the law itself was being used to stifle Negro rights, the young activists overcame the political inertia which had permitted segregated patterns to continue.

The Jehovah's Witnesses and civil rights cases illustrate two crucial elements about conscientious disobedience: (1) Disobedience is not simply the most efficient but often the only means of testing the validity of a challenged law; (2) Only when the Supreme Court has made a final ruling on a case do we know whether an act is illegal or not. Clearly, reformers from Father Cummings to Martin Luther King have known they were violating the law, but they took their chances in doing so and hoped to win their case by proving the law was in derogation of rights secured them under the Constitution.

Not only did these challengers vindicate themselves, but their actions brought about many of the proudest declarations of human freedom and political liberty ever made by the courts. Such deliberate defiance of law has led to dozens of important Supreme Court decisions in the field of civil rights and civil liberties, which have broadened the freedoms of all Americans.

The Susan Anthony trial and the Birmingham episode also show how good faith disobedience of law—whether or not finally sustained by the courts—can work as a focus for the political outgroups themselves; even if they lose (perhaps *because* they lose), their position vis-à-vis the government is more clearly defined. The defendants can then convey to their followers exactly how a governmental policy restricts their rights and on this basis marshal their forces for a broader political attack. As Otto Kirchheimer explains in his brilliant book on *Political Justice,* such tactics can give oppressed minorities a "new élan" at a time when it is most needed.

## Part Two

---

# THE RESISTANCE

# 7

## Perspective

We have seen that oppressed groups throughout American history have not let the law block their efforts at reform. From the Whiskey rebels to the civil rights activists, minority groups aggrieved by the law have taken their protest activities well past the line of legality. But their opposition to law led neither to crime waves nor to anarchy. Practically speaking, it was the *only* way to generate political action that would remove the evils they suffered under.

These illegal acts were generally "public claim[s] against the state . . . publicly acted out." Such behavior, writes Michael Walzer, always encompasses a "willingness . . . to offer explanations to other people" for the group complaint which inspired the action.[1] By educating the public with their problems, the aggrieved minority does not endanger the psychic balance of society by its lawlessness. The pressure to punish them is relieved by a recognition that the law has already unfairly oppressed them.

The significant units in a functioning democracy are not atomized individuals but defined groups of like-minded men who engage in complicated political bargaining to protect their members and advance their interests. Group cohesion and loyalty upon which the system relies can be carried to a point where it conflicts with allegiance to the state. When that happens, the bargaining may rise to a new level. But disobedience should be seen as a gambit within the process directed to a specific, intolerable evil—an unfair tax, an oppressive land tenure system, or an unnecessary draft law—which the larger society can be made to appreciate.*

Oppressed minorities, after all, have no lobbyists to represent their interests in Congress or the state legislatures. There comes a time when their sense of being abused by the larger society grows so strong that it overcomes the normal inertia of obedience to law. Their violations then put pressure on the government to do something about existing conditions. "Throwing a good scare into those in power is sometimes more beneficial to reform than following the time-worn punctilio of appearing at committee hearings to cajole recalcitrant Congressmen." [3] In recent years we have seen the government take initial steps to clear up the problems of urban ghettoes only after the summer riots of 1965, 1966, and 1967 had badly frightened the authorities. And college presidents woke up to the backwardness of their curricula and administration only after student rebels had forced them out of their offices.

Perhaps the clearest recent example of conscientious disobedience to law which led to beneficial political results is the draft resistance movement. An examination of the anti-draft activities of the past few years reveals the reluctance of any oppressed group to pass into illegality until it felt all its other options had been cancelled. It shows the close relation between repression and rebellion in today's society. The movement demonstrated in microcosm how conscientious men, by violating our society's accepted norms, could make it live up to its highest ideals.

"The composition of the criminal cases commenced in the [federal] district courts in 1969 changed considerably from that in 1968," reports the Administrative Office of the United States Courts in its latest annual statement. "Significant numerical and percentage increases appeared in Selective Service cases, up 81 percent to 3,305, the largest number since World War II." [4] The government statistics

* Michael Walzer writes: ". . . men have a prima facie obligation to honor the engagements they have explicity made, to defend the groups and uphold the ideals to which they have committed themselves, even against the state, so long as their disobedience of laws or legally authorized commands does not threaten the very existence of the larger society or endanger the lives of its citizens. It is obedience to the state, when one has a duty to disobey, that must be justified." [2]

showed the following change in draft cases during the past five fiscal
years:

| 1965 | 1966 | 1967 | 1968 | 1969 |
|------|------|------|------|------|
| 380  | 663  | 1336 | 1826 | 3305 |

The ten-fold increase in Selective Service violations since the escalation of the Vietnam War reflects the seriousness of the government's
draft resistance problem. Not only is the administration of justice
under severe pressure, but more important, the citizens' sense of
responsibility to the state is being challenged. Prosecutors are
swamped with draft law indictments, court calendars clogged with
Selective Service cases, and probation officers and prison officials worried about how they will cope with the flood of violators. Draft cases
now constitute almost 10 percent of all federal crimes reported, ex-
ceeded only by auto theft, forgery, and immigration violations. During fiscal year 1969 an average of almost three hundred cases per
month, or over nine per day, were filed. Preliminary figures from
December 1969 to June 1970 indicate that the rate of draft offenses
was still rising, with no leveling off in sight.

In addition, figures from the Selective Service System indicate that
violations were increasing just as the draft calls themselves were decreasing. In fiscal year 1966, 343,481 men were inducted, while only
663 prosecutions were instituted. In 1968, there were 341,404 inductions and 1,826 prosecutions commenced; and in 1969, 263,800 inductions and 3,305 prosecutions.[5] Thus, although the number of
inductions declined from 1966 to 1969 by over 80,000 men, the
number of prosecutions multiplied six-fold. It is one thing for violations to increase because the draft calls are higher, quite another
when the calls not only stay the same but actually go down.

At the same time that violations increased to the highest rates in
recent times, public opinion has come to regard the crime of draft
evasion as one of the most serious affronts to the government and the
legal order. To many Americans, any man who refuses to fight for
his country when thousands of his fellow citizens have already died in
Vietnam is a coward and a traitor. A typical comment comes from
a judge who sentenced a young draft resister to ten years in jail:
"We can't fool around with people like that. We are in a war, and a
man who is a citizen of this country ought to act as such." [6] Reflect-
ing this point of view, the sentences meted out for draft law convictions are longer than ever before in our history. At the height of World
War II, from July 1, 1944 to June 30, 1945, the average sentence for
draft violations was thirty-one months. The same level was reached
again in fiscal year 1952, during the Korean conflict. At no other

time did the average sentence reach thirty months. However, in fiscal year 1967, the average sentence for draft law violations stood at 32.1 months; in 1968 it went to 37.3 months, and in 1969 was at 36.3 months. Since the maximum sentence for such offenses is five years (or sixty months), a surprisingly large number of judges have been giving the stiffest penalties possible under the law. In 1968, of 580 men sent to jail, 104 received five year sentences—an unprecedented ratio—and an additional 301 were given three to five year terms.

This increase has taken place while sentences are decreasing for virtually all other criminal offenses. Draft law violators, moreover, are almost always first offenders (of 748 convicted in 1967, only five had prior felony records) and recommendations for parole were made in many cases.

Clearly, the increased tempo of violations means that an increased number of men have grave reservations about their military obligations to their country and the right of the government to demand compliance from them. They choose to ignore a law which supposedly embraces one of the basic responsibilities of a man toward the state and forms the basis of our national security. But like the Abolitionists, draft resisters refuse to violate their consciences and object to a law that potentially makes them do evil to others. Like the opponents of the Alien and Sedition Laws, the resisters and their allies claim the government oppresses them because they oppose an unpopular war in a vigorous way. Like the union organizers and farmer rebels of the nineteenth century, they consider their disobedience to be an effective political device to change what they see as the disastrous policies of the government. Draft resistance has become the compression chamber of our rebelling youth, in many cases a temporary proving ground and resting point between the stable middle-class life that society and their parents laid out for them and a revolutionary life-style whose final form we have yet to see.

# 8

# Background:
## Civil War—World War II

Draft resistance is nothing new in American history. The Civil War draft, the first passed by Congress, was opposed by substantial numbers in the Northern states. Blatantly class-oriented, the system allowed the rich middle class to buy their way out of the draft, creating bitter resentment among the workers and the poor. The March 1863 conscription law permitted any draftee to hire a substitute, or pay a $300 commutation fee which exempted him from all service requirements. To the lower class, such a law made the conflict into "a rich man's war and a poor man's fight." The poor man himself had little sympathy for the cause of Negro emancipation, fearing that freed blacks would only compete with him for jobs in Northern factories.

The middle class and small farmers also opposed the draft since it was the most serious claim the federal government had yet made upon its citizens. Although some compulsory military service existed previously in the state militias, men had been enrolled in local units under officers they had known throughout their lives. And the state officials who controlled the forces were subject to close electoral scrutiny. These safeguards ceased to exist when a remote federal authority reached out to draft men, impersonally and at random.

As a result, the government encountered the greatest difficulty in raising sufficient numbers for the Union Army. The law required that enrolling officers visit every home and obtain a military census of all eligible men. The provost marshal general who administered the draft reported: "Many men, on the approach of an enrolling officer, left their homes, and their wives, mothers, or children gave false names, or grossly misrepresented the age of the person to be enrolled." [1] Another report noted that opposition to enrollment took place in nearly every home that was visited. "Every imaginable artifice was adopted to deceive and defeat the enrolling officers. Open violence was sometimes met with. Several enrollers lost their lives. Some were crippled . . . In certain mining areas organized bodies of men openly opposed the enrollment." [2] Thirty-eight enrollers were killed and sixty wounded before the war ended.

The 1863 law exempted the physically disabled and certain classes of public officials. Malingering of every degree took place: self-mutilation, removing one's teeth, cutting off a trigger-finger. When fire brigades were declared exempt, some towns listed all their able-bodied men as fire-fighters. Many cities put up the $300 commutation fee to protect their citizens.[3]

The most convenient draft resistance technique was running away. This form of evasion became so frequent that a new word—"skedaddling"—was coined to describe it. New England farmers deserted their employers in such droves that crops rotted in the fields. Towns sprang up across the Canadian border as evaders from all parts of the country sought refuge. Many ran away to California or mining towns in the Rockies. In 1864, over 150,000 men crossed the Missouri River heading westward, and more sailed around Cape Horn. A large percentage of these travelers were liable for the draft.

The most drastic defiance took the form of armed uprisings. In the Pennsylvania anthracite fields (home of the Molly Maguires), full-strength regiments were required to enforce the draft against armed miners. A group called the Knights of the Golden Circle operated in Illinois, Ohio, and Indiana, hid individual evaders, and formed armed bodies to harass enrolling officers and other draft officials. The Union Army had to divert many experienced units to deal with this opposition.

In July 1863, thousands of draft opponents in New York City rioted at the first selection of names under the Enrollment Act. Thirteen regiments of troops were required to put down the week-long spree, which left 1,200 people dead (mostly blacks) and caused millions of dollars worth of property damage. Satellite riots took place in Troy, New York, and Boston in the same period. Practically every state had its history of "persistent, sullen, often virulent and sometimes violent resistance" to the Union-imposed draft.[4]

As a result the total number of men actually conscripted was negligible. Of the 2,666,999 men who served in the Union Army during the Civil War, only 46,347 were drafted. The total called was, of course, much higher. In the first draft of July 1863, 292,441 names were drawn for service. But 164,395 were found exempt for medical or other reasons; 53,288 paid the commutation fee; 26,002 substitutes were provided and only 9,881 were held to personal service. No fewer than 39,415 men who were ordered to report failed to show. The second draft—spring of 1864—called for 113,446 men, and only 3,416 were drafted. Twenty-seven thousand men failed to report without excuse. In the third call of July 1864, with the commutation exemption all but eliminated and substitutes accepted less frequently, 66,000 of the 231,918 called did not appear for service.

Of 776,829 men called to service during the Civil War, 315,509 were exempted; 86,724 paid the commutation fee; 73,679 provided a substitute; and 161,244 failed to report.[5]

The ratio of men failing to report thus averaged 20 percent throughout the war. In addition, approximately 200,000 men "skedaddled" and never appeared on the rolls to be called at all. Thus the percentage of illegal draft evaders during the Civil War may have been as high as 40 percent and certainly was not lower than 30 percent.

The next draft, during World War I, met with a higher degree of compliance. About 2,760,000 men were drafted over a period of twenty-four months. Under the 1917 Selective Draft Law, all men between ages twenty-one and thirty were obliged to register on June 5, 1917, and on subsequent registration days. If they failed to register, they were indicted in the civil courts, the offense treated as a misdemeanor punishable by not more than a year in jail. The government initiated 51,778 prosecutions for failing to register or making false statements to a draft board or assisting a registrant to evade service. But the great majority of men indicted subsequently agreed to comply with the law; by January 1920, only 3,748 young men had been tried, convicted, and sentenced for failing to register, and only 956 were sentenced for other types of offenses.[6]

After registration, however, the military assumed jurisdiction over all draft evaders. If a man registered but then failed to return his questionnaire or failed to report for a physical, the military would order him to appear for immediate induction. If he failed to report, he was treated as a deserter. When apprehended, he was tried by military court-martial rather than a regular court. Thus a simple failure to return a questionnaire on time could lead to trial by a military tribunal. The total reported desertions as of July 15, 1919 were 489,003, but 151,354 were found to have enlisted or otherwise were not subject to the draft, leaving a total of 331,649 draft-law violators.[7]

About three-quarters of the total deserters were men declared delinquent and ordered for priority induction. Included in this total were 129,268 aliens who were obliged to register but upon proper proof of alienage would have been declared exempt. Since they never registered, however, they were carried as delinquents and then as deserters. One-quarter of the total, about 80,000 men, were draft refusers who willfully failed to obey an initial order for induction. In his final report, the provost marshal general noted: "It therefore appears that out of a total registration of more than 23,000,000 men, but 1.41 per cent wrongfully sought to escape the military obligations imposed upon them by the selective-service law." [8] However, the proper base is not 23,000,000 (the total registered) but three million, the total number to whom a valid induction order was addressed (2,760,000 inducted plus 212,129 who were declared delinquent and then refused induction). Thus the ratio of draft resistance during World War I was about 7 percent (331,649 military delinquents plus 3,748 civil convictions, less 129,268 aliens, equalling 206,129 out of 3,000,000).

Special problems were presented by conscientious objectors. The law provided an exemption from combatant service for men who were members of "any well-recognized religious sect or organization . . . whose existing creed or principles forbid its members to participate in war in any form." But even Quakers, Mennonites, and members of other peace sects had to serve as non-combatants or were furloughed to work on farms. Many individual objectors who did not belong to an established church claimed a right to non-combatant status and refused military duties. A special Board of Inquiry with Harlan Fiske Stone as one of its members, went from camp to camp and inquired into the sincerity of thousands of objectors.* The board

---

* After the war was over, Stone wrote a famous article on the conscientious objector problem. Although he was discussing the problem of *religious* objectors in World War I, every word he wrote applies as well to the *humanitarian* objectors to the Vietnam War:

    It is the easy but undiscriminating and shallow way to dispose of the case of the conscientious objector by denouncing him as a coward and slacker. That many, if not most of his numbers, are muddle-headed and inconsistent in their theories of life increases the difficulty of the problem;

granted exemptions to the great majority of those brought before them (1,978 out of 2,294).[9]

But the army was particularly harsh with objectors who were found not sincere or who refused alternate non-combatant service. Of 504 tried by court-martial, only one was acquitted. Seventeen were sentenced to death and 142 were given life sentences. On review, the civilian authorities in the War Department reduced these sentences, but two men were given fifty-year terms; 186 received twenty-five- to fifty-year sentences, and 212 had ten- to twenty-five-year terms.*

Draft resistance in 1917–1918 never reached the dimensions of the Civil War, and outright armed resistance was extremely rare. The only notable instance of an armed uprising was the Green Corn Rebellion in the southern Canadian valley of Oklahoma, and even that episode had its roots more in the economic problems of the sharecroppers of the region than in any conscientious opposition to conscription. Over 80 percent of the farmers in eastern Oklahoma were tenant farmers. They operated one-crop farms (cotton), paid outrageous interest rates required by local banks, and were heavily mortgaged to their landlords or the general merchandise store that

---

but their evident sincerity and willingness to suffer to the end rather than to yield up their cherished illusion make impossible the wholesale condemnation of the conscientious objector as a coward and a slacker. That any considerable number of our citizens at a time when we were making our supreme national effort should defy our laws and refuse to participate in it is a serious matter; but the violation of the conscience of the individual by majority action is likewise a serious matter, and the statesmanship which would shut its eyes to facts and say that cowardice only is involved is singularly lacking in penetration and in any constructive policy.

The ultimate test of the course of action which the state should adopt will of course be the test of its own self-preservation; but with the limitation, at least in those countries where the political theory obtains that the ultimate end of the state is the highest good of its citizens, both morals and sound policy require that the state should not violate the conscience of the individual. All our history gives confirmation to the view that liberty of conscience has a moral and social value which makes it worthy of preservation at the hands of the state. So deep in its significance and vital, indeed, is it to the integrity of man's moral and spiritual nature that nothing short of the self-preservation of the state should warrant its violation; and it may well be questioned whether the state which preserves its life by a settled policy of violation of the conscience of the individual will not in fact ultimately lose it by the process. Every ethical and practical consideration which should lead the state to endeavor to avoid the violation of the conscience of its citizens should therefore lead a wise and humane government to seek some practical solution of this difficult problem.[10]

* When Franklin Roosevelt assumed the Presidency in 1933, there was still a small group of World War I draft resisters in the federal prison in Atlanta. He ordered them released immediately.

supplied them with their tools, seed, and clothing. Most of the farmers were illiterate and belonged to fundamentalist Protestant sects; many were Holy Rollers. The region had a reputation for being one of the most lawless in the country, with roughnecks from the oilfields, gamblers, bootleggers, and killers.[11]

Socialist or Wobbly organizers in Oklahoma and Arkansas had set up lodges under the aegis of an organization called the Working Class Union, and these became the center of social and political life of many tenant farmers, who were quite responsive to the anti-capitalist message of the I.W.W. Their knowledge of politics was rather vague, however, and the I.W.W. agitators put them off by advocating industrial sabotage. As the farmers saw the possibility of economic security in the brief period of prosperity following the outbreak of World War I, the lodges lost many of their members. The American declaration of war in April 1917 soon destroyed that vision. The combination of a fall in cotton prices, resentment against the unresponsive federal government which promised peace and then immediately declared war, and a return of the I.W.W. spellbinders to the region brought the farmers to the edge of revolution.

For a variety of reasons, the draft became the focus of the farmer's hostility. "Rube" Munson—a Wobbly organizer from Illinois—and his aides convinced many tenants that every able-bodied man would have to serve in the army and would be shipped to Germany to die. When registration day arrived—June 5, 1917—the Working Class Union passed out anti-war literature and convinced a number of farmers not to register. Arrests were made, but the authorities did not consider the local agitators a serious problem.

By July, Munson and the local W.C.U. leaders—Homer Spence, John Spears, Bill Benefield—were planning for revolution. They drew up a plan for a march on Washington to overthrow "Big Slick's"—Woodrow Wilson's—government and stop the war. The Oklahoma farmers would be joined by workers from other sections of the country, Munson claimed, lumberjacks and miners from the Far West, farm workers from Texas, Arkansas, and Missouri, and the disaffected everywhere. As they marched, they would destroy railroad bridges and telegraph lines, confiscate the property they needed, crush the few army troops left in the country, and subsist along the way on barbecued steers and green corn—thus giving the episode its name.

The rebellion was set for August 3. The main body of the revolutionaries (about one hundred men) gathered on a hill on John Spears' farm on August 2. Spears put himself in command and raised the red I.W.W. flag in front of his home. Fifty more men under Bill Benefield arrived around midnight and the force heard speeches denouncing Big Slick, which excited preparations for the march.

The next day the men set out barbecuing a steer and roasting a wagon-full of green corn ears. By the afternoon, they became lazy and lethargic from the big meal and the hot August sun. In the meantime, Sheriff Robert E. Duncan of Pontotoc County gathered a posse of twenty-five men to fight the insurrection, rumors of which had spread rapidly. The sheriff led his men to Spears' farm. Although the rebels occupied the top of the hill, had good cover, were well armed, and outnumbered the posse by five to one, they had no effective leadership to organize or direct them. The sheriff's men advanced without hesitation across an open field, presenting an easy target. But the farmers fired not a single shot; they broke and ran, and thirty were captured by the sheriff's men.

In succeeding days, this pattern reoccurred. Small posses dispersed larger groups of rebels who scattered at the first sight of the authorities. There was only one serious exchange of fire, at the small town of Four Corners in Hughes County where two deputies were wounded and W.C.U. leader Ed Blaylock killed. By August 5, only a few rebellious farmers had not been taken into custody. By August 16, 450 prisoners were held in the state penitentiary at McAlester.

The authorities soon realized that the rank and file of the rebels consisted of confused and illiterate tenant farmers who had fallen easy prey to the I.W.W. agitators. Many were released without trial, others given short sentences or small fines. The government's attitude toward the leaders was quite different. The federal judge presiding at the trial sentenced Munson, Spence, and Benefield to ten years in the federal penitentiary. Oklahoma was peaceful again and the farmers remained in the poverty from which the I.W.W. had promised to release them.

In Texas, the Farmers' and Laborers' Protective Association had urged its members to oppose the draft by force, but after one draft evader was killed by his patriotic neighbors, no organized resistance took place. An Irish organization in Butte, Montana, called the Pearce-Connally Club, organized a number of anti-conscription demonstrations, primarily because the Irish miners objected to fighting alongside the hated British. Police tried to break up one parade and several shots were fired. Many Arkansas farmers refused to be inducted and hid in the Ozarks. Armed skirmishes between the evaders and the authorities took place through 1917. The mountains of North Caro-

lina also served as a hiding place for native sons who refused to enter
the army. It was simply incomprehensible to them that they could be
called on to fight in a foreign land to make the world safe for
democracy. They would ambush the sheriffs and federal agents that
came into their territory to force them to serve. The provost marshal
described the difficulties in North Carolina as due "principally to the
ignorance and native suspicion of the mountaineers who could not at
first comprehend the importance of the draft." [12]

The Southern states had a higher percentage of draft delinquents
than the rest of the country. The ratio of deserters was highest in
Florida, with Alabama, Georgia, Mississippi, and Louisiana among
the leaders. The Southern farmers refused to serve not because they
had any political objection to the war, but because they traditionally
resented and resisted the claims of the government upon their pocket-
books or their persons. The Speaker of the House of Representatives,
Champ Clark, said when the administration's draft law was introduced, "I protest with all my heart and mind and soul against having
the slur of being a conscript placed upon the men of Missouri. In
the estimations of Missourians there is precious little difference between a conscript and a convict." [13] Many of his fellow Southerners
felt the same way.

Cutting across geographical divides were clusters of leftwing
groups who fought the draft out of political ideology. The Wobblies
had opposed World War I from the start as a conflict between capitalist, imperialist powers. When the United States declared war in
April 1917, the Executive Board of the I.W.W. debated long and
hard about the official organization policy. They knew that their
followers expected them to continue their antimilitarist position, but
they also knew that official opposition to the draft would mean
instantaneous repression of the organization by the government. The
leaders finally urged the Wobblies to register for the draft as "I.W.W.
opposed to war." [14]

Most of the Wobblies did in fact register, and many were inducted.
However, in Rockford, Illinois, 150 Wobblies and Socialists refused to
register and then voluntarily gave themselves up in a demonstration
before the city hall. Sixty of the men were aliens who had no obligations to serve but were required to register by law. They were beaten
in jail and then given maximum sentences by federal judge Kenesaw
Mountain Landis, one of the infamous "hanging" judges of World
War I who further insulted the defendants by calling them "cowards"
and "whining, belly-aching puppies." [15]

In the Mesabi iron fields of northern Minnesota, a group of
Finnish miners refused to register, less because of their I.W.W.

affiliation than their hatred of Russia, which had now become America's ally.*

The Socialist Party met in emergency session on April 7, 1917, the day after war was declared. They called on "the workers of all the countries to refuse to support their governments in their wars," and to support "all mass movements in opposition to conscription." [16] Their anti-draft and anti-war campaign met with stiff resistance from the authorities. Party leaders, including Eugene Debs, one-time Presidential candidate of the party, Charles T. Schenck, the general secretary, and Charles T. Ruthenberg, the Ohio state chairman, were arrested and convicted for discouraging or interfering with conscription.

Anarchist leaders were treated in the same way. Emma Goldman organized the No-Conscription League and issued a famous manifesto against the draft and the "militarization of America." After a few rallies were held by the organization in May and June of 1917, the government arrested Goldman and her co-leader Alexander Berkman. Both were sentenced to five years in jail. [17]

The bases for the prosecutions of the Socialists and the Anarchists were the Selective Draft Act of 1917 and the Espionage Act of 1917, both of which punished any form of obstructing the draft. A unanimous Supreme Court upheld the constitutionality of the 1917 laws in a number of decisions written by Oliver Wendell Holmes, including the famous Schenck case. Schenck had arranged for the distribution of leaflets which stated that conscription was despotism in its worst form and a monstrous wrong against humanity. Holmes first applied the clear and present danger test to uphold the law and found that mere distribution of the leaflets warranted the conviction:

. . . the document would not have been sent unless it had been intended to have some effect, and we do not see what effect it could be expected to have upon persons subject to the draft except to influence them to obstruct the carrying of it out. [18]

Holmes also affirmed the conviction of Eugene Debs under the Espionage Act for a speech against the war since his "opposition was so expressed that its natural and intended effect would be to obstruct recruiting." † [19]

---

* After the war was over, many of the aliens in the Rockford and Minnesota cases were deported under a new law making the committing of any offense involving "moral turpitude" the basis for a deportation order. The government took the position that failure to register showed the requisite moral failing to justify shipping the men back to their home country.

† Holmes had some misgivings about the Debs case, not concerning his opinion but the government's decision to prosecute. He wrote to Herbert

The government's treatment of draft opponents during World War I is one of the shabbiest episodes in our history. Innocent meetings called to protest the draft law were broken up by police and vigilante groups, the participants beaten, arrested, and often sentenced to long jail terms. Socialist literature suggesting the illegality of conscription was seized by the police and denied mailing privileges by the post office department. Any statement of opposition to the war could lead to indictment under the Espionage Act as encouragement to draft evaders.

In one case, Walter Matthey of Iowa attended a meeting where various anti-conscription remarks were made. He said nothing, but applauded the speakers. He was indicted for merely *appearing* at the gathering, found guilty, and sentenced to a year in jail. Twenty-seven farmers from South Dakota petitioned the governor of the state complaining that their county's draft quota was too high. They asked for a referendum on the war and threatened to vote against the governor if he did not support their position. They were sentenced to two years in jail, although their convictions were later reversed. Another South Dakota citizen was convicted under the espionage law for circulating a petition which called for the repeal of the draft law. The state secretary of the Minnesota Socialist Party was sent to jail for three years for suggesting the draft law was unconstitutional and there was no obligation to obey it.[21]

The government initiated thousands of cases under the Espionage Act to stifle criticism of the war. While few doubted Congress' power to raise an army and punish direct interference with the draft, using the law to throw dissenters into jail constituted a serious threat to the democratic process. No other legal club had—or has—as much potential to cut off debate in time of war. Any critical discussion of the government's conduct of a war might lead young men to refuse service. The nexus between criticism of the war and a refusal to serve must necessarily be vague. But to punish political opponents in wartime under the guise of protecting the draft machinery is a

---

Croly of the *New Republic*: "I hated to have to write the Debs case and still more of the other poor devils before us [Schenck, Frohwerk and others] the same day and the week before. I could not see the wisdom of pressing the cases, especially when the fighting was over and I think it is quite possible that if I had been on the jury I should have been for acquittal . . ." To Harold Laski he wrote: "I know that donkeys and knaves would resent us as concurring in the condemnation of Debs because he was a dangerous agitator . . . But on the only questions before us I could not doubt about the law. The federal judges seem to me . . . to have got hysterical about the war. I should think the President when he gets through with his present amusements might do some pardoning . . ."[20]

dangerous undertaking. The controversy over the Vietnam War was to recreate these problems in an aggravated form.

World War II enjoyed unprecedented popular support. Most of the nation's draft-eligible youth complied with their induction calls, and the rate of draft resistance fell to the lowest level in the country's history. Although over ten million men were inducted, there were only 348,217 reported delinquencies through June 30, 1945. Of these, 187,000 later complied with the law. Only 26,800 prosecutions were commenced and sixteen thousand convictions secured for draft offenses over a seven-year period ending in 1947. About six thousand of these were for minor derelictions, such as failure to return a draft questionnaire or to possess a registration certificate.[22]

No organized groups like the I.W.W. or the Socialists opposed the war or the draft; resisters generally operated as individuals, and they were not politically inspired. Although most of the publicized cases of draft evasion in World War II involved fraud—"draft dodgers" faking physical disabilities or claiming non-existent dependents—the most serious problems for the government were posed by conscientious objectors and Jehovah's Witnesses. In the course of the war, the Selective Service classified some 42,000 men as conscientious objectors. Quakers, Mennonites, and members of other peace sects were generally given non-combatant assignments, but the political pacifists who did not belong to an established church invoked little sympathy from prevailing public opinion which was fired up by the image of the fascist foes.

The Selective Training and Service Act of 1940 included provisions for conscientious objectors similar to those of World War I. No one could be classified as a C.O. unless his opposition to the war was grounded in "religious training and belief," and a form of alternate national service was required. After a series of discussions between leaders of the Historic Peace Churches (Mennonites, Friends, and Brethren) and administration officials, the government agreed to set up Civilian Public Service Camps for C.O.'s (paid for by the Churches but directed and controlled by the Selective Service System). In six years, 11,950 objectors worked in sixty-seven camps located in rural areas throughout the country. They engaged mainly in forestry and conservation work; some were allowed to work in mental health hospitals or served as guinea pigs in medical experiments.[23]

There were many complaints about the C.P.S. system. The men were not paid for their work, and their families endured great hardship as a result. Although Congress passed a law directing that military men in command of C.P.S. camps were to be regarded as civilians, pacifists resented the administrative control exercised by army officers in the camps. Many of the C.O.'s were professionals, yet their special skills were ignored. Dr. Don DeVault, a research chemist from Stanford, was conducting important research on penicillin molds in a homemade lab in his C.P.S. camp, but the Selective Service turned down his request to devote full-time to his experiments and finally sent him to jail when he refused to report for a ditch-digging detail. For most C.O.'s, serving in a military-run conservation corps proved no less compromising to their principles than killing "the enemy." [24]

Beginning in late 1942, more and more C.O.'s walked out of the C.P.S. camps or refused to accept work assignments. One departing pacifist, George Kingsley, announced that, "C.P.S. is a compromise I cannot tolerate: it is an insignificant witness against war and conscription." Another C.O., Corbett Bishop, left his C.P.S. camp, went to Washington, and announced to the Selective Service System and the Department of Justice that he had ceased to cooperate with them or the state. His non-cooperation went to the extreme of going limp during his trial for draft evasion: he had to be carried in and out of every court appearance.[25]

The government responded to these acts of conscience by indicting and jailing the C.O.'s who refused to remain in C.P.S. camps. In prison along with the walkouts were pacifists who refused to report to the camps and thousands of Jehovah's Witnesses who claimed ministerial exemptions and never even applied for C.O. status. Together they constituted 16 percent of all the men in federal prisons during World War II. Six thousand convictions for draft violations involved conscientious objector claims, including 4,411 Jehovah's Witnesses.[26]

The courts, moreover, were quite harsh on C.O.'s: the average sentence for C.O. draft offenders was thirty-six months, while for all others it was only fourteen months. According to a May 1944 report of the Bureau of Prisons, there were 4,199 Selective Service violators in federal prisons. These included 2,141 Jehovah's Witnesses who had been denied ministerial exemptions and another 648 who had applied for C.O. status and been turned down or had walked out of C.P.S. camps. Only 1,399 had never pressed any claim of conscience and could be considered "draft dodgers" as the public understood the term.[27] Thus, on the whole, the government responded to claims of conscience with the severest counter-measures. The most fraudulent and cowardly draft dodger stood a better chance before the courts than the most moral of pacifists.

# 9

# Origins

Five Beekman Place in lower Manhattan was for many years the headquarters of the War Resisters League (WRL), the Workshop in Nonviolence, and *Liberation* Magazine (edited by A. J. Muste and Dave Dellinger), and in 1967 it became the home of the Resistance —the center of anti-draft activity in the city. It was no accident that Vietnam draft resistance groups shared office space with long-established pacifist organizations, not only in New York City but throughout the country. For in many respects the Resistance was a continuation of the pacifist movement, drawing both ideology and tactics from the older organizations. At the same time, the new draft resisters—veterans of the civil rights drives of the early 1960's and the student rebellions immediately thereafter—brought their own spirit to the anti-war cause and took it far beyond the limits of traditional pacifism.

For the pacifists, resistance to conscription was part of a program of total opposition to militarism and war. In the 1950's, the Fellowship of Reconciliation, the Committee for Non-Violent Action (CNVA), and other peace groups mounted a campaign against the continuation of nuclear testing. They sailed ships into atomic testing areas in the South Pacific and tried to board the Polaris missile submarines docked at Groton, Connecticut. In 1959, when he was seventy-five years old, A. J. Muste, the spiritual leader of the American pacifists, twice climbed over a fence at an Air Force ICBM base in Mead, Nebraska and was arrested for trespassing. Dave Dellinger, Bayard Rustin, and members of the Catholic Workers regularly refused to take shelter during the air raid drills conducted in New York City.

Muste had always spoken out against the draft. In 1952, he wrote a book making a general appeal to the country's youth "to adopt and practice the great and urgent virtues of Holy Disobedience, non-conformity, resistance toward Conscription, Regimentation, and War." Opposition to conscription was required, in Muste's view, not only because the draft was a necessary instrument of the nation's war machine, but because of the coercion imposed on the nation's youth. "They may not have the slightest interest in the war; yet, they are made to kill by order. This is surely a fundamental violation of the human spirit which must cause the pacifist to shudder." Resistance—"Holy Disobedience"—was an "indispensable measure of spiritual self-preservation in a day when the impulse to conform, to acquiesce, to go along, is the instrument which is used to subject man to totalitarian rule." It was also a necessary political tactic to stop war.

For it becomes daily clearer that political and military leaders pay virtually no attention to protests against current foreign policy and pleas for peace when they know perfectly well that when it comes to a showdown, all but a handful will "go along" with the war to which the policy leads, all but a handful will submit to conscription. Few of the protesters will so much as risk their jobs in the cause of peace.[1]

Hundreds of pacifists responded to Muste's ideas and refused to enter the army. Between 1950 and 1960, an average of two hundred men per year went to jail for draft offenses. Well over half were either Jehovah's Witnesses or pacifists who could have been classified as conscientious objectors. David Mitchell, a member of CNVA, wrote to his draft board in 1961, long before the Vietnam War became an issue in the country, "I will not play any part in the conscription system. . . . I will not even play a part in seeking or serving alternate service, for then I would be contributing to an immoral system and hardening all men's acceptance of this system without dissent. . . . I pledge that my resistance to militarism shall be heard." In 1962, Mitchell helped form a small organization called "End the Draft," which hoped, rather quixotically, to gather opposition to the 1963 extension of the draft law. The organization declared in a pamphlet:

In allowing our government to place youth in military subjugation, we accept the insanity of nuclear war and the criminality of the so-called "limited wars." The power to draft allows government manipulation of world tensions. . . . It dismisses our rights and responsibilities by disrupting our lives and channeling us (deferments, enlistments) into military roles. . . . We support all who have and will boycott the draft.[2]

To help draft opponents, pacifist organizations, including the Central Committee for Conscientious Objectors (CCCO), the Fellowship of Reconciliation, and the War Resisters League, offered draft counseling throughout the Fifties and early Sixties. The CCCO, formed in 1952, put together a handbook on how to apply for C.O. status and how to deal with the objections of draft boards to a C.O. claim. Initially, only a small group of pacifists made use of the service. The first handbook published by the organization in 1952 was limited to eight thousand copies, but in 1965 twenty thousand copies were issued, and by 1968 the number reached one hundred thousand.

The pacifists also initiated active protests against the draft, most notably the draft-card burnings which were later adopted by the Vietnam resistance groups. As early as February 1947, Dwight MacDonald staged a card-burning ceremony on behalf of the WRL. Tom Cornell of the Catholic Worker movement burned his first card in a public ceremony during the Second World-Wide Strike for Peace in 1962 and organized another card burning in New York's Union Square the following year. Gene Keyes, a pacifist who had worked in the CNVA campaign against the Polaris submarines, burned his card in front of his Champaign, Illinois draft board on Christmas Eve of 1963. (His draft board then ordered him to report for a physical but on the date specified he was in an Albany, Georgia jail because of his civil rights activities.)

The civil rights drive of the early 1960's was itself a substantial force behind the draft resistance movement. Civil disobedience campaigns such as the sit-ins, freedom rides, and Birmingham-type demonstrations alerted many activists to the political effectiveness of defying what they saw as illegitimate authority. Many of the draft resistance leaders had their political baptism in the SNCC drives in Alabama or Mississippi or the 1964 Freedom Summer. The openness and camaraderie of those efforts, the verve and exhilaration they produced, the confrontation with genuine risk they demanded were all eagerly sought and regained in the Resistance. As Professor Staughton Lynd of Yale explained, "We were looking for something white radicals could do which would have the same spirit, ask as much of us, and challenge the system as fundamentally as had our work in Mississippi." [3]

The movement for Black Power in the spring of 1966 began the exclusion of white leadership participation in certain civil rights organizations. It coincided with the continued escalation of the Vietnam War and the growing national anger about the government's policies in Southeast Asia. White activists who found themselves ousted from the civil rights drive transferred their energies into the anti-war movement and particularly its anti-draft phase, which was both the most dangerous and the most rewarding.

Almost all the resistance leaders had also been active in Students for a Democratic Society (SDS), formed in 1960. In 1964 SDS worked with the Free Speech Movement at Berkeley—the first widespread student rebellion—to open the campus to speakers of all political persuasions. In these early efforts the student leaders developed many organizational skills which would prove useful in the later draft resistance movement—how to form effective working groups, how to draw the attention of the media to their projects, how to assemble small demonstrations and mass rallies.

By 1965, student activists were using the card-burning protest to voice their disapproval of the administration's foreign policy. On May 5, hundreds of Berkeley students attended a campus rally to object to American intervention in the Dominican Republic, and forty activists burned their cards in front of the local draft board. "It's purely a symbolic protest," one student explained. "We have been told we can get new cards if we apply for them." On July 29, 1965, a large rally was held at the Whitehall Street induction center in New York, and members of CNVA publicly burned their draft cards in a tin pot. Colonel Paul Akst, the director of the Selective Service for New York City, remarked to a *New York Times* reporter, "It's just a nuisance. They'll just come in to their local boards in a few days and get a duplicate card." [4]

But Congress was not as sanguine as Colonel Akst, especially when news coverage brought the events to public attention. On August 5, 1965, Representative L. Mendel Rivers introduced a bill to punish draft-card burning or mutilation with a five-year jail term. During subsequent Congressional debate, Representative William G. Bray of Indiana called the burners "beatniks and 'campus-cultists' " and their intellectual supporters—men like Professor Staughton Lynd of Yale and Dave Dellinger—were labeled "Communist stooges . . . and a filthy, sleazy, beatnik gang." The Armed Services Committee chief counsel said, "Now this is the answer, of course, to this attempted mass destruction of draft cards. These bums that are going around the country burning draft cards while people are dying in South Vietnam have brought about [this law]." [5]

For over twenty-five years, the message of the pacifists on the horrors of war had been all but ignored in America. But now the immediacy of the Vietnam War breathed new life into abstract pacifism and made it a compelling alternate to America's Asian adventure. The war bred a new generation of pacifists who took their ideological premises and activated them with astutely conceived tactics.

The anti-draft campaign began in earnest with the awakening of liberal opinion on the campuses and in the press to the terrible fiasco of our Vietnam policy coupled with the government's heavy-handed response to the protest movement.* After the bombing of North Vietnam began in February 1965, SDS called for a mammoth march on Washington in April. Liberals and intellectuals responded in their own way with a series of "teach-ins" (marathon seminars attacking American foreign policy). The first, organized by Arnold Kaufman, a philosophy professor at the University of Michigan, took place in Ann Arbor in late March 1965. In May, the Vietnam Day Committee was formed at Berkeley (with Jerry Rubin as one of its leaders) to arrange further demonstrations and teach-ins at the University of California. The VDC, an ad-hoc organization of all political shadings, prepared anti-draft literature which was distributed on many West Coast campuses. One pamphlet, entitled "Brief Notes on the Ways and Means of Beating the Draft," told students how to obtain C.O. classification, how to affect homosexuality or physical ailments, and recommended getting high on drugs before a medical examination. At a meeting in Bloomington, Illinois in September 1965, SDS made similar recommendations for "beating the system." It also proposed that anti-war literature be handed out at physical examination and induction centers, that recruiters be picketed on the campuses, and that draft boards be attacked as un-

* In the spring of 1964, the May 2nd Movement—a campus movement formed by the Maoist Progressive Labor Party—circulated the first "We Won't Go" statement, signed by a handful of students at Yale University and Haverford College (a Quaker institution): "Believing that United States participation in [the Vietnam] war is for the suppression of the Vietnamese struggle for national independence, we see no justification for our involvement. . . . Believing that we should not be asked to fight against the people of Vietnam, we herewith state our refusal to do so." [6] But it wasn't until 1965 that direct draft defiance gathered any momentum.

democratic and unrepresentative. But no call was yet made for outright draft refusal.

Nineteen sixty-five began with a draft call of only three thousand; by July, it rose to seventeen thousand after President Johnson announced large-scale shipments of American troops to Vietnam, and by October, thirty thousand men were being called per month. At this point, the entire anti-war movement focused on the draft. The VDC attempted to march ten thousand strong from Berkeley to the Oakland Army Base, but it was halted at the Oakland city line by three hundred policemen. The next day, October 16, 1965, a group of Hell's Angels joined the police in aborting another march. In New York City, David C. Miller of the Catholic Workers organization burned his draft card during a rally at Whitehall Street and was arrested two days later, the first offender under the new law. A group of thirty-nine students and professors from the University of Michigan invaded a draft board in Ann Arbor and refused to leave; they were arrested for trespass. (One of the students, Peter Wolff, was to figure in an important court case that resulted from the sit-in.) A large rally was held on Boston Common where hecklers managed to drown out most of the speakers attacking the government.

The reaction of the Johnson Administration to these activities gave a boost to the draft resistance movement. Even as late as 1965, it might have been possible to present the problems of the war and the draft in a way that would have minimized the friction between youth and government: by appealing to its idealism and patriotism, by recommending a more equitable system of selection, by treating opposition to the war as a serious matter to be considered and debated. Instead, Attorney General Nicholas Katzenbach charged that the anti-war rallies were Communist-infiltrated. President Johnson was "dismayed" by the demonstrations and warned that they would prolong the war by encouraging the Vietcong to continue fighting— an accusation repeatedly hurled against the opposition to government policy. For his part, General Lewis Hershey suggested that draft boards might reclassify demonstration participants as delinquents and induct them at the head of the line.*

* Hershey made his first public mention of the punitive use of the delinquency regulations in early Demember 1965, after the Ann Arbor sit-in and a well-publicized draft card-burning ceremony in Union Square, New York. (David McReynolds of the War Resisters League, Tom Cornell of the Catholic Workers, and three other young men, Marc Edelman, Roy Lisker, and David Wilson, burned their cards under the watchful eyes of A. J. Muste.) Hershey explained that committing a trespass or burning draft cards "were grounds for reclassification into 1-A and immediate induction . . . The government would be committing suicide if it deferred students who defied the Selective Service System." In answer to a complaint by Congressman Emanuel Celler that

Hershey's statements about punitive reclassification showed what tight control he had over the Selective Service System. Because of his strong support among the Congressional conservatives who sat on the House Armed Services Committee, Hershey did not hesitate to run the System in his own way and to oppose administration policies that he found objectionable.[8] Not only did he defend his organization as fair, efficient, and necessary, but he saw virtues in the draft method of selection extending far beyond national security: "I am convinced that this nation has paced the world's technological advance of recent years in large part because scores of thousands of people have become scientists, engineers, teachers and acquired and applied other technical skills because they were deferred [by the draft] to do so," he reported to a House Committee in 1966.

The year before, the Selective Service System had issued a semi-secret "Memorandum on Channeling" to its draft boards, describing in this very way the purpose underlying its system of deferments and exemptions. The draft was not simply a process for securing men for the armed forces: by using the "club of induction" the government could force other young men into studying and training themselves for occupations best suited to the needs of the nation. "Throughout his career as a student, the pressure—the threat of loss of deferment —continues." To maintain his freedom from the draft, he must complete his studies, and even after school is over, "he is impelled to pursue his skill rather than embark upon some less important enterprise, and is encouraged to apply his skill in an essential activity in the national interest." With great pride, the Memorandum concludes that "the psychology of granting wide choice under pressure to take action is the American or indirect way of achieving what is done by direction in foreign countries where choice is not allowed."

The Memorandum was a classic example of bureaucratic bungling. It implied that the United States was as tyrannical as any totalitarian government in dictating career choices to its citizens. It revealed an astonishing hypocrisy and cynicism about the government's role in the economic sphere and a boundless contempt for the nation's youth. Moreover, it exposed the subtle way in which each middle-class son is enticed to stay within the system. Needless to say, the Resistance

---

such reclassification violated the First Amendment, Hershey wrote, "Any deliberate, illegal obstruction of the administration of the law by registrants cannot be tolerated. We must always distinguish between young men who engage in a legal demonstration of political views and those who express those views by willfully violating the Selective Service laws, often with advance notice [that] they will violate the law at a particular time and place."[7] Hershey's letter to Cellar was released on the same day that four of the Union Square card-burners were indicted under the new law.

later seized on the Memorandum as "a prized captured enemy document and gleefully reprinted it in the hundreds of thousands as their basic recruiting leaflet." [9]

To young men troubled by Vietnam, their student deferments became an embarrassment. It was a reminder of their special immunity under the draft law, a middle-class privilege that separated them from the poor who could not buy their way into college. (SDS called the deferment system "divisive and class-racial-discriminatory.") They saw a II-S classification as a bribe to keep them quiet about the war as they docilely followed the career choices dictated by their parents or by Hershey's system of channeling. Above all, keeping one's student deferment meant tacit support of the military machine. David Zimmerman, later a Resistance leader, explained:

The Resistance movement, for all the diversity in motives and political sophistication, is essentially an attempt to find the appropriate response to General Hershey's technique of chanelling and all it implies about our society . . . Channelled college students only begin to throw off their oppression when they translate the social issues of the draft, the war it feeds, and the garrison state it sustains, into a personal problem. To return their draft cards and take the attendant risks may be the only way that the channelled can "seize control of their own lives," and initiate a process of political resistance to the source of *their* oppression.[10]

Michael Ferber wrote in the same vein:

We in the Resistance reasoned that if the deferment system is a kind of indirect totalitarianism then we no longer wanted our deferments, and we resolved to oppose not only the draft but the system of coercion it serves.

The first anti-war rallies in October 1965 did not lead to any widespread draft resistance. At that time, SDS dealt with the problem of conscription and the Vietnam War on a different level. Paul Booth, speaking for SDS on October 20, 1965, offered the following proposal:

We are fully prepared to volunteer for service to our country and to democracy . . . We volunteer to serve in hospitals and schools in the slums, in the Job Corps and VISTA, in the new Teachers Corps . . . We propose to the President that all those Americans who seek so vigorously to build instead of burn be given their chance to do so . . . Let us see what happens if service to democracy is made grounds for exemption from the military draft. I predict that almost every member of my generation would choose to build rather than burn; to teach, not to torture; to help, not to kill.

(In May 1966, Secretary of Defense Robert S. McNamara proposed that two years of civilian service to the nation, such as Peace Corps work, might be substituted for military duty. "It seems to me," he said in a speech in Montreal, "that we could move toward remedying . . . inequity [in the draft] by asking every young person in the United States to give two years of service to his country—whether in one of the military services, in the Peace Corps, or in some other voluntary development work at home or abroad." Key public figures praised the proposal but Congress never gave it serious consideration. Significantly, at a time when the government was accusing the peace movement of Communist infiltration and charging students— particularly SDS—with treason, no one acknowledged the fact that SDS had made an identical proposal six months earlier.)

In the spring of 1966, SDS issued a Freedom Draft Card which embodied Booth's proposal. "I want to work for democracy. I do not want to fight in Vietnam, because the war is destroying our hopes for democracy, both there and at home. I want to build, not burn. The efforts of many young Americans in civil rights and community organization are prime examples of what I want to do." The cards were handed out to students at many campuses, and many students signed petitions endorsing the plan.

SDS strenuously objected to Hershey's use of the delinquency regulations to induct anti-war protesters—a procedure later condemned by a unanimous Supreme Court decision. A second SDS petition was directed at the local draft boards, urging them "to pledge not to use the draft as a weapon of stifling political opposition to the war in Vietnam . . . This arbitrary use of power confirms our worst fear—that America, in time of war, will restrict the freedoms for which we are supposedly fighting."

A third SDS drive in the spring of 1966 focused on student deferments. The Selective Service System had dropped its nationwide qualification test for students in 1961, and subsequently draft boards relied on grades and class standing to determine whether a student was satisfactorily pursuing his college program. In March 1966, as draft calls continued around thirty thousand per month, Hershey decided to reinstate the test. Once again, Hershey's action reminded many college students of their privileged status in the prevailing system and of the compromises they were making to keep their deferments. Just before the test was to be given on May 15, a group of 350 students led by the local SDS chapter occupied the administration building at the University of Chicago to prevent testing. SDS-inspired rallies were held at Stanford, Buffalo, Brooklyn College, and City College of New York. CCNY quickly agreed not to send grades or ratings to Selective Service. In a short time schools throughout the country followed suit and refused to supply such information to the draft boards.

By the summer of 1966, however, the continuation of the war led SDS and other radical student organizations to escalate their campaigns beyond traditional protests. At their national convention at Clear Lake, Iowa, SDS denounced "demonstrations, electoral politics, lobbying the liberal establishment" and substituted organization of community-based draft resistance unions. At Yale, Staughton Lynd helped prepare a statement signed by a group of students in July 1966 calling for a turn-in of draft cards on November 16, 1966 "with a notice of our refusal to cooperate until American invasions are ended . . . We men of draft age disavow all military obligations to our government until it ceases wars against people seeking to determine their own destinies." The New Haven signers traveled around the Midwest during the summer of 1966 trying to find some way of launching a successful draft resistance campaign. They immediately saw the difficulties of planning a political movement which depended on the participants' willingness to go to jail. But wherever they went, they found support for an anti-draft stand.

A national conference on draft resistance was held in August at Des Moines, Iowa. The delegates decided that the New Haven plan for a November draft-card burning or turn-in demonstration required a network of local organizations—"We Won't Go" unions—to prepare young men to face the problems of civil disobedience. They saw the need to mobilize anti-draft sentiment in different schools, reach into the local communities, and carry the anti-war message to draft-age men through personal contact. Tom Bell of Cornell University, one of the participants at the August meeting, went back to Ithaca to initiate the program. He talked to three friends, who in turn talked to others, about the meaning of the war and their role in opposing it. Thereafter, as Bell describes,

We decided to make the same move as before; each person would talk to someone new, give him an understanding of what we were about, get him to talk to some of the other people already involved, and bring him to a meeting in two weeks.

The seven original organizers at Cornell agreed that they would never go into the army and that they would encourage others to do the same.

Everybody in the group had essentially taken on the job of being an organizer of the group. Our organizing had relied on long hours of soul-searching discussion and a healthy rejection of the press or already organized groups. The building of the draft resistance community had in no way challenged existing groups nor did it pretend to make decisions for anyone but those people participating in the resistance community.[11]

In the coming weeks the little group at Cornell held numerous meetings, with each member trying to determine his personal position toward the war and the draft. "One thing clearly emerged," according to Bell. "There is no 'right' way to handle one's position with the Selective Service System. Each person sees himself confronted with a set of alternatives *none* of which are satisfactory."

Interpersonal, one-to-one contact became the most effective method of organization for the resistance. To refuse military service was such a momentous decision in a man's life, particularly for those with middle-class backgrounds, that the deepest inquiry into all its implications was necessary. The rap sessions about the draft became a form of political group-therapy that probed all aspects of an individual's possible life-style and his relationship to society.

The Cornell group opened a draft counseling center in the local Unitarian parish house, although some of the militants on the campus objected to the move: they were afraid of being "in the liberal bag of simply trying to 'help' people in a specific and limited way."

In December 1966, one of the younger students in the group, eighteen-year-old Bruce Dancis, decided to tear up his draft card. Rallying support, five members of the Cornell group sent a letter to resistance groups and SDS chapters throughout the country in March 1967. They urged their brothers to make resisting the draft a common goal and called for a massive card-burning demonstration in New York City on April 15, 1967, at the Spring Mobilization rally against the war. The Cornell resisters pledged:

The armies of the United States have, through conscription, already oppressed or destroyed the lives and consciences of millions of Americans and Vietnamese. We have argued and demonstrated to stop this destruction. We have not succeeded. Murderers do not respond to reason. Powerful resistance is now demanded: radical, illegal, unpleasant, sustained. . . . In our own country, the war machine is directed specifically against the young, against blacks more than against whites, but ultimately against all.

Body and soul, we are oppressed in common. Body and soul, we must resist in common. The undersigned believe we should *begin* this mass resistance by publicly destroying our draft cards at the Spring Mobilization. We urge all people who have contemplated the act of destroying their draft cards to carry out this act on April 15, with the understanding that this pledge becomes binding only when 500 people have made it.

The letter stated that many church groups and student organizations had publicly supported draft resisters and that it would be difficult for the government to prosecute if thousands participated.

The Cornell group proceeded to collect pledges on their own campus. "Every day large crowds packed the Student Union lobby to listen to speeches, discuss the issues, and so forth," one participant reported. Tom Bell described the scene in a letter to Staughton Lynd as a "revival service" atmosphere. "Almost fifty Cornellians [ninety finally signed] have pledged to burn their draft cards, and I am afraid for many of them the decision comes from the emotion of the moment . . . We have speeches, a collection for the anti-war office, and on-the-spot conversions—signing pledges, plus a lot of personal witnesses." [12] Since the school administration and the student government opposed the solicitation, even ninety names were significant.

National SDS had discouraged the Cornell card-burning plan, although at the last minute *New Left Notes* ran a sympathetic story about them. At an anti-draft conference in New York in November 1966, one speaker claimed that acts "of individual protest had to be evaluated by the yardstick of how well they helped to bring people together." Young men could be radicalized only when they collectively challenged some aspect of established power and were then crushed by the authorities. SDS was also skeptical about college-oriented protests which seemed directed only to the middle class. In the December National Council meeting at Berkeley, they called for high school organizing and working with GI's to oppose the war. Direct action at draft boards or at induction centers seemed more likely to reach the mass of draft-age men than college draft-card burnings. Since the SDS focus was on building a radical political movement, what was important was the success of the organizing efforts. "We can speculate endlessly about how draft resistance might end the war," said one of the participants. "However, only talking about how resisting the draft will change people's lives can create a draft resistance movement."

But SDS endorsed the idea of local resistance groups—whether college-based or not—challenging the draft by putting their own bodies on the line. National Secretary Greg Calvert claimed that opposing the draft was part of the "revolutionary struggle which engages and claims the lives of those involved despite the seeming impossibility of revolutionary social change—the struggle which has the power to transform, to revolutionize human lives whether or not it can humanize the societal conditions of human existence." In other words, draft resistance was important not because it could create a revolution but because it could create revolutionaries.

During the winter and spring of 1966–1967, anti-draft groups sprang up spontaneously on colleges throughout the country, sometimes with and sometimes without the help of SDS. The first step was usually the signing of a "We Won't Go" petition. Seventy-six signed the first University of Chicago statement, twenty-four at Yale, sixty-six at Princeton, eighty-six at Harvard, thirty-three at Boston University, forty at Michigan State, thirty at Swarthmore, ninety-eight at the University of Wisconsin, 220 at Stanford. The signers then became the nucleus of a resistance committee who would talk to more students about avoiding the draft or refusing to go. The groups would offer draft counseling and legal assistance to their members and support anyone who declined army service by demonstrating at his induction center.

Intensive proselytizing was not necessary in the early "We Won't Go" unions. David Osher, later one of the leaders in New York Resistance, explained:

The words "attracted" or "came together" best describe the situation [in the resistance]. In spite of the hard work of organizers, individuals were not "organized" into resisting. The act preceded incorporation into the group in contradistinction to the classic view that organization precedes action. Sympathetic vibrations seemed to sweep campus and country. Only a small minority joined, but significantly a large part of that minority did not have to be "convinced" to act.

A "We Won't Go" conference was held in Chicago in December 1966—an outgrowth of the sit-ins against the college qualification tests of the previous spring. There were some five hundred participants, not SDS activists, but left-liberal college students trying to determine their own choices in the months to come. Speakers included David Mitchell and Jeff Segal (out on bail after a four-year sentence for draft evasion) as well as Staughton Lynd. There were workshops on legal problems, on the possibilities of escaping to Canada, and on the role of women in the movement.

As the April 15, 1967 rally approached, the adult organizers of Spring Mobilization put pressure on the Cornell students to burn their cards on some other day or at some other place. They feared that the newspapers would focus on the card burning and the larger message of the day would be lost. Even Dr. Benjamin Spock was reportedly against the card burning. But the students decided to go ahead, without the support of the older peace march leaders, and without the five hundred pledges they had hoped for. (One hundred and twenty had signed the pledge and only fifty-seven agreed to go through with it on the night before.) On a drizzly Saturday morning, they gathered on the rocks at Sheep Meadow in Central Park and 158 young men burned their cards in an empty Maxwell House Coffee can. One card burner attracting particular attention was Gary Rader, who appeared at the ceremony in a Green Beret uniform. (Rader had served six months on active duty and was assigned to a Green Beret reserve unit in Evanston, Illinois. He wore his reserve uniform to Central Park.) Within a week, he was arrested by the FBI for burning his card and wearing his uniform illegally. Released on bail, Rader became one of the leaders of the Chicago Area Draft Resistance (CADRE).

Also among the card burners was Martin Jezer, an editor and writer working for the New York Workshop in Nonviolence, who later wrote an eloquent statement of his position:

To destroy one's draft card, to place one's conscience before the dictates of one's government is in the highest tradition of human conduct. This country was not created by men subservient to law and government. It was created and made great by civil disobedients like Quakers who refused to compromise their religion to suit the Puritan theocracy; by Puritans who openly defied British authority; by provo-type Sons of Liberty who burned stamps to protest the Stamp Act and who dumped tea in Boston Harbor; by Abolitionists who ignored the Fugitive Slave Law, by slaves who refused to act like slaves; by workingmen who insisted, despite the law, on their right to organize; by black Americans who refused to ride in the back of the bus; and by the more than one hundred young Americans already in prison for refusing to acquiesce in the misguided actions of their government.[13]

The spring demonstrations coincided with widespread criticism of the existing draft system, due to expire in June. President Johnson had appointed a special committee to study possible changes in the law and its report was released in February 1967. Former Assistant Attorney General Burke Marshall headed the study group which included Kingman Brewster, President of Yale, Oveta Culp Hobby, former Secretary of HEW, other Eisenhower administration officials such as Thomas Gates and George Ready, and a number of professors, theologians, and businessmen.

Many respectable government leaders agreed that the existing system of student and occupational deferments favored the middle class —just as the Civil War commutation fees had done. The poor and the blacks were overrepresented in the draft, in the army, and, necessarily, in the casualty figures. Since a surplus of draft-eligible men existed, a fairer selection system was required. The Marshall Comission responded to this criticism in its final report, *In Pursuit of Equity: Who Serves When Not All Serve*. It recommended the abolition of all student and occupational deferments, and a random selection system based on national rather than state quotas with nineteen-year-olds being called first. The state-oriented draft board system should be eliminated, and a nationwide centralized organization established. It also supported the Supreme Court's decision in *United States* v. *Seeger* which widened the definition of conscientious objectors, not limiting the status to members of orthodox religious groups.

A minority on the commission favored the principle of selective conscientious objection being incorporated into a new draft law:

The classical doctrine on war widely held within the Christian community has been based on the moral premise that not all uses of military force are inherently immoral. The morality of war is indeed no more than a marginal morality, in view of the destruction, suffering and death that war always entails. Nevertheless, the tradition has maintained that certain uses of force for certain circumstances can be morally justified. In a word, a war may be just; it may also be unjust.

Translating the "Just War" doctrine to the present day, the minority continued:

Although the decision to make war is the prerogative of duly constituted government, responsible to its people, and constitutes a presumption for the citizen in favor of the legitimacy of the war, the citizen still is personally responsible for his own moral judgments on matters of public policy. He may not abdicate his own conscience into the hands of government. . . . In particular cases . . . it can happen that the conscientious moral judgment of the citizen is in conflict with the judgments made by government, either with regard to the justice of the nation's cause or with regard to the measure and mode in which military force is to be employed in the defense of the nation's vital interests. In such cases the citizen should not be compelled by government to act against his conscience by being forced to bear arms.[14]

The minority recommended that each objector should be obliged to state his case before a competent tribunal which would rule on whether his beliefs against the morality of a particular war were "truly held." This approach would raise the level of moral discourse about any war and keep the most moral young men of their generation from being faced with the alternatives of violating their consciences or going to jail.

But the majority of the commission did not go that far. They concluded that a decision about the morality of any particular war was a political one which must "be expressed through recognized democratic processes." Furthermore, "legal recognition of selective pacifism could open the doors to a general theory of selective disobedience to law, which could quickly tear down the fabric of government; the distinction is dim between a person conscientiously opposed to participation in a particular war and one conscientiously opposed to payment of a particular tax." Finally, a legal recognition of selective pacifism "could be disruptive to the morale and effectiveness of the Armed Forces."

The controversy within the commission echoed many of the arguments that surrounded conscientious disobedience to law throughout American history. Just as opponents of the Abolitionists argued that disobedience to the Fugitive Slave Law would lead to a general breakdown of law, so did the majority on the Marshall Commission see the possibility of the "fabric of government" being torn down by the recognition of the claims of conscience. To this claim, Theodore Parker in 1852 and the Marshall Commission minority in 1967 responded alike: that law must rest upon the conscientious beliefs of the people or it will ultimately fail.

If the minority position had been enacted into law, the draft resistance movement might have died in its earliest stages.

President Johnson, moving cautiously, sent only a few of the Marshall Commission recommendations to Congress. He proposed abolishing graduate school deferments (except for medical students), reversing the order of call so that the youngest rather than the oldest were called first, and he asked for a fair and impartial lottery system of selecting those eligible and available for the draft. Any change in the state headquarters system was to be subject to further study. Nothing was said by the President about the *Seeger* case or conscientious objectors.

Largely because Hershey objected to many of the new proposals, Congress made no significant changes in the prior law. It permitted the President to alter the order of call so that nineteen-year-olds could be called first, but it forbade any random selection system within age groups. In other areas it went backwards—restricting the definition of, and procedural safeguards for, conscientious objectors, making it more difficult for a registrant to challenge his classification in the courts, and giving Hershey greater power to punish draft offenders.[15] The *New York Times* commented editorially in June 1967 that the new law was "a small but regrettable victory for Representative [Mendel] Rivers of South Carolina and the know-nothing sentiment prevailing in the House Armed Services Committee . . . Nothing can undo the pettiness of Congress in yielding to the ugly spirit of its least enlightened members."

The victory of the Congressional conservatives turned out to be illusory. Not only did the failure to enact reforms in the law widen the gap between youth and the government and thus lead to greater defiance of the draft act, but the courts eventually invalidated or narrowly construed the changes made by Hershey and Rivers.* Still another opportunity was lost to assimilate legitimate dissent and thus foreclose wider resistance.

While Rivers was ramming the new draft law through, the government tried to reassure the public that draft offenses had not increased to any extent. A Selective Service spokesman announced that the number of prosecutions and delinquencies had remained about the same and that there had not been any appreciable increase in conscientious objector applications. But the authorities were worried. Rumors circulated around Washington that if college deferments were dropped, one out of four men called for service would not report. Tom Wicker wrote in the *New York Times* on May 2, 1967: "If 100,000 young men flatly refused to serve in the armed forces, regardless of their legal position, [the government's] real power to pursue the Vietnamese war or any other policy would be crippled if not destroyed. It would then be faced not with dissent but with civil disobedience on a scale amounting to revolt." The fear that draft resistance would reach the dimensions Wicker warned about may well have persuaded Congress not to tamper with the deferment system.

The spring of 1967 marked a crucial turning point for the resistance, when it went beyond the confines of SDS and other radical student groups and became the concern of all America's youth. Draft resistance no longer consisted of splinter groups growing by ones and twos, as in the Cornell episode, or of students making one-time theatrical gestures such as signing a "We Won't Go" petition while they held onto their 2-S deferments. It entered into what Staughton Lynd called its "classic period"—April 1967 to April 1968 —when it engaged the attention of the nation and played a vital role in the political revolution that brought down President Johnson.

* The key recommendations of the Marshall Commission—for a lottery and a youngest-first system—were enacted into law in 1969.

# 10

# The Classic Period:
## April 1967—April 1968

The wide publicity given the April 15 card burning spurred further draft resistance at college campuses—"We Won't Go" statements, anti-draft committees, and demonstrations. At the same time, a new organization called The Resistance hit upon a program that enlisted substantial nationwide support. The idea was that draft-age men throughout the country would turn in their draft cards, actually return them to the government, on a single day, October 16, 1967. The plan had been suggested by Staughton Lynd's Yale group the summer before, but rejected at the Des Moines conference. This time, the new Resistance organizers set a date far enough in advance so that local resistance groups could be formed and resisters marshaled for an impressive show of opposition.

The Resistance was the brainchild of four young men on the West Coast: David Harris, president of the Stanford University student government (and later husband of singer Joan Baez); Dennis Sweeney, a former SNCC activist, also from Stanford; Lenny Heller, a Berkeley student (once a fraternity man at the University of Connecticut); and Steve Hamilton, a veteran of the Free Speech Movement at Berkeley. The four represented different political viewpoints and entered draft resistance for different reasons.

Lenny Heller, the Berkeley activist, saw draft card turn-ins as the kind of action which could lead to a basic confrontation with the government. It was *doing* something about the draft and the war. "The Resistance has come to mean action . . . To change the course of this country and free ourselves, we must . . . begin to act against the system of oppression. That act must be with our lives. There is simply no other way." [1]

Steve Hamilton, who eventually left The Resistance because of what he saw as its apolitical character, wrote about the initial moral impulse behind it. "Here was something that certainly would make people stop and think. If thousands of middle-class young men turned in their draft cards and went off to jail for four or five years, the moral force that the government still conveys among most people would be severely shaken . . . we were still addressing . . . middle class liberals who might be edged just far enough left to create a strong national consensus against the war. Our goal was . . . public effect [which] could be created by a movement based on moral commitment." [2] (Hamilton concluded later in the year that political organization among the black and the white working class was the only way to effect any changes in government policy; he became one of the leaders of Stop the Draft Week in Oakland (October 16–21, 1967) and tried to organize blue collar workers in the San Francisco Bay Area.)

Dennis Sweeney thought of The Resistance primarily as an organizing vehicle. It was "a kind of net . . . which one could pull through the campuses of the country and thus collect the people with whom one wanted to make a [radical] movement." [3] Resistance was necessary not only to toughen the hard-core cadres that the new movement required, but to enhance their credibility among their potential allies, the poor and the black. Sweeney also saw the need for building a real community among the resisters: "communities of non-cooperators have been created around the country. These communities are building relationships based on sharing day to day lives, our futures and the risks of our movement . . . non-cooperation with the draft is a first step toward building a more inclusive community of resistance." [4]

David Harris shared Sweeney's view on the importance of the new Resistance community, but himself emphasized the moral impulse in the movement as it affected each individual resister. Everyone must live his life in an honest, uncompromising way that would necessarily reach members of his community. Of the four organizers, Harris alone went to jail for draft refusal, largely to keep faith with other resisters for whom he felt responsible. At his trial, Harris said:

my intention with that day [on which he refused induction] and with the other days was to somehow . . . with the limited tool of my life, begin to act in such a way as to really affirm the brotherhood I felt with people throughout this country and throughout the world . . . if men really accepted the principle that all men were their brothers and if men began to act that out on a day-to-day basis, really began to live that with their lives, there would be no necessity to force young men into taking up arms against other young men. In a world of brotherhood there is no such thing as an induction center.[5]

The program of The Resistance was explained in an early leaflet, entitled "We Refuse to Serve," which was distributed during the April 15, 1967 rally in San Francisco. Although the larger resistance movement was made up of many different strands, "We all agree on one point: the war in Vietnam is criminal and we must act together, at great individual risk, to stop it. Those involved must lead the American people, by their example, to understand the enormity of what their government is doing." If the student members of the resistance continued to go to school, kept their deferments, and protested the war in other ways, they would still not effect the consciousness of the country. "To cooperate with conscription is to perpetuate its existence, without which the government could not wage war. We have chosen to openly defy the draft and confront the government and its war directly."

A decision to refuse service was of great consequence in a man's life. "Each one realizes that refusing to cooperate with Selective Service may mean prison . . . we agree that to do anything but this is to effectively abet the war." The Resistance would actively support each of its members who would not serve. "We stand all-for-one, one-for-all. We are prepared to act together to support anyone singled out for arrest by every means possible, including civil disobedience and unified, public violations of the Selective Service Act." The Resistance pledged active measures to protest the war. "The aim of resistance is to provoke continual confrontations with the governmental institutions linked to the war. The Resistance confronts the government with an unresolvable dilemma; to prosecute and imprison us, which will generate new ways of protest and dissent, of unsurpassed intensity; or to set us free, which will provide greater impetus for the expansion of the movement."

The Resistance saw the war as the result of a basic dislocation in the American system. "It is becoming increasingly clear that peace cannot be attained unless some fundamental change is first affected

within American society, that there is something about the functioning of the American 'system' that does not permit it to respond other
than violently to the yearnings of the people it oppresses." The anti-
war movement must move from dissent to resistance and shake up the
society that had passively sanctioned the war. "If the normal day-to-
day pattern of American life were sufficiently disrupted, people in
large numbers would have to begin thinking about the nature of
their lives and the society around them." Resistance would thus
effect not only the individual lives of the young men refusing to be
inducted but the lives of all Americans. "Non-cooperation must be
seen in its larger context; a seizing of control of our own lives and a
conscious effort to redirect the movement of American society."
Finally, at the heart of the Resistance movement was the old adage,
"Wars will cease when men refuse to fight."

Until the spring of 1967, the "We Won't Go" groups had operated
on their own, without any coordination between them. The Resistance
proposed nationwide cooperation to maximize the public impact of
their protest rallies. October 16, 1967, was chosen for a demonstration of the strength of the movement:

ON OCTOBER 16, 1967, WE WILL PUBLICLY AND COLLEC-
TIVELY RETURN OUR DRAFT CARDS TO THE SELECTIVE
SERVICE SYSTEM IN MAJOR CITIES THROUGHOUT THE
COUNTRY. . . . By turning in rather than burning our cards, we
will be proudly giving our names to the public at large, and to the powers
that be. Our hope is that upon our example every young man in America
will realize that *he* must decide whether to resist or acquiesce to the
draft and the war. We are confident that many will resist.[6]

The particular form of protest called for by The Resistance—the
simple, nonviolent act of turning in one's draft card on October 16—
had tremendous symbolic and tactical value. It represented a rejection
of the channeling system designed, according to The Resistance, to
silence criticism of the government's war policy; it was a turning away
from the middle-class life patterns that so many were no longer able
to rationalize. It encouraged waverers about draft refusal by making
the act of saying no highly visible and publicly exposing how many
others were prepared to take a stand. Draft resistance organizers had
a specific date to work toward and a quantitative target—a specific
number of draft cards—to measure their success or failure. While not
everyone who turned in his card would necessarily refuse service when
ordered for induction, he would have taken a significant step toward
resistance.

It was college students to whom The Resistance particularly
spoke, and they responded in remarkable numbers. In New York,

Fred Rosen, a former Cornell student and then a graduate student at Adelphi; Paul Sanberg, a writer for *Rat*; Lenny Brody from the University of California; and David Zimmerman, a graduate student in philosophy at the University of Michigan, organized the Five Beekman Place branch of The Resistance (first called "Draft Denial"). They were spurred on by the April 15 card burning and by the encouragement of some members of the city's intellectual community. Paul Goodman in particular took an active interest in Resistance philosophy and organization, which he saw as the only hope for America. "If there is ever again going to be decency in America," he said, "it will be by open populist revolt. If formal democracy is not working, our action must be 'illegal' but it must be real democracy, making an open claim." [7]

Lenny Heller came to New York in the spring of 1967 with a Berkeley student, Dickie Harris (one of the few blacks in the movement), to encourage the idea of the October 16 nationwide rally. The young leaders made contact with anti-draft organizations in many of the city's colleges, and spoke with interested students at informal sessions or at public meetings. Where an autonomous organization was already functioning, The Resistance supplied draft counsellors and lawyers, and relayed information on upcoming rallies.

In Boston, two hundred students from Harvard, Tufts, and Boston University, led by Paul Hamburg and Phil Hunt, formed the Boston Draft Resistance Group in the spring. There was also an active branch of CNVA which participated in various demonstrations through 1966 and early 1967. On March 31, 1966, four young men had burned their draft cards on the steps of a Boston courthouse and had been immediately roughed up by counter-demonstrators. One of them, David Reed, a former SDS organizer at Harvard, was later sentenced to three years in prison for refusing induction. Another participant, David O'Brien, was arrested, tried, and convicted for draft-card burning. (He took his case to the Supreme Court, which upheld his conviction in June 1968 and declared that the card-burning law was a valid exercise of Congressional war power. Only Justice William O. Douglas dissented.)

In the summer of 1967, the New England Resistance was formed in Boston, an offshoot of the earlier antidraft groups, with Joel Kugelmass, Robert Talmanson, William Dowling, Alex Jack, and later Michael Ferber among its leaders. They too began to make plans for October 16, 1967, which was fast becoming the key date in the draft resistance movement.

On the West Coast, the original Stanford organizers went from campus to campus and city to city trying to enlist resisters for the

October rally. David Harris and Dennis Sweeney spent much of the summer of 1967 seeking non-cooperators. Their recruiting style was the same as that of the Cornell group six months before.

They . . . sought out one individual at a time, spending time with him, getting to know all sides of him, playing guitar and dropping acid besides talking politics. The first leaflet of the Bay Area Committee for Draft Resistance was simply six individual statements of noncooperation. This "open style" of organizing, in which one man tells another why he has decided to do something, seems to me inherently life-affirming, as opposed to the style which asks others to immolate themselves in a collective, impersonal destiny.[8]

Gary Rader in Chicago helped organize squads of workers to distribute leaflets at draft boards to young registrants. Other resisters proselytized at induction centers, while another squad telephoned I-A's whose names were posted for immediate induction. Demonstrations, sit-ins, protest meetings, and turn-ins were all organized under the auspices of CADRE.

Branches of The Resistance were formed everywhere—New Haven, Buffalo, Reed College (Oregon), Princeton, Syracuse, Philadelphia, Detroit, Ann Arbor, Minneapolis, Pittsburgh, Cincinnati, Kansas City (Missouri), Iowa City, San Jose, Santa Barbara, Denver, Chapel Hill (North Carolina), Antioch College (Ohio), and Los Angeles. Students at the University of Wisconsin, already active at induction centers, spawned a particularly strong Resistance group. On May 18, 1967, for example, eighty members came to the Milwaukee selective service center to demonstrate in support of three resisters called for physicals. Twelve went to the bus station with donuts and leaflets to talk to examinees. Fourteen others came into the examination center and gave speeches about the war and the draft as bewildered young men waited for the army doctors. (Eleven of the demonstrators were promptly arrested for disorderly conduct.) The three resisters who came for their physicals handed out leaflets and spoke unceasingly against the war and the draft. Forty other demonstrators picketed the center for three hours.

A similar demonstration with similar consequences took place in Oakland in late April 1967. In Cleveland, sixty resisters demonstrated in support of Phil Urbanski, who was refusing induction for a second time.

While draft resistance organizations sprang up spontaneously on different college campuses, the movement also won support from older members of the academic community who were part of the anti-war campaign. If anyone could be called the father, or at least faculty adviser, of The Resistance, it would be Staughton Lynd. A pacifist and non-combatant just after the Korean War, a civil rights activist during the early 1960's, and a teacher and historian with strong ties to SDS, Lynd participated in almost every significant event of the resistance movement. He was chairman and principal speaker at the April 1965 March on Washington and at the mass teach-in at Berkeley a month later. He was the organizer of the Assembly of Unrepresented People in August 1965 (a mass anti-war rally in Washington), and the picture of him and Dave Dellinger being splattered with red paint by hecklers during the demonstration perversely infuriated the Congressional conservatives who immediately thereafter passed the draft card burning law! He spoke at the December 1966 "We Won't Go" conference at Chicago and later draft resistance meetings at Madison, Wisconsin in August 1967 and Bloomington, Indiana in March 1969. When Tom Bell worried about the revival service tone of the resistance drive at Cornell, it was Lynd he commiserated with, and young resisters throughout the country followed his example.

On the West Coast, while teaching at Stanford in the spring of 1967, writer Mitchell Goodman met David Harris and other Resistance leaders. He composed a pledge of support for the young draft resisters and asked Stanford faculty members to sign. Forty-five of them, including the most distinguished members of the medical and science faculties, did so. Pledging themselves to "mass civil disobedience" to stop the war, they announced that, "the 'We Won't Go' Movement among draft-age youth represents an extreme, potentially effective and apparently infectious development in the society," and that there was "a great need for an analogous activity among those who are past draft age." In July, a seventy-member Committee for Draft Resistance was formed in the San Francisco area with a similar commitment to help draft resisters in every way possible.

Soon there were at least four separate support groups in operation on the East Coast: Support in Action, originated in New York by Paul Goodman, Karl Bissinger, and Grace Paley; Clergy and Laymen Concerned About the War in Vietnam, consisting of ministers, priests, and professors led by William Sloane Coffin; Resist, a body of New York and Boston intellectuals which included Noam Chomsky, Paul Lauter, Dwight MacDonald, and Robert Lowell; and Conscientious Resistance, the group organized by Mitchell Goodman, his wife, poet Denise Levertov, and their Maine neighbor, Henry Braun. The older intellectuals thought it important to establish their solidarity with the resisters. They prepared and signed complicity statements and anti-draft cards which pledged their support of the young men, demanding that they too be arrested for violating the draft law since they "counselled, aided and abetted" those who were refusing the draft. Complicity statements were collected with the draft cards of the resisters and tallies kept of both categories of draft opponents.

The older intellectuals gave their chief support by doing what intellectuals do best: articulating the reasons for the Vietnam opposition and mapping out a program for ending the war. They agonized over the precise wording of each manifesto. Mitchell Goodman worked with Henry Braun on his statement, "A Call to Conscientious Resistance to the War." The Clergy and Laymen organization issued "Conscience and Conscription," largely the work of Rev. Coffin, stating "We hereby publicly counsel all who in conscience cannot today serve in the armed forces to refuse such service by non-violent means." Marcus Raskin, co-director of the Institute for Policy Studies in Washington, collaborated with Arthur Waskow on a pronouncement which became the key document in the later Spock trial, "A Call to Resist Illegitimate Authority." The great French scholar of the Vietnam War, Bernard Fall, had reminded Raskin of the famous "Statement of the 121," the manifesto of the French intellectuals against the Algerian War. Raskin used it as the model for the Call which he and Waskow drafted in the spring of 1967, and then gave it to Noam Chomsky and others for comments. Revisions followed, and by the summer of 1967, the document was sent out for endorsement by Resist, over the signature of Dwight MacDonald, Dr. Spock, Rev. Coffin, and Chomsky.

The Call began with a declaration that the Vietnam War was "unconstitutional and illegal." Congress had not declared war, American presence in Vietnam violated the United Nations charter and the Geneva agreements of 1954, and American conduct of the war violated the Nuremberg principles and international treaties prohibiting atrocities against civilians.

Taking up the issue of the draft, the Call declared:

We also believe it is an unconstitutional denial of religious liberty and equal protection of the laws to withhold draft exemption from men whose religious or profound philosophical beliefs are opposed to what in the Western religious tradition have been long known as unjust wars.

The young men subject to the draft faced the "most excruciating choices." Resistance meant "separation from their families and their country, destruction of their careers, or loss of their freedom. Each young man must decide himself what path of resistance to choose; whether to seek conscientious objector status or whether to refuse service or, if in the army, to desert or disobey orders." The signers of the Call believed that each of these forms of resistance "against illegitimate authority" was "courageous and justified," and that "open resistance to the war and the draft" would be most likely to bring an end to the war. The statement continued:

We will continue to lend our support to those who undertake resistance to this war. We will raise funds to organize draft resistance unions, to supply legal defense and bail, to support families and otherwise aid resistance to the war in whatever ways may seem appropriate.

Mitchell Goodman picked up a copy of the Call in Noam Chomsky's Cambridge office in mid-September 1967. Knowing about The Resistance's plans for October 16, Goodman sought to devise appropriate supporting tactics for his generation. Chomsky suggested that he consult Bill Coffin at Yale. When Goodman went to New Haven, Coffin suggested, "Suppose we get the draft cards that are turned in from all over the country, take them to the Department of Justice and turn them over to the Attorney General?" Goodman agreed to the plan, set October 20 as the date, and called upon his peers to come to Washington for the demonstration. Among the first he contacted was Norman Mailer, who later used the telephone conversation with Goodman as the opening section of his brilliant book on the Pentagon confrontation, *Armies of the Night*.

In October, Resist—the sponsor of the Call—arranged for a press conference to announce the Washington plan. Herschel Kaminsky, a member of National Mobilization and one of the mysterious figures in the Spock conspiracy case,* called Dr. Spock, Rev. Coffin, Robert Lowell, Dwight MacDonald, and others for a press conference on October 2, 1967 at the New York Hilton. Included with the handful of newspapermen and onlookers at the conference was Lawrence Miller, a local agent of the F.B.I., which was now a close observer of The Resistance and all its support groups.

The October 16 demonstrations planned by The Resistance six months earlier took place as scheduled throughout the country. In New York, a protest rally was held before the federal court house in Foley Square. Three hundred young men participated, including twenty-five from the Union Theological Seminary. They handed in their draft cards (or duplicates and photostats) to the Resistance leaders, who tried to give them to United States Marshal Anthony

* Four of the five defendants in the Spock case (all but Ferber) testified that they were summoned to the press conference by Kaminsky, whom three had never met and never did meet. They simply accepted the word of an unknown voice on the telephone telling them to be at the Hilton on October 2. The newspapermen and defense lawyers at the trial told each other half jokingly that Kaminsky had to be an F.B.I. agent. In fact, he was a social worker and editor in New York City and a professional left-wing organizer.

Marasco. But a solid line of federal marshals prevented the resisters from entering the building. Finally, Marasco spoke to David Zimmerman and Fred Rosen, but would not accept the draft cards. The young men then marched in a joyful procession to a post office on Wall Street and mailed the package of material (over two hundred cards) to Attorney General Ramsey Clark.

In Washington, D.C., eleven cards were left at the national headquarters of the Selective Service System. Independence Hall in Philadelphia was the site of a card-collecting and -burning ceremony. Two hundred young men demonstrated in front of Selective Service headquarters in Portland, Oregon; two hundred came to the Cincinnati induction center, and hundreds more marched in Ithaca, New York. Gary Rader led 150 men in a rally before the Chicago federal court house; eight men invaded the building and were arrested for trespass. In Los Angeles on October 17, two hundred demonstrators sat in before the armed forces induction center. The police arrested nineteen.

Smaller rallies were held in Denver, Cedar Rapids, Iowa, St. Louis, Providence, Albany, Syracuse, and Atlanta. And the rally that was to have the greatest legal impact took place in Minneapolis, where twenty young men simply left their draft cards at the Federal building: one of the participants was David Earl Gutknecht, who would eventually be vindicated by a unanimous Supreme Court for the protest actions he took on that day.

The largest demonstration in the East occurred in Boston, with five thousand people gathering on Boston Common to hear ministers, professors, and young resisters speak. Professor Howard Zinn of Boston University declared that when he read "the U.S. Air Force has bombed again and again the residential areas of North Vietnamese cities . . . villages that are devoid of military significance . . . a hospital for lepers thirteen times, I am ashamed, and I want to dissociate myself from these acts." [9]

That afternoon, one of the most unusual religious ceremonies ever held in this country took place at the Arlington Street Church in downtown Boston. Early in September, Alex Jack and Michael Ferber decided to enlist the help of sympathetic members of the Boston clergy. They contacted Rev. Harold Frey, chairman of the Boston Committee of Religious Concern for Peace, which arranged for the use of the Arlington Street Church, once the center of Abolitionist activity in Boston, for October 16. Rev. Coffin agreed to officiate and be present for the afternoon ceremonies.

Rev. Dr. Jack Mendolsohn, the minister of the church, spoke, as did Dr. George H. Williams, Hollis Professor of Divinity at Harvard, and a Roman Catholic priest, Fr. Robert Cunnane. Coffin gave the main address. "Let us remember these men were not out to destroy the legal order. By accepting the legal punishment they actually upheld it. Nor were they disrespectful of the law. They broke it as a last, not a first resort. But they respected the law only, they did not worship it, and were determined to bend their every effort to the end that the law reflect and not reject their best understanding of justice and mercy."

Following the clergymen, Michael Ferber delivered his famous "A Time to Say No":

We must look at ourselves once more. We all have an impulse to purification and martyrdom and we should not be ashamed of it. But let us be certain that we have thought through the consequences of our action in the outside world, and that these consequences are what we want to bring about. Let us make sure we are ready to work hard and long with each other in the months to come, working to make it difficult and politically dangerous for the government to prosecute us, working to help anyone and everyone to find ways of avoiding the draft, to help disrupt the workings of the draft and the armed forces until the war is over. Let us make sure we can form a community. Let us make sure we can let others depend on us.

If we can say Yes to these things, and to the religious tradition that stands with us today, and to the fact that today marks not the End but a Beginning, and to the long hard dirty job ahead of us—if we can say Yes to all this, then let us come forward together to say No to the United States government.

Then let our Yes be the loudest No our government ever heard.

(Ferber's remarks were cited as one of the overt acts in the so-called Spock conspiracy. They later won a national award from the Unitarian Universalist Association as the oustanding sermon in the field of social action during 1967.)

After the sermons, 250 young men—far more than expected—walked up to the pulpit to hand their cards in to Ferber, Coffin, and the other clergymen. A Bach hymn, "Sheep May Safely Graze," played while fifty other men burned their cards in a William Ellery Channing candlestick and then deposited the ashes in a silver receptacle on a table. Coffin quietly shook hands with each of the men participating. Ferber had been chosen to take the draft cards to Washington for the October 20 rally, and Coffin said he would meet him later in the week. Although the two men were named as co-conspirators in the Spock case, this was the only contact they had ever had with each other.

In contrast to the quiet Boston ceremony, bedlam broke loose on the West Coast, at the Oakland induction center. To a group of seven young radicals from the San Francisco Bay Area, a peaceful turn-in of cards on October 16 was not an adequate way of protesting the war. They decided to block the streets to prevent inductees from getting to Oakland draft headquarters (the induction center for all of northern California), and in that way "to shut the mother down." Among the planners for the event was Steve Hamilton, one of the original Resistance organizers, who believed that the anti-war movement had to go beyond symbolic draft card turn-ins. Three of the other organizers were from Berkeley; two others were former SNCC workers.

They designated the entire week of October 16 as "Stop the Draft Week." If they could gather enough demonstrators on the streets in front of the induction center, army buses wouldn't get through to deposit inductees. Rather than sit-in and be quietly arrested, the participants were to move around the streets, defend themselves if necessary, and make it difficult for the police to arrest them. They hoped that their militancy would reach the lower-class draftees who had looked upon the Resistance as a weak, bourgeois game.

At 6:00 A.M. on October 16, two thousand demonstrators gathered in front of the induction center. About two hundred, including Joan Baez, sat down in front of the army headquarters and 119 were quickly arrested.* That evening a five-hour open rally took place at Berkeley to get the demonstrators primed for the coming encounters. (A tape of that rally was the key piece of evidence in the conspiracy trial of the Oakland Seven. The openness, vitality, and humor of the rally belied any idea that the later events were the carefully planned results of a secret conspiracy. All seven men were acquitted.) On Tuesday morning, three thousand demonstrators appeared and the police cleared them away with a brutal use of nightsticks and chemical Mace. Twenty were arrested and two hundred hospitalized. On Wednesday, the police used a flying wedge to clear the streets. On Thursday, the demonstrators rested, preparing for the final effort the next day. About ten thousand protesters appeared on the last day, October 20. Not only did they mill around the streets so that the army buses were successfully halted, but they built barricades against the counterattacks of the police and stood up to their clubs and Mace.

---

* Across the bay in San Francisco, David Harris led five hundred demonstrators outside the federal court building. "The assumption of young people being the bricks on which they will build an empire is a wrong assumption," he said. "We want life in America, not death." Hundreds of young men dropped their draft cards into a wicker basket that was passed among them. Harris tried to deliver the cards to Cecil Poole, the United States Attorney for the area, who refused to take them.

The street fighting became quite serious until police reinforcements arrived and the National Guard was alerted.

At almost the same time that fighting reached its height in Oakland on October 20, the rally planned by Mitch Goodman and Rev. Coffin was beginning in Washington. The demonstrators met at a local church around noon, heard some speeches, and then walked to the Justice Department for their confrontation with the authorities. (Two years later, at almost the same spot, a group of militant Weathermen from SDS would throw rocks at the Justice Department windows after the November 15, 1969, peace march and be dispersed by tear gas.)

Coffin again officiated. Norman Mailer, seeing him for the first time, called him "a winner." "He was one full example of the masculine principle at work in the cloth." Mitchell Goodman, Dwight MacDonald, Dr. Spock, and Robert Lowell spoke. Lowell had been asked by a reporter whether he had handed in his draft card and he answered: "When some of us pledge ourselves to counsel and aid and abet any young men who wish to turn in their cards, why then you may be certain we are aware of the possible consequences and do not try to hide behind the technicality of whether we literally have a draft card or not . . . we are not searching for tricks . . . and we will protest this war by every means available to our conscience . . ." [10]

Coffin made many of the same points that he had touched on during the October 16 Boston ceremony. Once again he used the specific words of the Selective Service law to underscore his purpose:

We hereby publicly counsel these young men to continue in their refusal to serve in the armed forces as long as the war in Vietnam continues, and we pledge ourselves to aid and abet them in all the ways we can. This means that if they are now arrested for failing to comply with a law that violates their consciences, we too must be arrested, for in the sight of that law we are now as guilty as they.

It is a longstanding tradition, sanctioned by American democracy, that the dictates of government must be tested on the anvil of individual conscience. This is what we now undertake to do—not as a first but as a last resort. And in accepting the legal punishment we are, in fact, supporting, not subverting, the legal order.

Still, to stand in this fashion against the law and before our fellow Americans is a difficult and even fearful thing. But in the face of what to us is insane and inhuman we can fall neither silent nor servile. Nor can we educate young men to be conscientious only to desert them in their hour of conscience. So we are resolved, as they are resolved, to speak out clearly and to pay up personally.[11]

The young men then turned in the draft cards brought from different sections of the country, putting them in a small Fabrikoid briefcase held by Coffin. Dickie Harris collected three hundred from San Francisco alone. (Mailer described Harris in *Armies of the Night*: ". . . a Negro with goatee and horn-rimmed glasses, not very tall, slim, wearing dungarees and a shirt open at the neck. He had a smile which spoke of a wry, sly humor, and his voice was easy and remarkably relaxed . . . he had the dash, the panache . . . of the old cadres in SNCC. . . .") Michael Ferber had 237 cards from Boston. David Zimmerman contributed two hundred cards from New York. The Chicago representative was Gary Rader, and John Sanno came from Rochester. Resistance leaders from Yale, Cornell, and other campuses went through the ritual of announcing the totals from each of their constituencies.

As these numbers were announced, the crowd being when all is said, good Americans, gave murmurs of pleasure . . . by handing in draft cards, these young men were committing their future either to prison, emigration, frustration, or at best, years when everything must be unknown, and that spoke of a readiness to take moral leaps which the acrobat must know when he flies off into space . . . They were young men with souls of interesting dimension, and their faces did nothing to disprove this. None of them looked alike; they had a surprising individuality in their appearance. Some were scholarly and slight, dressed conservatively, and looked like clerks, others were in dungarees . . . a few were sports and looked to have eight hobbies, custom cars, pot, draft cards, skiing, guitar, surfboard, chicks and scuba . . ." [12]

Lenny Heller did not go along with all this humor and camaraderie. He had just come from Oakland and his eyes were still smarting from the Mace attack on Tuesday. He told the older supporters: "You want to come along with us, that's okay, that's your thing, but we've got our thing, and we're going to do it alone whether you come with us or not."

It took thirty minutes for the resisters to pass by. Some turned in their own cards. Others apologized for turning in duplicates, photostats, discharge papers, expired registration cards, or 4-F classification cards. Since the burnings and turn-ins had been going on for years, it was rare for the Resistance leaders to have original, mint draft cards anymore. But the ritual continued to be played out.

When the last student had filed past, Coffin announced that 992 cards had been handed in. (The government said at the Spock trial that only 252 valid notices of classification were contained in the briefcase.) Coffin then picked a group of older supporters and four of the Resistance leaders to accompany him inside the Justice Department. The over-thirty group included Dr. Spock, Mitchell Goodman, Seymour Melman (a professor from Columbia), Richard Lewis (an English professor from Yale), Arthur Waskow, and Marcus Raskin of the Institute of Policy Studies. Representing the Resistance were Gary Rader, Dickie Harris, David Zimmerman, and John Sanno.

The eleven men walked into the Justice Department building and were directed to a conference room on the first floor. Greeting them were John McDonough, a deputy Assistant Attorney General, and John Van de Kamp, who supervised the assistant U.S. attorneys throughout the country. (McDonough, who was stocky, round-faced and looked like a well-fed businessman, once acted as dean of the Stanford Law School. Van de Kamp was a thin, high-strung lawyer who later ran as a Democrat for Congress against Barry Goldwater, Jr. and lost handily.) McDonough introduced himself in a nervous voice and asked his visitors to sit down around the long mahogany table. "Now, gentlemen, may I offer you some coffee?" Dickie Harris said, with a laugh: "Coffee! Oh man." When the coffee came, McDonough was so nervous he almost spilled it in his visitors' laps trying to pour.

He then asked Coffin whether he had anything to say. Coffin repeated in substance what he had said at the rally outside. He acknowledged that he and others were violating the law by counseling, aiding, and abetting young men who resisted the draft, but said that they felt obliged to show their support of the young resisters. Next to speak was Dr. Spock, who expressed his annoyance that Attorney General Ramsey Clark was not there to talk to them. Marcus Raskin said that he thought the draft was unconstitutional since the Vietnam War was illegal; therefore refusing to go into the army or turning in draft cards was not a crime. Raskin's colleague, Arthur Waskow, echoed that proposition. Gary Rader, the first resister to speak, said that young men like himself faced a terrible dilemma, but he and many others could not fight the "immoral" war in Vietnam. Seymour Melman added that the United States had violated the Geneva Agreement and other international treaties in its conduct of the war. Thus the war was illegal and the young men refusing to be drafted were justified in what they were doing.

Dickie Harris spoke next. "Man, you gonna hear me?" McDonough answered: "Yes, I'm listening to you." Harris said: "I didn't say listen, man, I said *hear* me!" He went on. "Man, you don't exist! You are a nothing, your boss is a nothing and his boss is a nothing." [13] He defended the resisters as creators of a new society in which there would be neither oppressor or oppressed, and where war would be impossible.

John Sanno spoke longer than any of them: It was wrong to be in a society where a draft card was a symbol of security and losing it put a young man in a position of insecurity. He also thought the war was illegal and that the United States should be spending the money it was wasting in Vietnam on domestic problems. The values of the country were perverted. For people like himself there was no choice but to repudiate the society, the war, and the draft.

David Zimmerman agreed. Mitch Goodman said that the young men represented by the draft cards turned in that day were only the "tip of the iceberg." More and more young people were losing respect for the values of the country and its laws. Society had to be changed to conform to the expectations of the young people, who made up more than half the population of the country. Richard Lewis said that it was important for the members of the older generation to associate themselves with what the young people were doing and to support them in every way possible.

After listening patiently to each person's statement, McDonough said he would convey their comments to the Attorney General. Coffin asked him whether he had anything to say to them. McDonough said yes and took a long typewritten sheet out of his pocket. "Man, you ain't gonna read that?" said Dickie Harris. When McDonough said he was, Harris answered: "Well, I ain't gonna listen." Harris and John Sanno then danced out of the room.

McDonough's paper contained the exact words of section 12(a) of the draft law which made it a crime to counsel, aid, or abet young men to violate the law. As he read the statement the briefcase containing the 992 cards and other papers was being pushed toward his end of the table. Coffin picked up the bag and handed it to McDonough. "Am I being tendered something?" he said. "You are *tenderly* being *tendered* these draft cards and statements of support," said Coffin. McDonough refused to accept the briefcase. Coffin tried again. McDonough turned away. At that point, Arthur Waskow lost his temper. He demanded that McDonough accept the cards. After all, a crime was being committed and he had an obligation as a representative of the Justice Department to accept evidence of the crime. He banged his fist loudly on the table.* "You are *required* to

* When McDonough testified at the Spock trial, he said Raskin had demanded that he accept the cards, but all the other witnesses agreed it was Waskow. This mistake in identity may have been the reason Raskin was indicted as the fifth defendant rather than his colleague.

accept this evidence. I demand a response." McDonough said he had
nothing more to say. The party then left the Andretta Room, leaving
the Fabrikoid briefcase on the top of the mahogany table.

The next day, one hundred thousand people marched on the Pentagon, and hundreds—including Mailer, Chomsky, and Dellinger—
were arrested for breach of the peace when they failed to obey police
orders to move. Soon after the October protests, a freelance writer
asked Attorney General Ramsey Clark whether he was planning to
take any action against the Spock-Coffin group for their support of
the resisters. He said no, they were merely exercising their First
Amendment rights. In the meantime, Resistance leaders continued to
organize opposition to the draft, generally satisfied with the October
turn-outs and turn-ins, but not exactly sure what impact they had on
the government's conduct of the war.

Within two weeks of the October rallies, however, the Resistance
received an unexpected and highly important boost which not only
guaranteed the continued vitality of the movement, but ultimately
removed one of the government's chief weapons against it. This great
boon came from the chief enemy and target of the Resistance, General
Lewis Hershey.

Two years earlier, after the October, 1965 anti-war demonstrations, Hershey had suggested that "illegal" protesters could be declared delinquent and become subject to immediate induction. Some
draft boards took the hint and began reclassifying students who had
invaded induction centers or sat-in at Selective Service headquarters.*
One of these students was Peter Wolff of New York, who had participated in the Ann Arbor demonstrations of October 15, 1965. He immediately brought a law suit against his local draft board, claiming
they had no right to declare him delinquent for behavior not connected with the draft, particularly not for political protest.

Early in 1967, a federal court of appeals in New York upheld his
claim. It said: ". . . the free expression of views on issues of critical
national importance . . . is jeopardized [by the draft board's ac-
tion] . . . the allegations of the complainant . . . that the draft
boards have unlawfully suppressed criticism must take precedence
over the policy of non-intervention in the affairs of the Selective
Service." [14] Hershey complained to Congress about the *Wolff* case
when they were considering the 1967 extension of the draft law. He

* Under Selective Service System regulation 1642.4(a) "whenever a registrant has failed to perform any duty . . . required of him under the selective
service law . . . the local board may declare him a delinquent." Such delinquents may be immediately ordered for induction under Regulation 1642.13.

said that an inductee could hold up his draft call for months if he had the right of judicial review. Congress endorsed Hershey's position by forbidding any draft registrant to challenge his classification in court before he responded to an induction notice one way or the other.\* But nothing was said in the new law about the proper use of the delinquency regulations.

With the new law to protect him, Hershey took the next step. On October 26, 1967, following the wave of demonstrations, he sent a local board memorandum and a letter to all 4,081 draft boards directing that they declare delinquent any registrant taking part in an "illegal" demonstration, reclassify him to 1-A status, and induct him as soon as possible. "Deferments are only given when they serve the national interest . . . Any action that violates the military selective service act or the regulations, or the related processes cannot be in the national interest. It follows that those who violate them should be denied deferment in the national interest." Those who turn in or mutilate their cards should be declared delinquent, "for failure to have the card in his possession," and taken first under the regulations. Even ministers or veterans should be reclassified, and 4-F's should be given another physical examination to see if they were acceptable.[15] (Hershey did not specify what constituted an "illegal" demonstration or what were "related processes" to the Selective Service Act. But at the least they included trespassing in draft boards or interfering with recruiting on campuses, since this prevented volunteering for the army.)

Not satisfied with a local board memorandum (which has no binding force but is generally followed), Hershey proposed that a Presidential Executive Order be issued to require implementation of his proposal. This step necessitated the approval of the Justice and Defense departments, which were well aware of the *Wolff* case. They concluded that the directive was unconstitutional, since it punished registrants without any judicial safeguards and furthermore inhibited lawful protest activity. When the controversy leaked to the press in early November, a great uproar arose against Hershey's use of the draft to suppress dissent. The *New York Times,* the National Council of Churches, and all civil liberties organizations joined in attacking the directive. Justice Abe Fortas called Hershey "a law unto himself," and college presidents throughout the country said they would not permit recruiters on campus if draft boards engaged in punitive

---

\* Under Section 10(b)3 of the law, "no judicial review shall be made of the classification . . . of any registrant . . . except as a defense to a criminal prosecution . . . after the registrant has responded either affirmatively or negatively to an order to report for induction."

induction of student demonstrators. Kingman Brewster of Yale called
it "an absolutely outrageous usurpation of power."

The resisters were delighted with the controversy. Michael Ferber
explained, "Every time he opens his mouth, he gets another couple
of hundred draft cards." The obviously repressive nature of Hershey's
memorandum confirmed the Resistance view that the government was
acting illegitimately both in Vietnam and at home. It spurred the resisters to greater efforts. If Hershey was trying so hard to stop them,
they must be doing something right.

While the controversy was raging in the press, New York Resistance made plans for its own "Stop the Draft Week" along the lines of
the Oakland demonstration. (David Harris came to New York to
help prepare for the encounter.) If enough protesters clogged the
streets around the New York induction center on Whitehall Street,
potential inductees would not be able to get into the building, and
the draft would be halted for a limited period. The week of December
4 was set for the new go-around with the government.

New York Resistance formed a coalition with the Fifth Avenue
Peace Parade Committee, the War Resisters League, and other organizations. For their part, the peace groups planned to sit illegally
on the sidewalk in front of the induction center as a symbolic ges-
ture of protest. On Monday, December 4, eighty-eight resisters
turned in their draft cards at a church in Brooklyn. Early the next
morning, a large crowd gathered in front of the Whitehall Street
induction center prepared for civil disobedience. Dave McReynolds
of WRL had negotiated with Mayor John V. Lindsay and police
representatives as to the exact place where the older group of
demonstrators would sit down in the street and be arrested. But
because the morning was so cold and dark, communications broke
down and the police at first blocked the demonstrators (including
Dr. Spock and Mitchell Goodman) as they tried to get past the
barriers. Finally they were allowed to assume their designated places
on the sidewalk, where they were duly arrested by the police. Most
pleaded guilty to obstructing traffic or disturbing the peace and paid
a small fine.

The resisters and the more militant peace demonstrators were trying to duplicate the Oakland tactics, but they failed on several counts.
First of all, they lacked the sheer numbers to make them effective.
The streets around Whitehall were narrow and winding, and draftees
could approach the induction center from many directions. (The
Oakland draftees were bussed in in large numbers to the induction
center.) When the mounted police used their horses to force the
demonstrators away from Whitehall, the protesters wandered around

the city for hours, meeting with harassment, beatings, and arrests wherever they went.

During the same week in Portland, Oregon, students from Reed and Portland State College held a torchlight parade contrary to a city ordinance. Twenty-six draft cards and seventy-six complicity statements were handed in. In Tucson, Arizona, demonstrators locked arms to block the local draft board and then sat down in front of a bus filled with inductees. Three hundred protesters converged on the Manchester, New Hampshire draft center and fifteen were arrested for disorderly conduct. A large rally was held in the Cambridge Common opposite Harvard College and a giant five-by-seven foot replica of a draft card was destroyed to the cheers of the crowd. One thousand students attended a teach-in at Sacramento State College and 250 demonstrated the next day at the local induction center. At Urbana, Illinois, an Air Force sergeant turned in his identification card along with six other resisters. Peaceful picketing and leafletting took place in Raleigh, North Carolina. Five resisters in Washington conferred with General Hershey for over an hour, while fifty protesters picketed outside national Selective Service headquarters.

On December 18 and 19, five hundred demonstrators sat down in the Oakland induction center and 290 were dragged off and arrested. Federal marshals also took five demonstrators into custody for not possessing their draft cards, but the local United States Attorney, Cecil Poole, upbraided the marshals and refused to prosecute the cases.

Again the demonstrations were met with counter-moves from the government. Although Hershey's October letter had been rejected by the Justice Department, the administration was under considerable Congressional pressure to do something about the new wave of protest. During the first week of December, Ramsey Clark and Hershey met to discuss what should be done about the older supporters as well as the young men who turned in their cards. On December 9, 1967, they issued a joint statement which seemed to answer the problem. A special unit was to be established in the criminal division of the Justice Department "to coordinate prompt prosecution of offenses against the Selective Service laws and related offenses . . . including prosecutions against those who counsel, aid, or abet registrants to refuse to register and serve . . ." [16] (In other words, an effort would be made to prosecute the Spock group.) However, they continued, "the lawful exercise of rights of free expression and peaceful assembly have incurred and will incur no penalty or other adverse action." The Justice Department took the position that any violation of a regulation by a registrant with respect to his own status made him a delinquent; that is, if he failed to appear for a physical or inform the draft board of a change in status. But any violation not touching his own relations to the draft (burning someone else's card or participating in an anti-war rally of any kind) could be handled only by criminal prosecution.

The joint statement was taken generally as a rebuke to Hershey. The Justice Department had rejected his theory of punitive induction and, in a quid-pro-quo, promised to move quickly to initiate criminal proceedings instead. No doubt it saw the step as a plus for civil liberties: Hershey's vague directive was undermined in exchange for a promise to enforce the law. However, within the week, Hershey insisted his October letter was still in force. Criminal prosecution was an alternative to rather than a substitute for reclassification and priority call-up of draft protesters. "Either one of the channels is open to the government," Hershey said.

In the meantime, the new Justice Department prosecution unit, headed by John Van de Kamp and launched with instructions to prosecute those who counseled, aided, or abetted draft resisters, began operations. Van de Kamp made no bones about the purpose of his unit. He told Jessica Mitford: "The prosecution [of Dr. Spock] came about as a result of our flap with Hershey about his October 26 letter to the draft boards. The prosecution of these five was thought to be a good way out—it was done to provide a graceful way out for General Hershey." The specific defendants were picked because of "their names and personalities." Also there was plenty of evidence available against them. "We wouldn't have indicted them except for the fact that there was so much evidence available on film. They made no great secret about what they were doing." [17]

In the meantime, many draft boards were putting Hershey's October 26 letter into operation. Not only were Resistance leaders, including Fred Rosen and David Zimmerman, reclassified for turning in their cards, but divinity students (given special exemptions by the draft law) were also declared delinquent and ordered for induction. Phil Beck, a veteran of six years (including two in Vietnam!) was reclassified as a delinquent; as was Henry Braun, a thirty-seven-year-old teacher with two children. Arthur Waskow, who was 4-F, was ordered for another physical examination. A totally disabled paraplegic was also called in for a physical review because he had sent in his draft card. Some students were reclassified for quietly marching in a peace parade and others for handing out anti-war leaflets during their physical examinations.

The Resistance reported that two thousand men had handed in their draft cards during the last three months of 1967—1,158 on

October 16, approximately 550 during the first week of December, and another 350 at other times. The available figures indicate that a large majority of those resisters were reclassified as delinquents. According to Selective Service records, there were 15,621 delinquents as of October 31, 1967. By February 29, 1968, the number had grown to 17,874, an increase of 2,200 in only four months—the sharpest rise of the year. By June 1968 (when The Resistance claimed that over four thousand men had handed in their cards since the previous October), there were 22,103 delinquents, an increase of almost seven thousand in the nine months after Hershey's directive.* [18] It seems logical to suppose that the major reason for the increase was the activities of The Resistance coupled with the impact of the October 26, 1967 letter.

Intellectuals in many different cities—writers, publishers, directors, teachers—continued to support the resisters despite the Spock indictments. They contributed money, spoke at rallies, and invited the resisters into their homes for meetings and study sessions. Sometimes they regretted their decisions. The mother of one prominent Broadway director with a large apartment on Central Park West was frightened out of her wits by a Resistance member called "Red Star" (because of the large red star he wore on his jacket). "Red Star" looked about the fine apartment with its beautiful view of the park and told her, "When we take over, the poor will live in this apartment and you and your kind will be out in the streets!" But there was a minimum of such trouble and the young resisters were grateful for the encouragement of the famous names that supported them. Robert Bly, for example, took his $1,000 check for winning the National Book Award for poetry in March 1968 and handed it over the edge of the stage to a representative of New York Resistance.

The last large-scale, national rally that involved draft card turn-ins took place on April 3, 1968. Once again Boston led the way. Almost ten thousand people appeared on Boston Common to listen to Staughton Lynd, Noam Chomsky, Mike Ferber, and others, after which 191 cards were collected. In Central Park, David Harris spoke, his wife Joan Baez sang, Ellen Schneider (David Mitchell's fiancée) read one of his letters from prison, and Mitchell Goodman tried to spark the crowd by denigrating the recent Kennedy and McCarthy peace candidacies. Eighty-two cards were returned. Throughout the country there were a total of more than 650 new resisters.

* As explained in the Appendix, delinquency totals are minimum figures since they show the number of delinquents as of a certain date. See the discussion at p. 184.

Yet it was disappointing for the organizers. None of the April rallies attracted the numbers or the enthusiasm that its sponsors had hoped for. Political events were moving too quickly for The Resistance to cope with, even though it was partly responsible for the changes that were taking place.

Six months before, on the same day that the Oakland demonstrators were having their final climactic battle with the police and Dickie Harris was baiting Assistant Attorney General McDonough in the Andretta Room, a political event occurred that was at once a victory for The Resistance and the chief cause of its decline. That morning— October 20, 1967—Senator Eugene McCarthy told Al Lowenstein at a Los Angeles breakfast that he would run for President on an anti-war ticket. On December 2, 1967, a few days before the second "Stop the Draft Week," he formally announced his candidacy. On March 31, 1968, three days before the April 3 rallies, President Johnson declared that he would not run for re-election.

McCarthy was by no means the Resistance candidate for President, although he was later to call for an amnesty for draft resisters and army deserters. Nor can it be said that McCarthy decided to run primarily because of Resistance activities. But during 1967, the anti-draft movement supplied crucial energizing force for the nation's anti-war sentiment upon which McCarthy based his candidacy. Resistance made vivid the meaning of the war, it brought home the terrible choices that American society had forced upon its youth, and triggered the dissatisfactions with the existing political structure which McCarthy was soon to attack. If the Vietnam War represented the gap between American ideals and the reality of its foreign adventures, the draft represented the practical claim on the citizenry to participate in and thus become responsible for the government's policies. The draft and the resistance it evoked took the issue of the war into every living room. The Resistance message, spread and amplified by its older intellectual supporters, created a new constituency that helped to force Johnson out of the White House. The Resistance organizers would have been horrified to think of themselves as another traditional political pressure group in American society, producing their own candidate within the system. That was certainly not their original purpose. But the American political machine has a way of assimilating even the most vociferous of its critics.

Thus, the McCarthy campaign soon drew away many of The Resistance's shock troops and followers. The Viet Cong's Tet offensive, followed by McCarthy's surprising showing in New Hampshire and President Johnson's startling announcement that he was stopping the bombing and would not run for another term, pulled the rug from under the radical anti-draft movement. What was the point of organizing people not to go into the army and risking many years in jail when it looked like the war might be over soon? The hoped-for political solution proved to be illusory. But the disillusionment with the war, which affected all America and which even Nixon and the Republicans were to tap, was in part a result of Resistance activity.

# 11

# The Resisters

While the October, December, and April demonstrations attracted widespread public attention, the message of The Resistance reached individual draft-age men every day of the year. In the San Francisco area thirty people a week were refusing to go into the army; in Los Angeles, seven. One out of five men called for induction in New York City failed to appear. In the first quarter of 1968, 609 men were indicted for Selective Service Act violations, a substantial increase over the last quarter of 1967 (347 indictments) and the corresponding period of the prior year (362 indictments). Draft opponents were further encouraged by the publicity and protest activity surrounding prosecution of the Spock group (Dr. Spock, Rev. Coffin, Mitchell Goodman, Michael Ferber, and Marcus Raskin) which commenced on January 5, 1968.

The Resistance organized support demonstrations at the induction centers whenever one of their number would say no. Over four hundred men came to cheer David Harris on when he refused induction on January 17, 1968. (There were songs, speeches, and a communal breakfast at the Oakland induction center.)[1] Six hundred and fifty attended Ray Mungo in Boston on the day that he did not take the symbolic step forward. New York Resistance organized two demonstrations a week to support draft refusers. Over two hundred friends of Mark Weintraub trekked out to Queens when he refused induction on January 29. (Among them were Grace Paley, Keith Lampe, and one of Weintraub's professors from Queens College.) Vinnie McGee, a student at Union Theological Seminary and one of the April 15 card burners, refused service on the same day at Whitehall, while two hundred seminarians and clergymen picketed. Emmet Schaefer, a Columbia student, refused on February 5, 1968, with his father, a Columbia dean, members of the Columbia faculty, and The Resistance in attendance. James Branigan of Wesleyan refused on February 20; Ron Moyer of Virginia Tech on February 26; Robert Payne of Bucknell on March 6; and Bob Kowollik of St. Peter's College in Jersey City on March 12. In Minneapolis, three resisters refused in one week (January 15), including Dave Gutknecht.

The style of the induction center demonstrations was generally the same. The resister would read a statement as to why he was refusing to go into the army, usually an attack on the repressive nature of American foreign and domestic policy. "America is using its great power for destruction and repression when it should be used to aid human progress," said Bob Kowollik. "The draft represents a prime violation of the ideals [of brotherhood, freedom, and self-determination] and is the tool with which this government executes its repressive . . . policy." The supporters would acknowledge that they had counseled, aided, and abetted the resister. An effort would be made to talk to other inductees, to convince them that alternatives to the army were available. Generally this was done with refreshments and sex. "Resistance girls are the prettiest and they were busy distributing flowers, donuts and coffee to the guys—volunteers and inductees— who had come to *accept* induction. Resistance men passed out leaflets explaining what the demonstration was all about. . . . At the beginning, some of the guys were wary of us. They expressed fear that we had put acid in the donuts and coffee and they didn't want to get involved with any Freak the Draft Week activities. But when it became apparent that our intentions were good, they started accepting our gifts graciously." The resister in this case, David Bolduc of Los Angeles, went into the induction center and three times refused to take the step forward. ". . . we waited, and while we waited soft, easy, human conversations began between Resistance members and inductees, onlookers, newsmen, and army personnel." On the same day that Bolduc refused induction, nine others did the same.[2]

Sometimes the resisters would engage in guerilla theater to make their point about the draft. When Jan Norris appeared for induction at Salem, Oregon, he chained himself to four other men and one girl. "We formed with Mr. Norris a literal 'chain of life' in the belief that all men are brothers and that we are all bound together by our common humanity. We made these feelings visible by padlock and chain." *

This form of metaphoric behavior became highly popular in The Resistance. James Wessner, a Harvard senior, wandered around the streets of Cincinnati (before his trial for draft refusal) dressed as the Grim Reaper, with a death skull mask, a black cape, and a scythe, to show his opposition to the war. After he was convicted and sentenced to four years, he literally became a non-cooperator, refusing to move, talk, or help the marshals take him to jail (just as Corbett Bishop had done twenty-five years earlier). He was carried to prison and lay motionless on the concrete floor of his cell. A few days later, the marshals carried him back to court where he waived his right of appeal.

When David Harris was sentenced, all the resisters in the courtroom stood up to show their solidarity and community with him. George Crocker, a Quaker from Minneapolis, demanded that the judge hearing his case either refuse to pass any sentence on him or give him the maximum. Judge Philip Neville began to answer him, but one of Crocker's supporters came up to the bench: "For what George Crocker has done, no man should be sentenced and imprisoned. But if he is to be imprisoned, he will not stand alone. I stand with him." Two other resisters started toward the judge, but were blocked by federal marshals. Some of the spectators started singing "Oh, Freedom," and soon the whole courtroom had joined in. The marshals tried to arrest some of the participants, but they all linked arms to block the officers. Finally, after the court had been cleared of most of the demonstrators, Judge Neville, who was generally lenient in draft cases, sentenced Crocker to four years in jail—an unusually heavy term for someone with his background.

In all these incidents, the resisters displayed what Professor Nevitt Sanford of Stanford called their "annoying purity"—their passion for consistent application of their ideals, no matter what the personal consequences. Most of the resisters could have stayed safely in college with their II-S deferments. Their initial choice was not between the army and jail, but between a comfortable college routine on the

* Many resisters also sought sanctuary in churches and synagogues to show that their disobedience was rooted more in a profound morality than intellectual political conviction.[3]

one hand and active draft resistance on the other, with far-reaching effects on their lives and careers. They would often ignore legal advice and demonstrate their continued recalcitrance, in the courtroom and later in jail, to their own practical disadvantage.

In addition, the resisters were driven to explain their behavior at every stage in the resistance process. Seldom in history has any group of lawbreakers devoted so much time and effort to declaring and justifying their violations. They spoke at great length at protest rallies and induction center demonstrations, stood up in court to debate with the judges, and directed an avalanche of mail to convince their draft boards to stop the war-waging machine. A typical letter came from a young man returning his card to his draft board in Peekskill, New York:

I am enclosing your latest attempt to classify me. I informed you many, many months ago that I rejected your right to keep people's names in your files, like a tally of so many lambs available for slaughter. You have no right to raise an army for this war, a war which is undeclared, unsanctioned this very day by the American people, against the Geneva Agreements whose pledge to the Vietnamese people was upheld by the United States government, and in the prosecution of which daily acts of violations against the Nuremberg Codes occur, committed by United States forces against civilian populations.

Thus, I continue to refuse to hold your card, whatever classification you choose to assign me. I have no classification, or label. I am a free man. I will defend this country, for I believe it is worth defense—but I shall not let evil men without conscience decide when and where I shall defend it. In fact, I am defending it this very moment, when I refuse to follow your orders. I also defend it when I plead with you to resign from your positions as members of the draft board, and join with me in trying to end this war by all means within your consciences.

Ray Mungo of the Liberation News Service sent along a ten-page denunciation of American policy in Vietnam when he sent back his card. Daniel Due of Santa Rosa, California, a worker in New York Resistance, had been declared a conscientious objector but he informed his draft board he would not undertake alternate service:

I have waited several weeks to write this to you, because I don't like to precipitate anything that will get me into trouble. During the thirty day period that you gave me to find an alternate service job, I tried to do so, and failed to find one that would meet both your demands and mine. During that time and since then, I have gradually been coming to feel that though I may not now be leading my life just as I want to, I can't allow it to be interrupted by an arbitrary, impersonal force that knows nothing of the demands and conditions of existence of my body and soul. I will no longer go along with Selective Service.

My draft cards are in my possession, but buried away in a drawer where I can forget them.

Two months later, Due wrote again:

Here are my draft cards. Since I really want nothing more to do with the draft, I don't feel right carrying them, or even keeping them.

I urge you to resign from the draft board. It must be very hard to justify morally the putting of young men in a position where they might easily have to kill or be killed. Resignation from the board really is the only way out of such a position.

The draft board ordered Due to report for alternate service but he refused:

I can't follow the order you gave me last week to report tomorrow for direction to a job of alternate service. I'm no longer cooperating with the draft because it's a machine that coerces young men to kill and die, and because its existence is destructive of a free society. . . .

In the interest of good feeling, some friends of mine and I thought it would be cheerful to send you some flowers. They should arrive tomorrow.

The next document in Due's draft file was a memorandum stating:

March 31, 1967: Flowers arrived from "The Flower Shop." Message: Sorry these are late. For peace and good will.

s/Daniel A. Due

Flowers refused by Mrs. Norma M. Niclaes, Chief Clerk.

On October 16, 1967, Due participated in the draft card turn-ins at Foley Square in New York. He wrote that same day to his board:

Dear Friends,
I'm sending you this letter today because today I'm standing with my friends who are publicly ceasing cooperation with the draft or reaffirming, like me, a position already taken.

I don't go along with the draft any more because it's wrong to co-operate with a machine that makes war—kills people. And it's simply wrong to cooperate with the inhibition of anyone's freedom . . . we can't make a community if we're taking our brothers' lives. Please stop sending young men into the army. It eliminates the possibility of freedom and love. Quit the draft board, it's no good.

As these letters and statements show, The Resistance program appealed to the most articulate and politically aware college students. Its message and approach were most appreciated by men who had read Gandhi, Tolstoi, and Thoreau and could agonize about a man's duties to his conscience, his fellow man, and the state. But it meant little to the poor and the blacks. In Chicago and Philadelphia particularly, the organizers tried to contact lower-class men who were 1-A and explain the alternatives to them. A handful did respond. But to most inhabitants of the central city slums, the army was a step up where a man could escape a closed circle of poverty. Saul Alinsky said that a meeting called in the Rochester slums about the war and the draft would attract twelve people—all middle-class white professionals who did not live in the area.

Many SDS professionals and other radical spokesmen sneered at The Resistance for their hyper-moral stance, their apolitical behavior, their *posing,* as it were, and above all, for their failure to engage the poor. Carl Davidson wrote in *New Left Notes* that noncooperation and voluntary imprisonment showed only guilt, masochism, and would-be martyrdom, typical middle-class reactions to the contradictions of American society. Such attitudes did nothing to resolve the problems and only led to the loss of a needed organizer.[4]

But Staughton Lynd points out that draft resistance was the first contemporary political movement in the North that actually required its participants to take serious risks and confront the apparatus of the state directly. The unique tone of The Resistance resulted from the existential test that its members had undergone, rites of passage that took them out of the American mainstream. They learned that they could face the nation's contempt and the heavy hand of the authorities.

The essential spirit of the resisters—their exhilaration, their moral assertiveness, their feelings of brotherhood, of shared work, and shared commitment—came from a sense of release. They had broken the deal that the government had made with them, rejected their special middle-class privileges, and accepted a life course that was dangerous, fulfilling, and theirs alone.

Nonetheless, there were many internal strains in The Resistance, conflicts between those who saw the movement as the "cutting edge" of a political revolution and others who still focused on the single crucial issue of the draft and the war. At a national draft resistance conference in Madison, Wisconsin in August 1967, deep differences in approach began to emerge. Bob Swartz of CADRE insisted that draft resistance was meant to "develop revolutionaries." The radical SDS wing thought it was unrealistic to think about depleting the army sufficiently to end the war. "Our focus should therefore be on building revolutionary consciousness," said Swartz.[5] Even among the radicals there were differences. Should they proselytize among the lower classes, organize immediate protests along economic lines, ally themselves with the black radicals, and get out of draft resistance altogether?

But many resisters felt that as resisters they served a special function in the radicalization of America. Specifically, The Resistance was building a sense of community and brotherhood among the youth of the country, who, having passed through the crisis of draft resistance, would stay together to solve the other problems of our society. America lost, or perhaps never had, that sense of community that was needed for the task ahead. The Vietnam War was a reflection of the atomization that was at the core of our troubles. David Harris explained at his trial for refusing induction: "When the society rejects that brotherhood as an organizing principle . . . ultimately they are going to be involved in the destruction of other societies and other men and Vietnam provides us with that example." But while The Resistance should be a broad political movement, politics is the way you live your life. From the start, the West Coast leaders saw the need for a life-style that was appropriate to the new political tactics of brotherhood and community—a total rejection of middle-class life patterns, community living where the new values could be learned, a willingness to experiment with new sensory experiences through drugs.

Many of the East Coast members were not so sure that communal living was the answer. In their eyes, the issue was primarily a political one. The important point was to reach as many draft-age men as possible, particularly middle-class students whose parents controlled the political machinery. Rather than getting out of the mainstream, the East Coasters wanted to inject it with more anti-draft sentiment. While they also saw the experience of draft resistance as a highly emotional act of personal liberation, they were anxious to carry as many others with them as possible, for whatever reasons they chose. Furthermore, the effort to reach the poor and the black would be more successful if the lower classes were not frightened off by the strangeness and uncertainties of the hippie culture. The greatest need, in their eyes, was for tactics that would increase the *numbers* of resisters, not the revolutionary fervor of the hard-core.

The conference in Madison produced endless talk about these problems, but no resolution. Since almost everyone agreed on the draft card turn-ins, few immediate difficulties were caused by the ideological differences behind the scenes. But as time went on, tactical disputes began to emerge. Should resisters evade jail under any circumstances, go underground, and so be available for revolutionary activities, or should they publicly accept the consequences of their refusal and thus impress the middle class with their personal witness against war? How much time and energy should go into other revolutionary activities—organizing anti-war G.I.'s or joining in student rebellions? Or is that effort better spent getting as many men as possible to refuse induction?

In New York, The Resistance decided to make use of the conditional pledge—potential resisters were asked to pledge themselves to refuse induction only when a certain number of other men likewise agreed. Much debate went on as to the number of pledges that would be binding. Should it be low enough so that it would be easily reached or high enough so that more men would be likely to join? The radicals ridiculed such ideas as the conditional pledge. What kind of revolutionary would promise to join the movement only if a certain number of his friends also decided to sign up.

In short, the internal Resistance conflicts reflected many of the strains that American society as a whole was beginning to show—between those who had some faith in the viability of electoral politics and those who saw the need for a wider restructuring of our institutions. The Resistance debate yielded no more definitive results than debates in other corners.

# 12

# The Denouement

The most important draft resistance event after the April 1968 demonstrations was the Spock trial in Boston. That the trial was held in the Massachusetts federal court gave it a special significance. One hundred and fourteen years before, another group of prominent professionals, teachers, writers, and clerics had been indicted by the government in the same court for encouraging resistance to a federal law. The parallels between the Theodore Parker episode (when he and others were prosecuted for interfering with the rendition of Anthony Burns) and the Spock case were remarkably striking. Not only was the same caliber of defendant accused of the same type of crime, but the evidence was almost identical. In both cases, intellectual supporters of active resisters to an unpopular federal enactment were accused of going beyond the permissible limits of dissent and inciting disobedience to law. Members of both groups applauded and supported each other's remarks at public meetings and distributed signed leaflets containing "insurrectionary rhetoric." In both cases, a highly unsympathetic judge was appointed to hear the case and in both cases the accused were ultimately vindicated.

The five defendants in the Spock trial were accused of conspiring to counsel registrants under the draft law to evade service and refuse to keep their draft cards in their possession, and generally to interfere with the administration of the draft. The acts which formed the basis of the prosecution included the preparation and signing of "A Call to Resist Illegitimate Authority"; the holding of press conferences to publicize their opposition to American policy; participation in anti-war demonstrations, and their presence at rallies where draft cards were turned in. The defendants were not accused of any substantive crime but merely *conspiring* to do so. Thus under traditional legal rules regarding conspiracy, the government could introduce a wide range of evidence, such as statements by alleged co-conspirators which would otherwise not be admissible. And the prosecution did not have to show that the defendants succeeded in persuading a single young man to turn in his draft card.

The gravamen of conspiracy is an "agreement" to perform an illegal act, whether subsequently accomplished or not, and "agreement" can be proved by demonstrating parallel conduct toward an illegal goal. Thus the government tried to show that the defendants encouraged each other in voicing opposition to the war and supporting draft resisters. Even applauding each other's remarks at public rallies became evidence of an illegal conspiracy. Jessica Mitford, in her brilliant book on the trial, exposes the government's stance: "At the Spock trial, the government's message came over loud and clear: You are not as free as you think you are. Yes, of course you may sign a peace petition, you may have your name on a newspaper advertisement supporting draft resisters. . . . However, if you do these things, you will be 'kept under surveillance by the FBI' . . . and should it suit the government's purpose, you will then be prosecuted, and the petition, the advertisement, the mass meeting, and your applause will be solemnly paraded before the jury against you." [1]

The trial itself was a great disappointment to the anti-war movement. Sidney Zion of the *New York Times* quoted an anonymous peace leader as saying: "It could have been a great trial. Instead it was pallid, dull, and carping. They should have admitted all the truthful facts proudly instead of trimming on the question of whom they sought to influence. They should have thunderously denounced the war and said it was their legal right and moral obligation to urge all the kids to stay out." [2]

Coffin insisted that his anti-war activity was designed to elicit a test case which would challenge the legality of the Vietnam War and the constitutionality of the draft. But the federal judge in Boston, eighty-four-year-old Francis Ford, ruled these matters irrelevant. The defendants were charged with conspiracy and were forced to conduct a narrow, legalistic defense denying criminal agreement among them, or any attempt to influence the young resisters. All their efforts, they said, were intended to comfort and support resisters already committed. Coffin testified that he only supported "those who had already in conscience decided not to serve in the Armed Forces as long as the war in Vietnam continued."

Dr. Spock said: "It was against my professional principles to try to persuade anybody to do anything that he is not ready to do himself, and actually, in addition, it is well known professionally if you try to persuade somebody who hasn't made up his mind, you only push him in the other direction. No one can do it until they are ready." Goodman told the court: "I intended, as I always intended, that they should make up their own decision," and Ferber said that he did not intend to attract any uncommitted people by his sermons and speeches. Noam Chomsky, Paul Lauter, and Florence Howe showed how easy it was to attack this approach. "If their support for resisters really did encourage men to refuse the draft, then they were guilty of inciting young men to violate the law and go to prison; or, if their statements were ineffective in extending resistance, then their whole enterprise was a public relations gambit and a sham." [3]

Their position offered the prosecution an easy target for ridicule. U.S. Attorney John Wall asked Coffin about the Arlington Street Church ceremony: ". . . did it not occur to you that in those circumstances, in that house of worship, . . . in clerical garb, you . . . might move some of those that had less iron in their spine than others to act on their convictions and turn in their draft cards?" When Coffin answered, "I would not seek to get converts to my view," it is unlikely the jury believed him. How could the defendants make such strong statements against the war if they were not trying to persuade others, including draft-age young men, to oppose the war? Wall said in his summation to the jury, with heavy sarcasm: " 'Son, I can't ask you to make a decison like that, can't ask you to do it; it's too serious, it's too noble, the demand is too much. You will have to make it yourself. But once you have made it, I will stand beside you right into the gates of jail, if that's what happens.' "

The defendants, highly articulate men, never adequately explained their position at the trial. Ferber did testify that the draft cards collected in Boston on October 16 were held until the last minute in case anyone changed his mind and wanted his card returned. In fact one law student did ask for his back, and received it. At other times the defendants stated that the same compassion that made them want to share the fate of the young resisters did not permit them to urge such a drastic step upon these boys—leading to perhaps five years in jail, loss of many professional opportunities, and the contempt of most of the country. To assume that The Resistance was organized and directed by the older intellectuals was foolish. If anything, the reverse was true—the support groups were a response to The Resistance. It was not the urging of the other professionals that led to draft refusal. "What has led young men to resist is unquestionably the information presented in the press and on television, in books, lectures and teach-ins, and discussions on and off campus during the past three years." [4]

Despite their disclaimers, the judge certainly believed the defendants had perpetuated The Resistance. When he sentenced each of the four defendants found guilty (Marcus Raskin was acquitted) to two years in jail, Judge Ford summed up:

It is the view of this court that it is reasonably inferrable that the defendants have played some material part in inciting certain draft evaders to flout the law.

It would be preposterous to sentence young men to jail for violation of the Selective Service Act and allow those who, as the jury found, conspired to incite Selective Service registrants to take action to violate the law and who, it is reasonable to conclude, were instrumental in inciting them to do so, to escape under the guise of free speech.

But the government overreached once again. Judge Ford had shown so much hostility to the defendants during the trial that even the U.S. Attorneys responsible for the case, particularly John Van de Kamp, thought there was a good chance the appeal court might reverse. To preserve the guilty verdict, they thought it would be desirable to isolate any error by submitting special findings to the jury. If any error was made in one aspect of the case, the special findings by the jury could show that it did not infect the entire proceedings. As the judge explained to the lawyers, "Suppose they find them guilty, and so forth, and found them guilty of counseling. I may be wrong on the definition of aiding and abetting, but if they found them guilty of counseling, that would be enough to sustain the verdict." The government lawyers, however, had not done their homework. It took twenty minutes for an A.C.L.U. lawyer and David Rosenberg (a young lawyer working in the office of Leonard Boudin, Dr. Spock's counsel) to discover that the submission of special findings to a jury in a criminal case against the wishes of the

defendants was itself reversible error. They prepared a legal memorandum on the point; this was handed up to Judge Ford, who rejected
it.

A year later, the Federal Court of Appeals for the First Circuit
declared that Judge Ford was wrong. Not only did the three appellate court judges conclude that there was not sufficient evidence to
prove that Dr. Spock and Michael Ferber had conspired to violate
the draft act, but they held that by asking the jury to focus on special
questions its general conclusion might have been affected. "There is
no easier way to reach, and perhaps force, a verdict of guilty than to
approach it step by step. . . . By a progression of questions each
of which seems to require an answer unfavorable to the defendant, a
reluctant juror may be led to vote for a conviction which, in the large,
he would have resisted." [5] The conviction was reversed with directions
for a new trial for Coffin and Goodman; the government has made no
effort to retry the case.

The *Spock* decision was not the only case in which the courts
upbraided the government's handling of the draft resistance problem.
One of the young men who handed in his draft card at the Arlington
Street Church on October 16, 1967 was James J. Oestereich, a divinity
student at the Andover-Newton Theological School in Newton,
Massachusetts. When his card reached his draft board in Cheyenne,
Wyoming, they reclassified him I-A for failing to have it in his
possession and ordered him to report for induction. Thereupon he
sought the help of the American Civil Liberties Union, which initiated
an action in the courts to regain Oestereich's IV-D (divinity student)
status.

Unfortunately, the 1967 changes in the draft law clearly specified
that registrants could not challenge a draft board decision on their
status by a civil action before responding to the induction order.
When the lower federal courts dismissed Oestereich's complaint, a
petition for certiorari was filed in the Supreme Court, and Solicitor
General Erwin Griswold, after consulting with Ramsey Clark, confessed error. The strong Congressional policy in favor of divinity
school exemptions required the opportunity for pre-induction judicial
review in cases such as Oestereich's.

General Hershey was furious about Griswold's concession. He
immediately lodged a document with the Supreme Court giving his
view of the law: judicial review was not provided for in the statute
and the case must be dismissed. The Court then ordered full argument on the case. On December 16, 1968, the Supreme Court declared that the action of the draft board in taking away Oestereich's
statutory exemption was "basically lawless." Justice Douglas wrote

for the Court: "Once a person registers and qualifies for a statutory exemption, we find no legislative authority to deprive him of that exemption because of conduct unrelated to the merits of granting or continuing that exemption. The Solicitor General confesses error on the use by Selective Service of delinquency proceedings for that purpose." [6]

The decision was important for two reasons: first, it seriously eroded Hershey's attempt to insulate draft board decisions from review by the courts before the date set for induction. If a draft board went clearly beyond its statutory authority, the courts could reexamine its actions. Thus one of the chief retrogressive features of the 1967 law was judicially repealed.

Second, the Court cast doubt on the entire delinquency procedure established by Hershey to meet the tactics of The Resistance, particularly his letter of October 26, 1967. Within a short period many new cases were filed relying on the *Oestereich* decision. The lawyers challenged the revocation of any deferment or exemption because a person handed in his draft card. One case went even further. David Gutknecht of Minneapolis attacked the right of a draft board to accelerate his induction for turning in his card even though he was classified 1-A at the time. Gutknecht's lawyers said that no penalty of any kind could be imposed by a draft board, even changing the order of call of the 1-A's who were supposed to be inducted "oldest first."

In January 1970, the Supreme Court declared unconstitutional the entire delinquency structure established by Hershey. It unanimously held that Gutknecht's turning in of his draft card could have no effect whatsoever on his draft status: "The power under the regulations to declare a registrant 'delinquent' has no statutory standard or even guidelines. The power is exercised entirely at the discretion of the local board. It is a broad, roving authority, a type of administrative absolutism not congenial to our law-making traditions. . . . We search the Act in vain for any clues that Congress desired the Act to have punitive sanctions apart from the criminal prosecutions specifically authorized." [7]

A week after the *Gutknecht* decision, the Supreme Court refined it by adding that any registrant whose deferment was taken away under the delinquency regulations could obtain pre-induction judicial review of the draft board action.[8] (The case was brought by Timothy Breen, a student at the Berkeley School of Music in Boston, who had handed in his card during a rally in November 1967.)

These decisions were particularly important for the organizers of The Resistance. Hundreds of them had handed in their cards at an early stage of the anti-draft movement and had been ordered for induction as delinquents. Now their draft boards' actions were held illegal. Many of the resisters had passed the age of twenty-six and could no longer be taken into the army. Thus they escaped all criminal prosecution and neither did they have to worry about military service. Those young men who never turned in their draft cards, were never declared delinquent, but refused service nevertheless, had no such legal defense. For once, it paid off to be a militant in America.

By the time the Supreme Court had issued its *Breen* ruling in early 1970, the resistance movement had virtually ceased to exist. The drama had been taken out of draft refusal and the radicals and the media were concerned with the Chicago trial, the Black Panthers, and the rash of bombings in New York and other cities. The quiet willingness to say no to the army seemed quixotic and dated. New York Resistance closed its office in October 1969 and the major Resistance headquarters elsewhere also stopped operating (except in Philadelphia where a vigorous organization still functions). At a national Resistance meeting in Bloomington in March 1969, Staughton Lynd called for a broader, multi-issue orientation by Resistance members which would encompass other problems of American society, such as racism and capitalism. The G.I. movement, high-school student rebellions, and women's liberation offered further outlets for meaningful radical activity.[9] The Resistance, as a special organizing vehicle for the middle-class students objecting to the war in Vietnam and the oppression of the draft, was over.*

What had it done in the three years of its existence? The number of resisters had never grown sufficiently to jeopardize the flow of troops to Vietnam. General Hershey contemptuously told Jessica Mitford that the resistance movement had had no effect at all on the draft. "They stopped them [inductees] for some *minutes* in Oakland, that was all." [10] But despite the lack of recent resistance activity, the number of resisters has steadily increased and the final plateau is not yet in sight. From June to December 1969, over three hundred prosecutions per month were initiated for draft law violations. The rate in the first months of 1970 went even higher. With the problems of initiating the new lottery system combined with increased draft refusals, the Selective Service System failed to meet its quota for the

* Following the invasion of Cambodia and the Kent State killings in May, 1970, a call for a new draft resistance movement emerged from many college campuses. A nationwide conference was held in Princeton and a new organization, UNDO (Union for National Draft Opposition), was formed. The tactics, ideas, goals and supporters of the new movement were identical to those of The Resistance.

first quarter of 1970. On December 31, 1969, there were 33,960 delinquents—people who had refused to perform some duty required of them under the Selective Service System—and 23,598 conscientious objectors. These totals were the highest since the Korean War and the highest rates since World War I. The students who signed the "We Won't Go" petitions in 1967 and 1968 were fulfilling their promises in 1969 and 1970. One by one, without fanfare, they were refusing to lend themselves to the government's Vietnam policy.

The Resistance attack on our involvement in Vietnam had been so widely accepted by 1970 that President Nixon was searching for a face-saving device to get the troops back home. As far as the draft itself was concerned, Nixon appointed a blue-ribbon committee in March 1969 (headed by Thomas Gates, former Secretary of Defense) to study the feasibility of an all-volunteer army. In February 1970, it issued its report, calling for the elimination of the draft by July 1971. The Gates Commission criticized a conscription system in words that not even SDS had used in 1965 and 1966: "It has been a costly, inequitable, and divisive procedure for recruiting men for the armed forces. It has imposed heavy burdens on a small minority of young men while easing slightly the tax burden on the rest of us . . . It has weakened the political fabric of our society and impaired the delicate web of shared values that alone enables a free society to exist." Furthermore, the Commission—composed of two ex-generals, four big businessmen, and four college presidents—declared: "Compelling service through a draft undermines respect for government by forcing an individual to serve when and in the manner the government decides, regardless of his own values and talents." Discussing The Resistance in highly sympathetic terms, the report noted that "the draft erodes ideals of patriotism and service by alienating many of the young who bear the burden. American youths are raised in an atmosphere where freedom and justice are held dear. It is difficult for them to cope with a situation which falls far short of these ideals just as they enter adulthood. The draft undermines identification with society just at the age when young men begin to assume social responsibilities. It thwarts the natural desire of youths to commit themselves to society." [11]

Elimination of the draft was certainly a chief feature of the original Resistance program since it was the clearest form of oppression that this society had imposed on them directly. Their refusal to obey the law that oppressed them had helped to create sufficient public sentiment to make the end of the draft a reality—just as the Whiskey rebels found resistance to be the most effective way of opposing the excise tax, and the Helderberg farmers, the feudal rent payments.

The Resistance message made its impact throughout American society. By exposing the channelling of draft-age men, they helped others to see the thousand ways in which they too were being channelled. By challenging the government's illegitimate authority, they stimulated resistance by very different types of citizens—in the army, the schools, and the streets. By confronting the state's coercive power, they desanctified the institutions that had brought us into Vietnam.

The defense lawyers at the Chicago Seven Conspiracy trial advanced a novel legal argument to justify their clients' clash with the police during the 1968 Democratic convention. Recalling the 1770 Boston Massacre when British troops fired at a hostile crowd which had taunted them with the insult "lobster-back" (the eighteenth-century equivalent of "pig"), the lawyers claimed that the founding fathers anticipated defiance of constituted authority *as a legal right*. When they framed the Constitution and passed the First Amendment, the early leaders took into account the possibility that the state power would be misused to clog the political machinery, as the British had done in the colonial period (and as the Chicago police did in 1968). If the political institutions were not properly functioning and if the government engaged in repression of dissenting groups, otherwise "illegal" acts became proper and legal until the forms were set straight again. In short, a revolutionary right of petition was written into the Constitution and the Bill of Rights which required acquittal of the Chicago defendants.[12]

The idea that "illegal" acts can become legal depending on the purpose or motive of the perpetrator has received much attention recently. Harrop A. Freeman of the Cornell Law School has flatly declared that "civil disobedience is within the protection of the First Amendment." The citizenry must have access to what the Supreme Court called "the Poor Man's Forum," the right to "push doorbells, to talk in the park, to parade in the streets . . . to call his case, by whatever means he is able to use—even civil disobedience—to the attention of the people." [13] When an "illegal" act—like the refusal to serve in the army—is based on conscientious beliefs akin to religious faith, many commentators and a few judges have suggested that the free exercise clause of the First Amendment may completely excuse the "criminal." Judge Charles Wyzanski decided in the *Sisson* case that a young draft resister's conscientious beliefs—"as real, pervasive, durable and commendable a marshalling of priorities as a formal religion" [14]—justified his refusal to be inducted to fight in Vietnam.

Placing the principle in broader terms, lawyer J. Morris Clark has written: "when an individual because of compelling conscientious belief refuses to perform any duty of positive action established by the state, there exists a constitutional presumption that the state can satisfy its needs" in some alternate way.[15] Clark justifies this view because of the free speech purpose of conscientious behavior (its capacity to persuade others to new political ideas or actions) and because "religious or conscientious values frequently represent an idealism which serves a valuable function in society even though the idealist's conclusions may be rejected." Furthermore, to punish a conscientious man for acting according to his beliefs "often works an exceptional harm to him which, unless justified by the most stringent social needs, constitutes a moral wrong in and of itself." [16]

A New York University Law School professor, Norman Redlich, and a student at the school, Kenneth Feinberg, have suggested still another legal defense of draft resistance: "the right not to kill." They assert "where no threat to the homeland exists (as evidenced by a declaration of war or other emergency measures), the person who conscientiously refused to kill in an undeclared war overseas should be tested in the same constitutional crucible which, we are confident, would justify the refusal of a citizen to be a public executioner." [17]

It is premature to assume these legal arguments will have any substantial chance of succeeding in the courts. We are still in the backwash of the legal realism of the English utilitarians and Oliver Wendell Holmes which focused on the conduct rather than the motives of an accused man. Our legal philosophy and institutions are geared to ignore intent except in certain well-defined situations. When nine militant "ultra-resisters" from Baltimore (including poet-priest Daniel Berrigan) were tried for destroying some Catonsville, Maryland, draft board files with homemade napalm, they argued that their actions were designed "to stop the machine of death" and therefore were legally protected. But the court ignored their plea. "Their sincerity is beyond question," said Judge Simon Sobeloff, joined by Judge Clement F. Haynsworth. "It implies no disparagement of their idealism to say that society will not tolerate the means they chose to register their opposition to the war." The reason the court advanced was the same that has always met conscientious disobedience of law. "If these defendants were to be absolved from guilt because of their moral certainty that the war in Vietnam is wrong, would not others who might commit breaches of the law to demonstrate their sincere belief that the country is not prosecuting the war vigorously enough be entitled to acquittal? Both must answer for their acts." [18]

Many judges and public officials have claimed that conscientious lawbreaking on the left will only encourage conscientious lawbreaking on the right and throughout society, which would lead to crime and violence on the one hand or anarchy and fascism on the other. A New York City judge sent thirty-five white students to jail for disrupting their school with demands for admission of one thousand Negroes and Puerto Ricans: "When you decide that you're going to change Brooklyn College on your own . . . why shouldn't the kid who needs some money snatch a pocketbook?" Judge Jacob Mishler commented, as he sentenced a draft resister to four years in jail: "If democracy won't work and if many people violate the laws, society will demand order from a more repressive form of government." And Sidney Hook angrily told Justice William O. Douglas at a law school symposium about his book *Points of Rebellion*: "Those who resort to violence or write apologies for rebellion are preparing the way for the very police state they fear."

These statements reflect an emotional current that is impossible to ignore. Our society finally rests on a delicate equilibrium of prizes and penalties, on a sense that virtue will somehow be rewarded and evil somehow punished: our notions of justice and fairness are threatened when law-violators go free. Not only does unpunished crime undermine our idea of how society should operate, but it offers too great an inducement to our own criminal impulses. We need jails and judges as a terrifying example for our own superegos so that we will not be tempted to transgress. The more "lawlessness" we see, the more repression we need to reestablish our internal equilibrium.

But when conscientious men disobey a law for a political or moral purpose, different considerations apply. Violating the law to show one's opposition to Vietnam—by refusing to be inducted or by burning draft files—is simply not the same as a man committing arson or rape for his personal gain or as a Southern extremist disobeying the law on school disegregation. The difference is not only in the criminal act but in society's reaction to it. If the danger is that the people will themselves be threatened or tempted by a breakdown in law enforcement, then their reaction to each different situation is crucial. If they accept opposition to Vietnam as moral though misguided, but violent opposition to integration as unfair and dangerous, there is no difficulty in saying that the former violation is legitimate but the second is not.* Furthermore, there is a moral difference be-

---

* "A society which cares about itself requires a citizenry that is ready to see a moral difference between one who protests against the killing in a place such as Vietnam and one who protests to prevent black children from getting a decent education. To abdicate that responsibility is only to begin the march in law-abiding lockstep toward moral oblivion." [19]

tween the two forms of conduct which is recognized by everyone but the most literal-minded defenders of law and order. Most important, conscientious lawlessness has always been useful "in constantly reminding citizens and the government of the depth and urgency of our problems, in making them aware of possible solutions, and in bringing pressure to bear for the adoption of these solutions."[20]

This analysis suggests new criteria for evaluating disobedience of authority. Where a defined interest group complains about a specific evil which the government refuses to correct after many peaceful entreaties, its members are justified in escalating their protest to the point of illegal resistance as part of their political efforts. So long as the disobedience is directed toward the specific oppression and is not disproportionate to the situation, there is no danger of a breakdown of law and order and no threat to the democratic process. The historic examples described here show that American rebels have seldom been revolutionary (attacked the state as such), that they generally shared the basic values of the larger society (the militant Black Panther Party insists on its constitutional rights), but that their grievances can reach the point where peaceful petition is not enough.

By far the greatest threat to an open society is not disorder and disobedience but the loss of its legitimacy. Only when the mass of the citizens accept the authority of its institutions and accord them respect can a government properly conduct its business. "Legitimacy is earned by the ability of those who conduct the power of the state to represent and reflect a broad consensus. . . . It cannot be claimed or granted by mere technicality of law; it must be won by the success of state institutions in cultivating and meeting expectations." [21]

The point is, finally, that our system has had more viability than either the radicals or the Establishment has been willing to admit. The current militants insist that our democracy is a sham and our institutions make reform impossible; but this society has shown a remarkable ability to assimilate and respond to the most severe— and illegal—attacks of its critics. Government leaders react with horror to any violations of law, but disobedience has played the most significant role in political and social change since the earliest days of the republic. It is the rebels who are the greatest support of our traditions and values. Under their pressure, our institutions may yet prove adaptive enough to survive.

# Appendix A

## Statistics on Draft Resistance

| Fiscal Year | Total Registered | Calls | Inducted | FBI Delinquency Investigations | New Delinquents |
|---|---|---|---|---|---|
| 1918 | | | ( ) | | ( ) |
| 1919 | | | (2,760,000) | | (337,649) |
| 1920 | | | ( ) | | ( ) |
| 1940 | 16,316,906 | | | | |
| 1941 | 16,565,037 | 651,151 | 622,775 | | 31,640 |
| 1942 | 28,952,160 | 1,474,184 | 1,410,480 | | 80,069 |
| 1943 | 23,076,133 | 4,355,043 | 4,037,200 | | 119,984 |
| 1944 | 22,212,562 | 3,227,707 | 2,379,594 | | 85,789 |
| 1945 | 22,028,772 | 1,257,100 | 1,182,118 | | 30,735 |
| 1946 | 9,279,114 | 780,800 | 471,164 | | |
| 1947 | * | 59,500 | 19,306 | | |
| 1948 | * | — | — | | |
| 1949 | * | 35,000 | 30,129 | | |
| 1950 | * | — | 1,637 | | |
| 1951 | 11,142,168 | 550,379 | 587,444 | | ( 20,072) |
| 1952 | 13,225,218 | 367,288 | 381,006 | | ( ) |
| 1953 | 14,446,108 | 523,000 | 560,798 | 15,538 | 11,730 |
| 1954 | 15,598,758 | 251,000 | 268,018 | 20,600 | 17,600 |
| 1955 | 16,701,965 | 211,000 | 213,716 | 22,080 | 20,362 |
| 1956 | 17,816,273 | 136,000 | 136,580 | 13,461 | 10,430 |
| 1957 | 18,969,850 | 175,000 | 179,321 | 11,178 | 12,003 |
| 1958 | 20,200,664 | 124,958 | 126,369 | 11,472 | 13,848 |
| 1959 | 21,480,369 | 109,000 | 111,889 | 17,881 | 14,495 |
| 1960 | 22,829,879 | 89,500 | 90,549 | 10,892 | 9,708 |
| 1961 | 24,332,138 | 58,000 | 61,070 | 16,988 | * |
| 1962 | 25,808,555 | 147,500 | 157,465 | 20,433 | * |
| 1963 | 27,278,763 | 70,000 | 71,744 | 19,190 | * |
| 1964 | 28,735,389 | 145,000 | 150,808 | 26,279 | * |
| 1965 | 30,676,300 | 101,300 | 103,328 | 21,452 | * |
| 1966 | 32,638,305 | 336,530 | 343,481 | 26,830 | * |
| 1967 | 34,523,326 | 288,900 | 298,559 | 29,218 | * |
| Dec. 31, 1967 | | | | | |
| 1968 | 36,410,077 | 343,300 | 341,404 | 29,485 | * |
| Dec. 31, 1968 | | | | 15,772 | |
| 1969 | 37,953,210 | 263,800 | 262,046 | 32,000† | * |
| Dec. 31, 1969 | | | | 18,000† | |
| 1970 | 40,303,654 | 209,300 | 203,576 | 36,000† | * |

* Not available
† Estimated

| Fiscal Year | Total Delinquents as of June 30 | Failed to report for Induction | Conscientious Objectors (as of June 30) | | |
|---|---|---|---|---|---|
| | | | IV-E or I-O | I-W | I-W released |
| 1918 | | | | ( ) | |
| 1919 | | | | (56,830) | |
| 1920 | | | | ( ) | |
| 1940 | | | | | |
| 1941 | | | 3,692 | | |
| 1942 | | | 7,302 | | |
| 1943 | | | 10,747 | | |
| 1944 | | | 10,297 | | |
| 1945 | | | 8,576 | | |
| 1946 | | | 4,940 | | |
| 1947 | | | 2,061 | | |
| 1948 | | | | | |
| 1949 | | | | | |
| 1950 | | | 9,916 | | |
| 1951 | | (12,542) | 8,609 | | |
| 1952 | | ( ) | 7,602 | 5 | |
| 1953 | 14,800 | 11,730 | 3,783 | 2,763 | 6 |
| 1954 | 11,810 | 7,500 | 4,071 | 4,322 | 212 |
| 1955 | 11,528 | 6,546 | 5,081 | 3,277 | 2,439 |
| 1956 | 8,497 | 3,572 | 5,441 | 2,632 | 3,773 |
| 1957 | 7,299 | 4,098 | 5,105 | 2,105 | 4,769 |
| 1958 | 9,675 | 4,156 | 7,513 | 1,784 | 5,403 |
| 1959 | 6,677 | 4,972 | 8,311 | 1,875 | 5,506 |
| 1960 | 5,493 | 2,920 | 8,791 | 1,800 | 5,687 |
| 1961 | * | * | 9,278 | 1,638 | 5,818 |
| 1962 | * | * | 9,722 | 2,118 | 5,668 |
| 1963 | * | * | 9,097 | 2,162 | 5,507 |
| 1964 | * | * | 9,775 | 2,270 | 5,875 |
| 1965 | * | * | 11,492 | 2,448 | 5,721 |
| 1966 | 12,661 | * | 9,031 | 4,378 | 5,995 |
| 1967 | 13,084 | 19,774 | 10,364 | 6,415 | 5,954 |
| Dec. 31, 1967 | 16,655 | | 11,041 | 6,367 | 6,830 |
| 1968 | 21,759 | 21,331 | 12,178 | 6,072 | 8,100 |
| Dec. 31, 1968 | 23,422 | | 13,341 | 6,402 | 9,262 |
| 1969 | 26,776 | 27,444 | 14,585 | 7,279 | 9,913 |
| Dec. 31, 1969 | 33,960 | | 15,812 | 8,212 | 10,530 |
| 1970 | 22,201 | 26,475 | 19,714 | 9,189 | 11,743 |

| Fiscal Year | | Prosecuted | Total Defendants | Dismissal | Total Convicted |
|---|---|---|---|---|---|
| 1918 | | 12,074 | | 1,205 | 8,422 |
| 1919 | | 15,262 | | 1,711 | 5,923 |
| 1920 | | 19,790 | | 558 | 503 |
| 1940 | | | | | |
| 1941 | | | | (35.2% of total) | 303 |
| | | | | ( indicted ) | |
| 1942 | | 3,333 | | (1941–45 dis- ) | 1,611 |
| | | | | (missed ) | |
| 1943 | | 7,819 | | ( ) | |
| | | | | ( ) | |
| 1944 | | 6,622 | | ( ) | 4,756 |
| | | | | ( ) | |
| 1945 | | 4,301 | 4,287 | (1,399 ) | 2,838 |
| 1946 | | 2,157 | 2,651 | 953 | 1,652 |
| 1947 | | 1,188 | 2,074 | 908 | 1,137 |
| 1948 | | 470 | 833 | 511 | 304 |
| 1949 | | 355 | 506 | 202 | 292 |
| 1950 | | 207 | 449 | 272 | 175 |
| 1951 | | 338 | 368 | 202 | 156 |
| 1952 | | 659 | 561 | 222 | 313 |
| 1953 | | 771 | 630 | 236 | 345 |
| 1954 | | 1,015 | 822 | 278 | 424 |
| 1955 | | 477 | 719 | 367 | 289 |
| 1956 | | 251 | 371 | 167 | 186 |
| 1957 | | 303 | 357 | 75 | 262 |
| 1958 | | 311 | 325 | 66 | 229 |
| 1959 | | 258 | 258 | 44 | 202 |
| 1960 | | 200 | 239 | 65 | 166 |
| 1961 | | 236 | 244 | 37 | 199 |
| 1962 | | 321 | 274 | 46 | 225 |
| 1963 | | 320 | 338 | 66 | 265 |
| 1964 | | 287 | 276 | 63 | 206 |
| 1965 | | 380 | 341 | 88 | 242 |
| 1966 | | 663 | 516 | 132 | 371 |
| | 1967 | 1,335 | 996 | 224 | 748 |
| Dec. 31, | 1967 | | | | |
| | 1968 | 1,826 | 1,192 | 353 | 784 |
| Dec. 31, | 1968 | | | | |
| | 1969 | 3,305 | 1,744 | 747 | 900 |
| Dec. 31, | 1969 | | | | |
| | 1970 | 3,886 | | | |

| Fiscal Year | Guilty Plea | Convicted | | Acquitted | | Average Sentence (Months) |
|---|---|---|---|---|---|---|
| | | Court | Jury | Court | Jury | |
| 1918 | | | | 400 | | |
| 1919 | | | | 265 | | |
| 1920 | | | | 52 | | |
| 1940 | | | | | | |
| 1941 | | | | | | 12.9 |
| 1942 | | | | | | 15.4 |
| 1943 | | | | | | 24.0 |
| 1944 | | | | | | 28.5 |
| 1945 | 1,823 | 319 | 696 | 25 | 25 | 31.9 |
| 1946 | 1,130 | 222 | 300 | 26 | 20 | 20.6 |
| 1947 | 898 | 178 | 61 | 18 | 11 | 14.3 |
| 1948 | 264 | 11 | 29 | 7 | 11 | 14.1 |
| 1949 | 263 | 20 | 9 | 3 | 9 | 14.6 |
| 1950 | 156 | 6 | 13 | 1 | 1 | 13.4 |
| 1951 | 105 | 24 | 27 | 6 | 4 | 29.6 |
| 1952 | 160 | 97 | 56 | 16 | 10 | 30.5 |
| 1953 | 185 | 129 | 31 | 39 | 10 | 29.3 |
| 1954 | 194 | 185 | 45 | 116 | 4 | 26.4 |
| 1955 | 157 | 106 | 26 | 57 | 6 | 24.8 |
| 1956 | 109 | 67 | 10 | 16 | 2 | 24.0 |
| 1957 | 183 | 70 | 9 | 17 | 3 | 23.7 |
| 1958 | 154 | 66 | 9 | 26 | 4 | 21.6 |
| 1959 | 159 | 39 | 4 | 11 | 1 | 23.2 |
| 1960 | 131 | 31 | 4 | 7 | 1 | 21.5 |
| 1961 | 160 | 33 | 6 | 8 | — | 22.6 |
| 1962 | 182 | 31 | 12 | 2 | 1 | 21.6 |
| 1963 | 212 | 46 | 7 | 7 | — | 21.5 |
| 1964 | 161 | 32 | 13 | 6 | 1 | 20.8 |
| 1965 | 197 | 28 | 17 | 8 | 3 | 21.0 |
| 1966 | 265 | 74 | 32 | 11 | 2 | 26.4 |
| 1967 | 538 | 141 | 69 | 22 | 2 | 32.1 |
| Dec. 31, 1967 | | | | | | |
| 1968 | 520 | 196 | 68 | 49 | 6 | 37.3 |
| Dec. 31, 1968 | | | | | | |
| 1969 | 511 | 252 | 137 | 88 | 9 | 36.3 |
| Dec. 31, 1969 | | | | | | |
| 1970 | | | | | | |

| Fiscal Year | Draft Prisoners Received from Courts | Total Draft Violators in Federal Prisons |
|---|---|---|
| 1918 | | |
| 1919 | | |
| 1920 | | |
| 1940 | | |
| 1941 | | |
| 1942 | 1,049 | |
| 1943 | 3,145 | 2,650 |
| 1944 | 3,930 | 4,679 |
| 1945 | 2,613 | 4,703 |
| 1946 | 1,446 | 2,797 |
| 1947 | 883 | 829 |
| 1948 | 236 | 328 |
| 1949 | 226 | 227 |
| 1950 | 136 | 102 |
| 1951 | 124 | 116 |
| 1952 | 281 | 237 |
| 1953 | 279 | 251 |
| 1954 | 342 | 300 |
| 1955 | 214 | 204 |
| 1956 | 136 | 137 |
| 1957 | 194 | 211 |
| 1958 | 197 | 175 |
| 1959 | 164 | 132 |
| 1960 | 135 | 112 |
| 1961 | 129 | 122 |
| 1962 | 153 | 143 |
| 1963 | 193 | 171 |
| 1964 | 145 | 148 |
| 1965 | 173 | 157 |
| 1966 | 266 | 256 |
| 1967 | 598 | 663 |
| Dec. 31, 1967 | | |
| 1968 | 521 | 739 |
| Dec. 31, 1968 | | 648 |
| 1969 | | 577 |
| Dec. 31, 1969 | | 537 |
| 1970 | | 499 |

The above figures show the extent of draft resistance during the Vietnam War in comparison to other wars and peacetime periods. In recent years, neither the Selective Service System nor the Justice Department have revealed exact figures on draft refusal. The Justice Department does issue prosecution statistics for draft offenses. The great majority are for refusing induction or, in the case of conscientious objectors, for refusing civilian work. (There have been only about thirty-five prosecutions for draft-card burnings and a small number for refusing to report for a physical or to keep the draft board informed of a registrant's address or status.)

However, prosecution figures are not identical to draft refusals. The Selective Service System recommended 27,444 prosecutions for failure to report for induction in fiscal year 1969* while only 3,305 cases were in fact initiated.[1] The reason for this discrepancy is that, in most cases, a draft board may have issued an induction order after a registrant was declared delinquent because his whereabouts were unknown. Once the F.B.I. located the young man, he often would agree to obey Selective Service orders. In other instances a man might initially refuse service but after an interview with the F.B.I. (which assigns individual agents to talk to every draft refuser before indictment) he would decide to go in.

On the other hand, not every registrant who refuses to report even after his F.B.I. interview is prosecuted. In many cases the local federal attorney will refuse to bring charges because he finds the draft board acted improperly in issuing the induction order, and he will send the case back for further action by Selective Service. Or because of the huge backlog of cases in certain areas or because some federal attorneys are themselves sympathetic to the resisters, no action at all is taken for indefinite periods. The best estimates in individual cities indicate that for every prosecution there is at least one other registrant who refused to go and was not prosecuted for doing so.

In any event, there is often a long lag between draft refusal and prosecution. Many men indicted in 1969 may have refused service in late 1967 or early 1968. Thus, prosecution figures in any given year may both overstate draft refusals (in that they reflect refusals from prior years) and understate them (in that they do not include many resisters who

---

* The resistance rate in 1970 was running considerably higher than in 1969. The Supreme Court's decision in the *Gutknecht* case protected any delinquent registrant from accelerated induction, and many draftees subject to the delinquency regulations were refusing to go in. The Oakland induction center reported that from October 1, 1969, to March 31, 1970, 2,380 men refused to report for induction out of 4,463 called, over 50 percent. However, these figures are atypical since many young men planning to refuse service transfer their induction to Oakland so they will be tried in the San Francisco area where the judges have the reputation of being more lenient. See the discussion at p. 186. In New York City, Selective Service was calling twice as many men as it needed to meet its quota. In April 1970, 753 men received notices and 326 did not show up. Nationwide, of 66,000 men called for induction in March and April 1970, 3,278 did not report on time. About 1,300 had no excuses and could not be found.

were not indicted). From July 1, 1965, when the draft calls began to increase significantly until December 31, 1969, there were approximately nine thousand prosecutions. It is safe to assume there were at least twice as many actual refusals. Using eighteen thousand as the basic refusal figure would mean a draft resistance rate of 1.3 percent (eighteen thousand resisters since July 1, 1965/1,355,880 inductions since July 1, 1965).

The totals may in fact be higher if analysis is based on the number of delinquents, i.e., those refusing to fulfill some duty required of them under the Selective Service regulations. Here also the number of delinquents each year is not public, but they roughly correspond to the delinquency investigations made annually by the F.B.I. During 1969, there were approximately thirty thousand such F.B.I. investigations and 113,305 since July 1, 1965. In World War I, all delinquents were immediately ordered for induction and considered deserters if they failed to report. If one treats the Vietnam War delinquents in the same way, the resistance figure would be 8.3 percent (113,305 delinquents/1,355,880 inductions), well above the World War I rate (see p. 108).

The number of conscientious objectors also increased as a result of the Vietnam War. The rate for World War II was 0.04 percent of the total registrants and through the 1950's and early 1960's, between 0.06 and 0.07 percent. In 1969, it had risen to 0.09 percent. The rate was therefore twice what it was in World War II, and the total number of C.O.'s in 1970 was almost twice the 1964 figure. There is no doubt that the increase was inspired by the Vietnam War. (Often a draft board would classify as a C.O. a Vietnam War protester who made a favorable impression on them).

In addition, thousands of young men with draft obligations have moved to Canada. Estimates of the resisters in Canada vary from 950 (the Justice Department official figure on fugitive warrants outstanding) to sixty thousand (the figure offered by the Toronto Anti-Draft Program). The best independent estimates put the total at twenty thousand of whom three thousand to five thousand may be army deserters.* Many of the Canadian immigrant resisters are carried by their draft boards as delinquents, leading to the great increase in that category. Adding the emigrants to the increased number of C.O.'s, delinquents, and draft-refusers, the percentage of those resisting or conscientiously objecting to the war may be over 10 percent, making the Vietnam War second only to the Civil War in unpopularity.

Of course, not every man refusing to serve could be considered a conscientious draft resister. There were hundreds of Jehovah's Witnesses who would not accept induction (claiming they were entitled to ministerial

* About eighty thousand servicemen were classified as deserters in 1969, that is, they were away from their posts more than thirty days without authorization. The desertion rate in 1969 was 29.1 per thousand troops, higher than the Korean War figure of 22.5, but lower than the World War II rate of 63 per thousand.

exemptions), as well as drifters or "draft dodgers" who tried for personal reasons to avoid unpleasant army duty. But an examination of newspaper accounts, Resistance literature, and court cases shows that the majority of those refusing service since July 1, 1965, are Resistance members, primarily middle-class college students who would not go because they object to the war in Vietnam.

At the beginning of the Vietnam War, it was extremely difficult to win a draft case in the courts. (Many indictments are dismissed before trial when a registrant decides he will go into the Army.) Through the early 1960's only 4.7 of those tried were acquitted. However, the rate went up to 6 percent in 1967, 6.5 percent in 1968 and 9.7 percent in 1969. On the appellate level, the rate has been higher. From July 1, 1965 to October 1, 1970, the Supreme Court found for the defendant or registrant in eight of the nine draft cases that were fully argued before it (*Oestereich, McKart, Gutknecht, Breen, Toussie, Walsh, Mulloy,* and *Sisson*) and upheld the government only in the draft-card burning case (*O'Brien*).[2] At the Court of Appeals level, more draft cases are reversed than virtually any other type of criminal action. And on the basis of these appellate decisions, many defendants have similar cases dismissed by the district court even before trial.

One reason for the growing success in draft cases was the formation of an extremely sophisticated bar of draft law attorneys in the major cities where the largest number of cases are heard. Panels of lawyers were formed in San Francisco, Los Angeles, New York, Chicago, Boston, Philadelphia, Seattle, and Denver; they instituted workshops, held lectures, and kept each other informed of the latest developments in the law. The lawyers learned to scrutinize every Selective Service regulation and every draft board action to see whether some error or inconsistency could be shown to the courts. One of the leading lawyers in the field remarked, "If we applied all this energy and ingenuity to the tax laws, we could revamp the whole revenue policy of the government."

Another reason for the increase in acquittals was a growing lack of sympathy on the part of many federal judges with questionable Selective Service procedures. The rules forbidding registrants to appear with a lawyer before a draft board or giving draft boards broad discretionary powers in determining delinquency or conscientious objectors have been criticized by many courts. While the judges from the South and Midwest continue to reflect their areas' support of Selective Service, the judiciary in the larger cities have been casting a careful eye on the draft cases coming before it. The acquittal rate in New York City was 14 percent in 1968 and in the San Francisco area it approached 20 percent during 1969. In the New England area, of ten cases going to trial in 1968 there were five acquittals and five convictions. And the Court of Appeals in those areas have likewise been reversing a high percentage of cases.

The sentences given by the judges also vary according to geographic areas. In the Sixth Circuit area (Kentucky, Michigan, Ohio, and

Tennessee), 36 percent of the draft resisters found guilty were given maximum five-year sentences during 1968. (In southern Texas, fourteen of sixteen resisters also received the maximum and in Eastern Missouri, seven out of seven.) In the New England area, not a single five-year term was handed out in the five years since 1965. In the Fifth Circuit during 1968, only 9.5 percent of the defendants were given probation, while in the Third Circuit 44.5 percent of defendants were given suspended sentences. Some judges automatically gave five-year sentences to every resister that came before them, regardless of their backgrounds or reasons for refusing service. (Some did so on the erroneous idea that all resisters would be paroled after serving one-third of their sentences. See Note, "Sentencing Selective Service Violators: A Judicial Wheel of Fortune," 5 *Columbia Journal of Law and Social Problems* 164, 175 [August 1969].)

For a long time the federal judges in San Francisco were credited with being the most lenient in the country, and hundreds of resisters transferred their induction to the Oakland Army Base so that they would be tried in the Bay Area courts. (In 1968, there were twenty-nine probation sentences out of forty-six convictions. No one received a five-year term and only one man was given three years or more.) However, the sentence rate increased in 1969 as the Bay Area judges responded to the flood of cases coming before them.

The attitude of many federal judges to the draft resisters is a combination of outraged patriotism and legal righteousness. Draft resisters are twice cursed—once for shirking their patriotic duty to defend their country and again for doing it so deliberately and willfully. One judge explained, "Of course they don't threaten society in the same sense as do—for example—professional bank robbers. They probably threaten it more in the long run, by making law violation fashionable and suggesting that every man is free to obey or disobey the law, as it pleases him."[3] On the other side have been the large number of judges giving suspended or short-term sentences described above. One federal judge in Puerto Rico thought that draft resistance was so inconsequential an offense for individuals in his jurisdiction that he sentenced one young man to one hour in custody as his punishment.[4]

With the large number of draft prosecutions and the long sentences handed out, one might think that the jails would now be overcrowded with draft resisters. On the contrary, the number of draft offenders in jail has been steadily decreasing since the high point in the spring of 1968 (739 draft offenders in jail on June 20, 1968 and 537 on December 20, 1969).[5]

Part of the reason for the decline lies in the ability of draft lawyers to win cases on appeal, or at the least to delay proceedings for months or years. Again the sympathy of some federal attorneys aids in the delay in pressing cases to a conclusion.

In addition, the special position of Jehovah's Witnesses contributes to the decrease. Since World War II, there has been a steady percentage of Witnesses who refuse service and then go to jail. While they would be readily entitled to C.O. status, many refuse to apply for it on the ground that the request itself constitutes unacceptable cooperation with secular authority, forbidden by their religion. A federal judge in Oregon, Gus Solomon, discovered that if he suspended the sentence of a JW on the condition that he perform civilian work in a hospital or similar institution (the same duty required from a C.O.) he would agree to do so. As a result, many federal judges began ordering Witnesses to undertake equivalent civilian work instead of sending them to jail. In addition, JW's have been released on parole much more often than political draft resisters. In 1968, for example, 224 of the 321 JW's up for parole were released (70 percent) but only 71 of 235 other resisters were paroled (30 percent). Thus the number of Witnesses in federal prison declined from 574 on June 20, 1968, to 335 on October 30, 1969.

On the other hand, the number of political draft resisters has steadily increased. In 1965, only 71 non-JW's were committed. In 1968, the number increased to 303. There were 103 non-religious prisoners incarcerated on June 20, 1968, and 182 on October 30, 1969. The political resisters with long sentences are seldom parolled until they have served two years—the government's crude way of equalizing army service and prison time. Dr. Willard Gaylin has recently described the plight of *War Resisters in Prison* and shows how the most idealistic men of their generation survive the most degrading experience their country can offer them.

# Appendix B

## The Sentencing of David Harris

*David Harris, one of the founders of The Resistance, was tried for draft refusal in June 1968 in San Francisco. The jury found him guilty (after deliberating eight hours) and the federal judge, Oliver Carter, immediately passed sentence. The transcript of proceedings follows. (Harris' lawyer was Francis Heisler of Carmel, California, a well-known civil liberties attorney.)*

(The following proceedings were had in open court out of the presence of the jury.)

THE COURT: Now, Mr. Harris and Mr. Heisler, or Mr. Heisler and Mr. Harris, as the case may be, I don't know what you want to do about judgment and sentence. I am ready to proceed now if Mr. Harris is ready to proceed now, or I will proceed at some later day if he desires to proceed at some later day.

MR. HEISLER: If Your Honor please, I would like to submit to the Court a motion for a new trial.

THE COURT: Certainly, you have a right to make it and I would be glad to hear it; even after judgment, you have a right to make it then.

MR. HEISLER: I understand, Your Honor. I would like to consult with Mr. Harris and want to find out from him what his desires are in the matter, what Your Honor suggested, whether he wants to stand up now to hear sentence or whether he wants to ask the Court for a postponement.

THE COURT: The rule simply says it shall be done as quickly as possible.

MR. HEISLER: Exactly, but it doesn't mean at 9:15.

THE COURT: I agree with that and I am giving him his choice. I am not suggesting that he must do anything.

(*Defendant and his counsel conferring.*)

MR. HEISLER: Mr. Harris is ready to face the Court and, Your Honor, I almost used the words "Your Honor's pleasure," but I can't be sure it would be proper for me to use that word—for judgment.

THE COURT: I have anticipated that that probably would be his decision and I am ready to proceed if that is what he wants.

Mr. Harris, you have been found guilty of the offense with which you were charged, you're aware of the penalty that can be involved here. It calls for a maximum imprisonment of five years in prison, $10,000 fine, or both.

(*Whereupon most of audience arose.*)

THE COURT: Is this an act of some form of dissent in the courtroom?

THE DEFENDANT: No, I think it is simply an act of people who feel very much involved in the same thing I am involved in and wish to share—

THE COURT: Let them behave like other people do and be seated and welcome here to be part of the public trial and not to make it a type of proceeding in which they are converting it from a court proceeding into some sort of a rally. I recognize that they are proceeding from good motives, and they are not guilty of any offense, but I think we should proceed with dignity and do the best we can under the circumstances.

I have no relish for this, but I must do what I must do and I intend to do it to the best of my ability.

I have simply advised you as to what the penalty is and I'm sure you're aware of the maximum. You have the right to say to me what you desire because what you say may be of some importance.

I have a few observations that I would like to express to you before you speak to me because I think that for the dialog to mean anything there should be some communication.

A present sentence in this kind of a situation insofar as being a reformatory type of sentence and having any rehabilitative purpose is of no value whatsoever as far as you are concerned because you don't have to be rehabilitated and you don't want to be rehabilitated and you won't be rehabilitated, and I don't know that there is any reason that you should be rehabilitated in the sense of the fact that you lead a dissolute type of life as in other types of law violators. So the sole purpose of the penalty here is punitive, if I can characterize it. It is punitive in two senses, as I see it; punitive to you to say that you shall not do this without suffering a penalty, and secondly, to be a warning to others that they will be punished if they do the same. It is punitive in those senses and it has to be stark and real in those words and just as hard and tough as you are.

Now, what do you have to say? You understand the purpose of judgment in this case?

THE DEFENDANT: I understand. Well, I'd say what I said before in my testimony which I think ultimately that thing that judges myself and ultimately judges you, also ultimately judges all those people that have been engaged in judgment upon me in this Court. All those people around the world today who, although I have to serve a prison term, have to serve a much greater sentence than that.

What I can say is if my act has made their suffering any less then there in fact is no penalty involved.

What I can say further than that, is that the only way what we call civilization will ever cease to punish those people for the simple act of being human beings is when the rest of civilization decides that they, too, must be human beings, and the decision to be that human being is really a decision beyond the law, a decision beyond all the instruments of the law. It is a decision which, it seems to me, ultimately to lie in the hearts of myself and everyone else in this courtroom. What I think the judgment here today gives witness to, if nothing else, is the fact that I have made that decision and I can't help but express the hope that people all around the country will join me in that decision. And I think what is involved is not a negation and is not simply a statement of displeasure or disapproval. What's involved, I think, is perhaps the largest affirmation any of us could make with his life and that is the affirmation of all that life surrounds us. Even at this point I stand convinced that without us making that statement that it will never happen and there can be no us making that statement unless I make that statement.

What I had hoped would come out of this trial would be to the people in this courtroom would be forced to face that same decision that I had to face and I will continue to have to face and that all of us will have to face. And I hope through the process of this trial they begin to understand what it is that I faced and what it is the people around the. world face and I think that is the sole allegiance that I owe and that any man owes is to the face of those men. And I think ultimately those people around the world find me innocent and that is the only judgment that I can recognize.

THE COURT: Mr. Harris, only you can make that decision, no one can make it for you. I can't make it for you, no power on earth can make it, only you can make it.

THE DEFENDANT: I have made it.

THE COURT: You have made it and let it be said that you made it, no one else. You have made it from the very beginning and you were going to be here or in some other court in this kind of a situation, if I may use a term, come hell or high water.

THE DEFENDANT: Here's hoping high water comes first.

THE COURT: But I don't have any animosity in my heart nor do I have any feeling that there should be any unusual punishment, but I do think the purpose of the law has to be carried out. In this District we have had not unusually heavy criminal penal sentences for violations of the Selective Service laws. We have had penal sentences and it is quite difficult to say within the degree of discretion that the Court has what is a right sentence or what is a wrong sentence, because anything that you say can be just as wrong as it is right. I wish I could speak with assurance and conviction in this area.

May I say experience teaches me that without order in society there will be no society. You may have another kind of society, but I'm sure it will flounder in its own mess. Maybe the other one will too, but you show me a better one.

THE DEFENDANT: I tried.

THE COURT: You have the right to try, you go ahead.

THE DEFENDANT: I may be back here again.

THE COURT: You better show me, that's all I will say. But it has to have some form of order. What I want to see is your form of order, that's what I want to see, and I haven't seen it yet, and I want to see what develops.

THE DEFENDANT: You don't get much chance being in Court so often.

THE COURT: I realize that. Your people will have the chance. But I want to see the people that are now under 30 when they get over 30 the people who are then 30 say don't trust a person over 30, what the present people under 30 will be saying. This goes on, you know, and has gone on since time immemorial and this matter of who is going to be hostile to who—time will take care of you people. It's that certain. You won't always be in this arrogant position of being young.

THE DEFENDANT: I readily admit that.

THE COURT: All right. So having said that, now comes the matter of the problem that is before me.

I think that I must impose a prison sentence. The best I can arrive at under the circumstances, and before I do this, however, I should give your counsel a chance to say what should be said on your behalf. Now, Mr. Heisler, you have had many years of experience here. You may be able to contribute something. I hope you can.

MR. HEISLER: I tried my best, Your Honor.

THE COURT: I know you did.

MR. HEISLER: And I think that my best was overcome by Your Honor's course of instructions to the jury, if I may put it that way, but I would like to say that I appreciate whatever Your Honor is facing because I know it is not an easy thing. I would like to say to the Court, and I hope that not because of arrogance on my part, but I wouldn't want to change my place with Your Honor and that is not in any kind of depredation of the position Your Honor is in on the bench.

I would like to say, Your Honor, before you go any further, that the Court said and I'm sure that it wouldn't have been said except for the fact that the Court was convinced that David Harris was acting with good motives.

THE COURT: I'm sure he was. I think he believes in what he is doing and I think that stems from what he believes to be high motives and as far as I can see he hasn't been guilty of any chicanery or phoniness in this proposition and I respect him for it and I have said that to him and I say so publicly.

MR. HEISLER: And Your Honor knows that he refused to hide behind a technicality and I am convinced beyond any shadow of a doubt that the Court would have followed the other Courts as they have looked upon these things and I know that there is an error in the whole case when the draft board failed to grant him the right to appeal and every Court has decided that that is deprivation of due process.

THE COURT: He is entitled to the due process, but he waived that.

MR. HEISLER: Sure, he did, but I just wanted Your Honor to know—

THE COURT: I don't know that it was a good point, and Mr. Langford is sitting over there kind of shaking his head and I'm sure he believes it is not a good point, but I am not going to get into that argument.

MR. HEISLER: I don't want to, either.

THE COURT: And Mr. Harris doesn't want to raise it.

MR. HEISLER: I just wanted to point out he was not engaged in any kind of hiding behind technicalities.

THE COURT: I am aware of that.

MR. HEISLER: Now, Your Honor also said that we have a society and Mr. Harris is challenged to show a better one and I'm submitting, Your

Honor, that probably we ought to permit these young people to try, whether they can make a better society, because I know and my son who is in the courtroom agrees with me, because I referred to my generation as a generation of failures because we failed these young people, Your Honor. I did, I know. Because we just never were able to give up that which was offered to us by a comfortable living in whatever profession we may have been in later and we were giving too little attention, sometimes no attention whatsoever to the social problems and we permitted—we, and I don't want to be personal, but I saw a few days ago a statement made by our Secretary of Defense, Your Honor, Mr. Clark M. Clifford, who said: "The obligations imposed on us by the NATO alliance are far more important than the kind of government they have in Greece or what we think of it. If our military aid to our allies was determined by the kind of government they maintained at the moment then NATO would disintegrate into nothingness."

This kind of immorality expressed by our Secretary of State—

THE COURT: Defense.

MR. HEISLER: I beg your pardon?

THE COURT: Secretary of Defense.

MR. HEISLER: Of Defense. Oh, I am sorry, Your Honor. It makes little difference.

THE COURT: It makes no difference.

MR. HEISLER: Not for me. I saw the same kind of immorality—as a matter of fact, the Secretary of State said that while our citizens must be moral, the State does not have to be, the State cannot be and if that is true, and I don't believe it is true and these young people don't believe it is true, then the State has no right to exist if it has to deny morality. And probably I am trying to flatter these young people so that they should not be too hard on me because I was a failure, that I failed them. I agree with them that if the State must take the position from China down to Albania because of their right to exist requires to be immoral, unethical, then probably the State ought to be excused for it and I just hope for the sake of this country that this is not going to be the accepted precept.

Some days ago, Your Honor, I was leafing through the book of Gibbons on the *Decline and Fall of the Roman Empire*. I did not read it through because I didn't have the time, I had to defend too many young people in the Courts, but I was frightened when I saw the parallel when that mighty empire abandoned any claim for morality or to morality, when the State believed it can exist without the requirement what Dave Harris was talking about, the concern for our fellow man, then there was a beginning of the decline and fall. And I was frightened by seeing some of the parallel which exists in our country.

I would like to say, as I told it so many times to my friends and enemies among the psychiatrists when they were trying to retrain people and I asked them you are retraining them for what, to go back into a sick society? And this is not my word, it was said by a wiser man than

I am. The sick society needs these young people and because of that I believe, Your Honor, that any kind of a prison sentence given to David Harris would be not punitive but it would be vindictive and I'm sure that Your Honor would like to be free of any possibility of the charge, if I may put it that way, that the Court was vindictive.

THE COURT: Except I am not vindictive.

MR. HEISLER: I understand, Your Honor, that is the reason I am saying it, that in this case—

THE COURT: I may be, but I try not to be.

MR. HEISLER: No, I did not for a moment—

THE COURT: I know you are not suggesting that I am vindictive. You made the distinction.

MR. HEISLER: I want to make it very, very earnest in this distinction, but I also say, Your Honor, that as Dr. Sanford said this morning, these young people feel what we don't feel, that they don't have time, that if they are going to be able to accomplish anything to save us, save our society that they must be given all their time, and to take the time, Your Honor, in the form of locking this young man up is going to take away just a small possibility of the chance that there is a redemption for us, and we need redemption very badly.

Therefore, I suggest to Your Honor that Dave Harris, I'm sure, accepted the finding of the jury with grace, or without it, and he knows that he's found guilty of a felony. He knows that he is going to be deprived of certain rights. He may not be able to run for President of the United States for the next few years. I don't know whether—yes, he is already of age, so that he can vote, but that would be taken away from him, too, if he wants to vote in any other state than California.

However, I very earnestly suggest to the Court that it would be worth considering that since redemption is not going to be in place with Dave Harris, vindictiveness is again not in place and probably the Court is going to find that justice is served particularly because the case was on a knife's edge, Your Honor. That jury, as I said before they retired, could have come back with a not guilty and Dave Harris would not have been any different if the finding had been otherwise, and now that he is found guilty he is still no different from what he was ten minutes, fifteen minutes ago. He is not going to change and he is going to keep on trying to bring about the kind of society that he is dreaming of. Dreams are very necessary, Your Honor. We older people, we forget how to dream and without dreams mankind is lost.

THE COURT: Thank you, Mr. Heisler.

Mr. Harris, do you have anything further to say? I recognize that this is never an easy nor a nice task and I never appreciate or enjoy the task of sending anyone to prison. It is a most distasteful thing. But it is one of the necessary parts of doing this kind of work. In some cases you do have the justification of saying that person ought to be in prison, but in your case I am not saying that there is any remedial purpose to be accomplished in that respect.

The purpose of the law, when you get down to it, is punitive in the respect I have indicated and I have always hesitated against the punitive and entirely punitive sentences because I have great reservations as to their value. I think very little of the deterring effect of prison sentences personally. Others disagree with me. I recognize that there is a difference of opinion and I have had men tell me that they were deterred from doing certain things because there was a law against it. In other words, I have had men say I would have committed murder but for the death penalty, and mean it. And I am opposed to the death penalty. I have had numerous kinds of examples of the meaning of deterrents, yet I have great difficulty in accepting the notion of straight deterrents and the personal punitive nature of this penalty is of dubious value, if any. But it has the requirement that you pretty much have to cut the cloth to suit the situation. You preached the penalty yourself. You have expected and anticipated if you were found guilty that you would be sent to prison and I am not about to impale you on some of the statements you have made, but I simply say that because I take it that you have given consideration to this and this is what you have expected.

Now, I am trying to arrive at what is a most reasonable time I can come to grips with in view of the degree of the violation. In other words, insofar as being a wilful violator you are one of the most wilful violators I have ever known in my life and I think you say hurray to that.

THE DEFENDANT: Thank you.

THE COURT: I think you agree with that. In that sense you are a deliberate, obstinate, recalcitrant violator of the law and I have no other alternative but to follow this remedy. Mr. Heisler has tried to suggest another, but I don't think that is sufficient, so if there is nothing further to be said I will get to what I have to do.

THE DEFENDANT: I would like to make one short comment.

THE COURT: You may, sir.

THE DEFENDANT: Which is I think what the court ought to understand, really, that I come here representing something more than myself and I think it is only fair from your preceding comment for me to say that what I represent obviously cannot be stopped by prisons and that the organization of human love and of real brotherhood will never be put behind bars and that work will always continue.

THE COURT: Mr. Harris, while you may speak for others I wish you would speak for yourself. Will you be sure and do that?

THE DEFENDANT: I will be sure and do that.

THE COURT: I just want to be sure you are speaking for Mr. Harris.

THE DEFENDANT: I am speaking for Mr. Harris.

THE COURT: All right. And if there is nothing further to be said I will pronounce judgment and sentence. If there is nothing further to be said it will the judgment and sentence of the Court that you be imprisoned in an institution to be designated by the Attorney General for a period of three years.

# Notes

### INTRODUCTION

1. "Racial Discrimination and the Federal Law," in *Southern Justice*, ed. Leon Friedman (New York, 1965), p. 257.
2. *Public Papers of the Presidents, John F. Kennedy*, 1962, pp. 726–27.
3. (New York, 1955), pp. 5–6.
4. *Democracy and the Student Left* (Boston, 1968), p. 15.
5. For a history of the Dorr War in Rhode Island in the 1840's which led to a new suffrage program, see Arthur Mowry, *The Dorr War* (New York, 1970).

### CHAPTER 1

1. Robert Green McCloskey, ed., *The Works of James Wilson* (Cambridge, 1967), vol. I, p. 132.
2. Ibid., p. 184.
3. Ibid., pp. 242–243.
4. Ibid., p. 246.
5. Ibid., p. 186.
6. Quoted in Bernard Bailyn, *The Ideological Origins of the American Revolution* (Cambridge, 1967), p. 305.
7. Ibid., p. 306.
8. The problem of conscience continued to play a key role in colonial political thought. To the colonial statesmen, no society deserved a man's allegiance if his right to freedom of conscience was not respected. Since man enjoyed this freedom in the state of nature, he kept it upon entering society. William Livingston, one of the great political pamphleteers of the colonies, wrote: "Did men in their aboriginal condition ever suffer persecution for conscience sake? The most frantic enthusiast will not pretend it. Why then should members of society be supposed, on their entering into it, to have had in contemplation the reforming an abuse which never existed?" Quoted in Clinton Rossiter, *The Political Thought of the American Revolution* (New York, 1963), p. 114.
9. Cicero, *De Legibus* (Muller ed.), vol. 1, p. 23, quoted in Edward

S. Corwin, *The Higher Law Background of American Constitutional Law* (Ithaca, 1955), p. 10.

10. James Otis, *Rights of the British Colonies Asserted and Proved* (1764), p. 70.

11. John Adams, *Life and Works,* vol. VI, p. 62.

12. Max Farrand, *Records of the Federal Convention* (New Haven, 1911), vol. I, p. 431.

13. In the Virginia ratifying convention of June 1788, Madison declared: "On a candid examination of history, we shall find that turbulence, violence and abuse of power, by the majority trampling on the rights of the minority, have produced factions and commotions which, in republics, have more frequently than any other cause, produced despotism." Quoted in Madison, *The Forging of American Federalism,* ed. Saul K. Padover (New York, 1965), p. 47.

14. *The Papers of Thomas Jefferson,* ed. Julian P. Boyd et al. (Princeton, 1955), vol. XII, p. 278.

15. See Peter Brock, *Pacifism in the United States* (Princeton, 1968), p. 200.

16. Ibid., p. 278 ff.

17. *1 Annals of Congress,* 1st Cong., 1st Sess., 750.

18. *2 Annals of Congress,* 1st Cong., 2d Sess., 1818.

19. Edmond Dumbauld, *The Bill of Rights and What It Means Today* (New York, 1957), p. 46. See also Leon Friedman, "Conscription and the Constitution: The Original Understanding," 67 *Michigan Law Review* 1493, 1536 (1969).

20. Benson argued: "If this stands part of the Constitution, it will be a question before the Judiciary on every regulation you make with respect to the organization of the militia. . . . I have no reason to believe but the [state] Legislature will always possess humanity enough to indulge this class of citizens in a matter they are so desirous of; but they ought to be left to their discretion." Annals of Congress, 1st Cong., 1st Sess., 751.

21. *2 Annals of Congress,* 1st Cong., 2d Sess., 1818.

22. Ibid.

23. Ibid., 1824.

24. Ibid., 1827.

25. See W. W. Crosskey, *Politics and the Constitution* (Chicago, 1953), vol. II, p. 971.

26. 3 Dallas 386, 388 (1798).

27. Corwin, op. cit., p. 89.


CHAPTER 2


1. *Writings of Albert Gallatin* (New York, 1960), pp. 3–6.

2. See John C. Miller, *The Federalist Era* (New York, 1960), p. 161; *Writings of George Washington* (Sparks ed. 1894), vol. XII, p. 454.

3. Jacob E. Cooke in a recent article, "The Whiskey Insurrection: A Re-evaluation," 30 *Penna. History* 316 (1963), claims the subpoenas were issued by District Judge Richard Peters on May 13, 1794, and Hamilton had no role in the fiasco that followed. But it is difficult to see why no effort was made to serve the subpoenas until July if someone in the government did not see a reason for delay, namely, to provoke the farmers after they thought relief was on its way. Hamilton wrote to a friend later in the year: "The insurrection will do us a great deal of good and add to the solidity of everything in the country." Ibid., p. 338.

4. Ibid., p. 338, Leland D. Baldwin, *Whiskey Rebels* (Pittsburgh, 1968), p. 110 ff.

5. Ibid., p. 141.

6. *American State Papers, Miscellaneous* (1794), vol. 1, pp. 87–88.

7. *Writings of Albert Gallatin*, pp .7–8.

8. *United States* v. *Insurgents*, 26 Fed. Cases 499 (C.C. Pa., 1795); *United States* v. *Mitchell*, 26 Fed. Cases 1277 (C.C. Pa., 1795); *United States* v. *Vigol*, 28 Fed. Cases 376 (C.C. Pa., 1795).

9. Washington called the societies "self-created bodies, forming themselves into permanent censors, and under the shade of night in a conclave resolving that acts of Congress, which have undergone the most deliberate and solemn discussion by the representatives of the people [are unconstitutional] . . . endeavoring . . . to form their will into laws for the government of the whole." *Writings of George Washington* (Sparks ed., 1894), vol. X, p. 437.

10. *Annals of Congress,* 3rd Cong., p. 915. See Charles A. Beard, *Economic Origins of Jeffersonian Democracy* (New York, 1915), pp. 262–63.

11. *Writings of James Madison* (G. Hunt ed., 1906), vol. VI, p. 221.

12. *Writings of Thomas Jefferson* (Lipscomb ed., 1904), vol. IX, pp. 294–95.

13. "The Consent of the Governed," 44 *Virginia Quarterly Review* 513, 515–16 (Autumn 1968).

14. *United States* v. *Worrall,* 2 Dallas 384 (1798).

15. See James Morton Smith, *Freedom's Fetters* (*Ithaca,* 1956), p. 226.

16. An earlier Massachusetts case involved Thomas Adams, editor of the *Boston Independent Chronicle.* Not only did Adams (no kin to the President) attack the Alien and Sedition Laws, but he added up all the money the Adams family—including the President's son, John Quincy Adams—had taken from the public treasury over a five-year period. Abigail Adams, wife of the President, considered him worse than Bache: "I think impudent as Bache is, the *Chronicle* has more of the true spirit of Satan, for he not only collects the Billingsgate of all the Jacobin papers, but he add[s] to it the Lies, falsehoods . . . and bitterness of his own." A federal grand jury in Boston indicted Adams in October, 1798, for violation of the Sedition Law, but he too died before the charges could be heard. See Smith, op. cit., p. 247 ff.

17. Ibid., p. 262.

18. In 1817 Jefferson was to write to Baron von Humboldt: "The first principle of republicanism is, the *lex majoris partis* [the law of the majority] is the fundamental law of every society of individuals of equal rights; to consider the will of the society enounced by the majority of a single vote as sacred as if unanimous, is the first of all lessons in importance, yet the last which is thoroughly learned. This law once disregarded, no other remains but that of force, which ends necessarily in military despotism." *Writings of Thomas Jefferson* (Lipsomb ed., 1904), vol. XVI, p. 127.

19. See Adrienne Koch, *Jefferson and Madison* (New York, 1964), p. 189.

20. *The Papers of Thomas Jefferson* (Princeton ed.), vol. XII, p. 356; vol. XI, p. 93; *Writings of Thomas Jefferson* (Lipscomb ed, 1904), vol. XII, p. 183.

21. Kentucky Resolution of 1798, J. Elliot; *Debates* (1835), 540.

22. Ibid., p. 528.

23. Ibid., p. 533.

24. As early as June 7, 1798, when the laws were first under debate in Congress, Jefferson wrote to Madison: "They have brought into the lower house a sedition bill, which among other enormities, undertakes to make printing certain matters criminal, tho' one of the amendments to the Constitution has so expressly taken religion, printing presses, etc. out of their coercion. Indeed this bill and the alien bill both are so palpably in the teeth of the Constitution as to show they mean to pay no respect to it." *Writings of Thomas Jefferson* (Ford ed., 1892) vol. VII, p. 266.

25. J. Elliot; *Debates*, pp. 546, 575.

26. Ibid., p. 576.

27. "Against Nullification," in *The American Enlightenment,* ed. Adrienne Koch (New York, 1965) pp. 532–33.


CHAPTER 3


1. *The Writings and Speeches of Daniel Webster* (National ed., 1903) vol. IV, p. 275–76.

2. See Gilbert H. Barnes, *The Anti-Slavery Impulse* (New York, 1933); Dwight Lowell Dumond, *Antislavery* (New York, 1961); Louis Filler, *The Crusade Against Slavery* (New York, 1960).

3. Postmaster General Amos Kendall, a member of President Andrew Jackson's "kitchen cabinet" and a slaveowner himself, supported Southern postmasters who refused to deliver Abolitionist literature. "We owe an obligation to the laws," he said in a public statement, "but we owe a higher one to the communities in which we live, and if the former be perverted to destroy the latter, it is patriotism to disregard them." President Jackson himself called the attention of Congress to the "painful excitement produced in the South by attempts to circulate through the mails inflammatory appeals addressed to the passions of the slaves, in

prints and various sorts of publications, calculated to stimulate them to insurrection and to produce all the horrors of a servile war." The solution, said Jackson, lay in a law which would "prohibit, under severe penalties, the circulation in the Southern States, through the mail, of incendiary publications intended to instigate the slaves to insurrection." Congress did nothing, however, to pass such a law. Dumond, op. cit., p. 206 ff.

4. Even so, the gag-rule was hardly ever effective. The few Abolitionist congressmen, through a series of ingenious parliamentary devices, managed to bring the problem of slavery before the floor numerous times. Joshua R. Giddings, elected in 1838, introduced petitions on the annexation of Texas, protection of the Abolitionists in the Deep South, and changes in the citizenship and naturalization laws to benefit the Negro. It was impossible to discuss such matters without focusing on the slavery question. When Adams attempted to present a memorial directly from a group of slaves, Southerners insisted that even free Negroes could not petition Congress. At another time Adams introduced a resolution from some New York Lutheran ministers asking that Congress implement the Declaration of Independence in the District of Columbia: " 'This says nothing of slaves,' said Mr. Adams . . . 'It does not come within the rule.' 'But it does, though,' said Mr. Speaker Polk. [The Speaker then asked the House] whether such a memorial comes within the rule. 'But what is the memorial?' asked Mr. A. 'You have not read it. The House has not seen it. . . . He compelled the Speaker to read the petition so that the House might know on what they were to vote. And there he sat, half-rabid and half laughing . . . He had had his way even with the opposition of two hundred to one." Barnes, op. cit., p. 123.

5. See "Speech of William Gaston," *United States Catholic Historical Society* (1926), vol. XVII, pp. 189–244. Russel B. Nye, *Fettered Freedom* (Lansing, 1963), p. 155 ff.

6. *Prigg* v. *Pennsylvania*, 16 Pet. 539 (1842). Justice Joseph Story, who was sympathetic to the anti-slavery cause, claimed that his opinion was a "triumph of freedom" because it pointed the way to complete state abdication from fugitive hunting. The year before, he had written the Court's opinion in the *Amistad* case, (1841) 15 Pet. 518, holding that slaves who were brought to this country illegally from Africa and subsequently killed or captured their abductors were free. Under international law, they were regarded as kidnapped persons who had regained their freedom. John Quincy Adams, then seventy-four years old, argued the case for the blacks.

7. 2 *McLean's Reports* 611 (C.C.D. Ohio, 1843).

8. 5 How. 215 (1847); In *Moore* v. *Illinois*, 14 How. 13 (1852) the Supreme Court upheld an Illinois Law making it a crime to harbor a fugitive. McLean dissented from that decision, but he and every other Supreme Court Justice upheld the federal Fugitive Slave Laws whenever the question of their validity was brought before them.

9. James G. Birney had run as the presidential candidate of the

Liberty Party in 1840 and gathered only a few thousand votes. In 1844 he was a candidate once again and took away enough votes from Henry Clay in New York to throw the election to James K. Polk. The annexation of Texas in 1845, the Mexican War from 1846 to 1848, and the accession of a wide swath of territory from the Rio Grande to California raised the possibility of more slave states being admitted to the Union and stirred antislavery impulses in much of the nation. In 1848, Martin Van Buren, once a notorious Southern sympathizer, ran for President as a candidate of the Free Soil party, dedicated to keeping the new territories free from slavery; he won 10 percent of the vote. A new group of antislavery congressmen came to Washington—Salmon P. Chase, John Hale, Charles Sumner, and William Seward to the Senate, and Thaddeus Stevens, George Julian, and Owen Lovejoy to the House.

10. See Nye, op. cit., p. 277.

11. *Congressional Globe*, 31st Cong., 2d Sess., pp. 15–16.

12. *The Duty of Disobedience to Wicked Laws* (Cincinnati, 1851) p. 12.

13. Henry Steele Commager, *Theodore Parker* (Boston, 1960), pp. 208–09.

14. Ibid., pp. 211–12.

15. See W. Freeman Galpin, "The Jerry Rescue," 26 *New York History* 19 (1945); Earl E. Sperry, *The Jerry Rescue* (Syracuse, 1924).

16. *Charge to Grand Jury,* 30 Fed. Cases 1013 (C.C.N.D. N.Y. 1851).

17. *United States* v. *Cobb*, 25 Fed. Cases 481, 482 (C.C.N.D. N.Y. 1851)

18. Frederick Wilkins (who had taken the name "Shadrach") escaped from Virginia and was working as a waiter in a Boston coffee house. Two federal marshals entered the restaurant, ordered a meal from Shadrach, and after eating, seized him as a fugitive. He was held at the Boston Court House, since Massachusetts did not allow the use of its jails for escaped slaves.

19. *The Journal of Richard Henry Dana* (Cambridge, 1968), vol. II, p. 412.

20. *United States* v. *Morris,* 26 Fed. Cases 1323, 1336 (C.C.D. Mass. 1852).

21. *Journals*, vol. II, p. 424.

22. Commager, op. cit., p. 221.

23. Ibid., p. 234.

24. T. W. Higginson, "Cheerful Yesterdays," *Atlantic Monthly* (March 1897), pp. 350–52.

25. *Journals*, vol. II, pp. 629–30.

26. Commager, op. cit., p. 244.

27. Ibid.

28. Ibid., pp. 245–46.

29. *Journals*, vol. II, pp. 628, 638.

30. Hans L. Trefousse, *The Radical Republicans* (New York, 1969), p. 80.

31. Filler, op. cit., p. 274.

32. *Reminiscences of Levi Coffin* (Cincinnati, 1876), p. 550.

33. William C. Cochran, *The Western Reserve and the Fugitive Slave Law* (Cleveland, 1920), p. 152.

34. In Painesville, Ohio, the following proposal was adopted:

The Fugitive Slave Law is not only clearly unconstitutional, but is also so repugnant to every principle of Justice and Humanity that no Constitution or Compact can make it binding; and so derogatory to the moral sense and self respect of a free and honorable people, that it deserves no argument, but only execration and contempt.

Ibid. p. 175.

35. Ibid., p. 178.

36. Allan Nevins, *The Emergence of Lincoln* (New York, 1950) vol. I, p. 31.

37. *Oliver* v. *Kauffman, Weakley and Breckbill,* 18 Fed. Cases 657 (C.C.E.D. Pa. 1853).

38. William Parker, "The Freedman's Story," Atlantic Monthly (March 1866). See also *United States* v. *Hanway,* 26 Fed. Cases 105 (C.C.E.D. Pa. 1851).

39. *Ex Parte Jenkins,* 15 Fed. Cases 445 (C.C.E.D. Pa. 1853). See also *Van Metre* v. *Mitchell,* 28 Fed. Cases 1036 (C.C.W.D. Pa. 1853).

40. See Charles Warren, *The Supreme Court in United States History,* (Boston, 1926) vol. II, p. 332 ff.; Nevins op. cit., p. 29, n. 36.

41. For example, the great Massachusetts Senator Charles Sumner said, "By the Supreme Law which commands me to do no injustice; by the comprehensive Christian law of brotherhood; by the Constitution which I have sworn to support, I AM BOUND TO DISOBEY THIS ACT." "Freedom National, Slavery Sectional," *Works of Charles Sumner* (1886 ed.), vol. III, p. 194.

42. "The Higher Law," *Speeches of William Seward in the United States Senate* (1902 ed.), p. 66.

43. Larry Gara, *The Liberty Line* (Lexington, 1967), p. 82.

44. Nye, op. cit., p. 276.

45. Nevins, op cit., vol. II, p. 25.

46. Ibid., p. 78 ff.

47. Ibid., p. 99.

48. Nevins, op. cit. vol. I, p. 381.

49. In Staughton Lynd, ed., *Nonviolence in America, A Documentary History* (Indianapolis, 1966), p. 67.

CHAPTER 4

1. Walter Nelles, "The First American Labor Case," 4 *Yale Law Journal* 165, 167 (1931).

2. W. Hawkins, *A Treatise of the Pleas of the Crown.* 1st ed.

(London, 1716), bk. 1, c. 72, quoted in Richard Morris, "Criminal Conspiracy and Early Labor Combinations in New York," 52 *Political Science Quarterly* 51, 55 (1937).

3. Nelles, op. cit., p. 190.

4. The New York authorities prosecuted another group of cordwainers for striking to pressure their master into firing a nonunion apprentice. Mayor Jacob Ratcliffe of New York, presiding in the case, distinguished between a combination to commit an unlawful act and a combination to commit a lawful act by unlawful means. Ratcliffe suggested that striking for higher wages might not be unlawful. However, since the journeymen refused to work with nonmembers and tried to coerce other workmen and their employers to submit to their rules and regulations, they were guilty of using improper means. Workers could not use means "of a nature too arbitrary and coercive, and which went to deprive their fellow citizens of rights as precious as any they contend for," Ratcliffe said. Because of the novelty of the legal question, the cordwainers were fined only one dollar. *People* v. *Melvin,* 2 *Wheeler Criminal Cases* 256, 279, 281 (New York, 1810). See also Joseph G. Rayback, *A History of American Labor* (New York, 1966), pp. 56, 57.

5. Rayback, op. cit., p. 86.

6. Ibid., p. 81.

7. Ibid., p. 82.

8. Walter Nelles, "Commonwealth v. Hunt," 32 *Columbia Law Review,* 1128, 1145 (1932).

9. Ibid., p. 1157.

10. Leonard M. Levy, *The Law of the Commonwealth and Chief Justice Shaw* (New York, 1967), p. 187.

11. "Early American Labor Cases," 35 *Yale Law Journal,* 829, 837 (1926).

12. Wayne Broehl, *The Molly Maguires* (Cambridge, 1966), p. 188.

13. Ibid., p. 210 ff.

14. Louis Adamic, *Dynamite* (New York, 1970), p. 20.

15. Sidney Lens, *Radicalism in America* (New York, 1969), p. 146.

16. Rayback, op. cit., p. 167; Adamic, op. cit., p. 68 ff.

17. Louis Adamic offered one possible reason for the change in orders. "Palpably, the Inspector had orders from someone more powerful in the Police Department than the Mayor; from some one no doubt, who wanted a riot." *Dynamite,* p. 72. The someone was possibly Capt. Michael J. Schaak, the chief anarchist-hunter in the police department who would conveniently find dynamite in every labor leader's home he searched.

18. Rayback, op. cit., p. 168.

19. Governor John P. Altgeld pardoned the three remaining prisoners. See Ray Ginger, *Altgeld's America* (Chicago, 1965).

20. See Leon Wolff, *Lockout* (New York, 1964).

21. See Almont Lindsey, *The Pullman Strike* (Chicago, 1964), p. 161 ff.

22. Altgeld telegraphed President Cleveland: "As Governor of . . . Illinois, I protest against this [dispatch of troops] and ask the immediate withdrawal of Federal troops." Adamic, op. cit., p. 120.

23. *In re Debs,* 158 U.S. 564 (1895).

24. Lindsey, op. cit., p. 295.

25. Ibid., p. 353–54.

26. *Springfield Spinning Co.* v. *Riley,* L. R., 6 Equity 551 (1868). See Felix Frankfurter and Nathan Greene, *The Labor Injunction* (New York, 1930), p. 20 ff.

27. Frankfurter and Greene, op. cit., p. 63 ff. In fifty-eight of those cases the order was based only on the bill of complaint, submitted without supporting affidavits and expressing only general conventional formulas about the danger of violence. Frankfurter and Greene wrote: "An un-supported one-sided complaint in general terms is an incantation, and not a rational solicitation for judgment." Ibid., p. 65. Nevertheless, manage-ment could generally secure an immediate court order against union activity merely by asking for it.

28. Ibid., p. 80.

29. *Atchison, Topeka & Santa Fe Ry. Co.* v. *Gee,* 139 Fed. 582, 584 (S.D. Ia. 1905).

30. *Loewe* v. *Lawlor,* 208 U.S. 274 (1908).

31. *Duplex Printing Press Co.* v. *Deering,* 254 U.S. 443 (1921).

32. See, for example, *Adair* v. *United States,* 208 U.S. 161 (1908); *Coppage* v. *Kansas,* 236 U.S. 1 (1915); *Adkins* v. *Children's Hospital,* 261 U.S. 525 (1921); *Hammer* v. *Dagengart,* 247 U.S. 251 (1918); *Truax* v. *Corrigan,* 257 U.S. 312 (1922); *Bedford Cut Stone Co.* v. *Journeymen Stone Cutters Association,* 274 U.S. 37 (1927).

33. *Truax* v. *Corrigan,* 257 U.S. at 357.

34. Frankfurter and Greene, op. cit., p. 131.

35. *Great Northern Ry. Co.* v. *Local G.F.L. of I.A. of M.,* 283 Fed. 557, 562 (D. Mont. 1922).

36. Philip Taft and Philip Ross, "American Labor Violence: Its Causes, Character and Outcome," from *Violence in America,* issued by the National Commission on the Causes and Prevention of Violence (New York, 1969).

37. Ibid., p. 362.

38. Adamic, op. cit., p. 465.

39. Bruce Peck, "Radical Disobedience and Its Justification," in Hugo Adam Bedau, ed., *Civil Disobedience: Theory and Practice* (New York, 1968).

40. Taft and Ross, op. cit., p. 360.


CHAPTER 5


1. For the best account of the down-rent movement, see Henry Christmas, *Tin Horns and Calico* (New York, 1945).

2. Ibid., p. 93 ff.

3. Ibid., pp. 170–71.

4. Ibid., pp. 214–15.

5. Ibid., p. 242.

6. Allan G. Bogue, *From Prairie to Cornbelt* (Chicago, 1963), pp. 31–39.

7. David S. Terry was a former Chief Justice of the California Supreme Court and a leader of the bar in the 1870's and 1880's. His renown in history, however, is due to the manner of his death. He had married one Sarah Hill who had been pressing a claim against the estate of her alleged husband Senator William Sharon. Justice Stephen J. Field of the United States Supreme Court eventually decided against the Terrys, who swore revenge against him. When they accidentally met in a railroad station at Lathrop, California in August 1889, Terry attacked Field and was shot to death by a federal marshal, David Neagle, who was protecting Field. One year earlier, Mrs. Terry had physically attacked Circuit Judge Lorenzo Sawyer (the federal judge who decided the *Mussel Slough* case) also for ruling against her in the same case.

8. Frank Norris's powerful novel *The Octopus* (1901) was based on the Mussel Slough incident. See Oscar Cargill's "Afterword" in the Signet edition (1964).

9. James O. Nall, *The Tobacco Night Riders of Kentucky and Tennessee* (Louisville, 1939), p. 52 ff.

10. James O. Nall in his excellent history of the affair states:

> There is no reason to believe that the tobacco situation, in general, would have been any better in 1907–08 than it had been in 1903–04 if it had not been for the Planters' Protective Association. Likewise, there is no reason to believe that the association would have been able to control the majority of growers if it had not been for the Night Riders. They had forced the majority of Hill Billies into the association and so blasted the only foundation on which the trust could oppose the association satisfactorily. If the Hill Billies had not been so held in line they would have wrecked the association and, thus, all betterment of prices. Association growers would have left the association in order to get the better prices paid the Hill Billies and there is every reason to believe that the association would have been a failure and that tobacco prices would again have gone as low as in 1903, or lower. The Night Riders saved the day (even though they worked at night), and, if it had not been for them, general business conditions in the Black Patch would have been in chaos.

Ibid., p. 124.

11. Ibid., p. 125.

12. Although the Republican candidate for governor in Kentucky, Augustus E. Willson, was elected in 1907 on a law-and-order platform, promising to deal harshly with the rebelling farmers, the state legislature

went in the other direction and passed laws favoring the Association. Troops were occasionally dispatched by the governor, especially after the dynamite raids each December, but the authorities did not attempt to suppress the movement or punish the night riders except in extraordinary cases. One of the few indictments that was returned involved Dr. Amoss, who was tried in March 1911 for conspiring to destroy the property of others in the Hopkinsville raid of 1907. A group of night rider traitors testified that he was the commanding general of the organization and had led the raid that destroyed two tobacco factories. Amoss denied any role in the affair, claimed he was home eating dinner that night, and produced a number of alibi witnesses. The trial judge gave a favorable charge for the doctor, and the jury deliberated only a few minutes before finding him not guilty.

13. John L. Shover, *Cornbelt Rebellion: The Farmers' Holiday Association* (Urbana, 1965), p. 41.

14. Ibid., p. 142. See also Arthur M. Schlesinger, Jr., *The Coming of the New Deal* (Boston ,1959), pp. 42–43.

## CHAPTER 6

1. The Supreme Court has permitted declaratory actions or affirmative suits to test criminal laws only in certain special situations. See *Dombrowski* v. *Pfister,* 380 U.S. 479 (1965).

2. Charles L. Black, Jr., "The Problem of the Compatibility of Civil Disobedience with American Institutions of Government," 43 *Texas Law Review* 492, 499 (1965).

3. In the nineteenth century, the Supreme Court already upheld challenges to repressive laws passed against two diverse minority groups, Confederate sympathizers and Chinese immigrants. In an attempt to punish Confederate supporters who returned to their homes in the North after the war, many states passed laws requiring lawyers, teachers, ministers, and others to take an oath that they had not supported, aided, or favored the Confederacy. A Catholic priest in Missouri, Father Cummings, refused to take the oath while continuing to practice his profession. He appealed his subsequent conviction to the Supreme Court, which held that the test oath statutes were unconstitutional as ex post facto laws; that is, they punished past conduct which was not illegal at the time the actions were committed. Furthermore, the test oaths were bills of attainder—punishment decreed by a legislature rather than a court. The Constitution, declared the Court, "intended that the rights of the citizen should be secure against deprivation for past conduct by legislative enactment, under any form, however disguised." *Cummings* v. *Missouri*, 4 Wall. 227, 324 (1867).

In 1886 the Supreme Court made another significant decision precipitated by a deliberate violation of law. San Francisco had passed an ordinance requiring a license for the operation of a laundry in a wooden building. The law was designed to control the large number of Chinese laundries in the city, since these were almost always housed in wooden structures. All the white laundries were awarded the appropriate licenses, but 200 of the 240 Chinese applicants were denied permits. Yick Wo, a Chinese laundryman, kept his shop operating without a license and was convicted for disobeying the law. The Supreme Court finally reversed his conviction, however. Justice Stanley Matthews wrote for the Court: "Though the law itself be fair on its face and impartial in appearance, yet if it is applied and administered by public authority with an evil eye and an unequal hand, so as practically to make unjust and illegal discriminations between persons in similar circumstances, material to their rights, the denial of equal justice is still within the prohibition of the Constitution." This unequal and oppressive application of the ordinance "amount[s] to a practical denial by the State of that equal protection of the laws which is secured . . . by the broad and benign provisions of the Fourteenth Amendment." *Yick Wo* v. *Hopkins,* 118 U.S. 356, 373 (1886). This case was the starting point for the broad reading of the equal protection clause, a vital defense against the abuse of personal liberty within the legal system.

4. *Free Speech in the United States* (Cambridge, 1941), p. 399.

5. *Lovell* v. *Griffin,* 303 U.S. 444, 451, 452 (1938).

6. *Cantwell* v. *Connecticut,* 310 U.S. 296, 310 (1940).

7. *Minersville School District* v. *Gobitis,* 310 U.S. 586, 595 (1940).

8. *Harlan Fiske Stone: Pillar of the Law* (New York, 1956), p. 533.

9. *West Virginia State Board of Education* v. *Barnette,* 319 U.S. 624, 638, 640, 641, 642 (1943).

10. *Martin* v. *Struthers,* 319 U.S. 141 (1943).

11. *Murdock* v. *Pennsylvania,* 319 U.S. 105 (1943).

12. *Marsh* v. *Alabama,* 326 U.S. 510 (1946).

13. *Niemotko* v. *Maryland,* 340 U.S. 268 (1951); *Fowler* v. *Rhode Island,* 345 U.S. 67 (1953).

14. *Cox* v. *New Hampshire,* 312 U.S. 569 (1941).

15. *Chaplinsky* v. *New Hampshire,* 315 U.S. 568 (1942).

16. *Prince* v. *Massachusetts,* 321 U.S. 158 (1944).

17. Milton Konvitz has described the actions of the Witnesses as follows: "Two decades before the civil rights movement got under way, Jehovah's Witnesses went on our city streets and into our public parks to preach and to distribute their literature. They tested the laws passed or interpreted to thwart their efforts by peacefully yet intentionally doing the acts they were prohibited from doing. . . . Like the Negroes who followed them on the streets and in other public places, they went to the courts for the vindication of their constitutional liberties." *Expanding Liberties,* (New York, 1966), p. 15. In other free speech cases involving the same principles as in JW cases, the Court invalidated restrictions on the use of sound trucks without the permission of the chief of police,

*Saia* v. *New York,* 334 U.S. 558 (1948). Such a law, the Court said, amounted to censorship in its baldest form. The Court also voided other laws which required a permit from the police before outdoor religious meetings could be held, *Kunz* v. *New York,* 340 U.S. 290 (1951). In all of these instances, just as in the Jehovah's Witnesses cases, the restraints were challenged by deliberate and conscientious lawbreakers who refused to follow a duly enacted statute by the state or city involved. Yet each of them was eventually vindicated by the Supreme Court.

18. *De Jonge* v. *Oregon,* 229 U.S. 353, 365 (1937).

19. *Herndon* v. *Lowry,* 301 U.S. 242, 258, 259( 1937).

20. Katherine Susan Anthony, *Susan B. Anthony* (New York, 1954), p. 284.

21. *United States* v. *Susan B. Anthony,* 24 Fed. Cases 829 (C.C.W.D. N.Y. 1873).

22. Katherine Susan Anthony, op. cit., p. 296–97.

23. Ibid., p. 299.

24. *Thomas* v. *Collins,* 323 U.S. 516, 539 (1945). Labor unions were also protected by the Court under circumstances similar to the Jehovah's Witnesses cases. The state of Alabama passed a law in the 1930's forbidding picketing in conjunction with a labor dispute. Six members of an A.F. of L. local refused to obey the law and continued to picket a wood preserving company in Tuscaloosa. They were arrested, tried, and found guilty. The Supreme Court, through Justice Frank Murphy, reversed. "The freedom of speech and of the press guaranteed by the Constitution," the Court said, "embraces at the least the liberty to discuss publicly and truthfully all matters of public concern without previous restraint or fear of subsequent punishment. . . . In the circumstances of our times the dissemination of information concerning the facts of a labor dispute must be regarded as within that area of free discussion that is guaranteed by the Constitution." *Thornhill* v. *Alabama,* 310 U.S. 88, 101–102 (1940). In a later case, the Supreme Court struck down other laws which required a permit before a union organizer might solicit membership. *Staub* v. *City of Baxley,* 355 U.S. 313 (1958).

25. *Boynton* v. *Virginia,* 364 U.S. 454 (1960).

26. *Edwards* v. *South Carolina,* 372 U.S. 229 (1963).

27. *Peterson* v. *City of Greenville,* 373 U.S. 244 (1963).

28. *Lombard* v. *Lousiana,* 373 U.S. 267 (1963). During the same period, young Negro boys tried to use various segregated parks in the South. When a small group invaded a public park in Savannah, Georgia, to play basketball, the police asked them to leave and then arrested them for refusing to do so. The Supreme Court reversed the convictions on the grounds that "one cannot be punished for failure to obey the command of an officer if that command is itself violative of the Constitution." *Wright* v. *Georgia,* 373 U.S. 284, 291–292 (1963).

29. King wrote to eight fellow clergymen from Alabama who had complained of his advocating disobedience of law:

You express a great deal of anxiety over our willingness to break laws. This is certainly a legitimate concern. Since we so diligently urge people to obey the Supreme Court's decision of 1954 outlawing segregation in the public schools, at first glance it may seem rather paradoxical for us consciously to break laws. One may well ask: "How can you advocate breaking some laws and obeying others?" The answer lies in the fact that there are two types of laws: just and unjust. I would be the first to advocate obeying just laws. One has not only a legal but a moral responsibility to obey just laws. Conversely, one has a moral responsibility to disobey unjust laws. I would agree with St. Augustine that "an unjust law is no law at all."

Now, what is the difference between the two? How does one determine whether a law is just or unjust? A just law is a man-made code that squares with the moral law or the law of God. An unjust law is a code that is out of harmony with the moral law. To put it in the terms of St. Thomas Aquinas: An unjust law is a human law that is not rooted in eternal law and natural law. Any law that uplifts human personality is just. Any law that degrades human personality is unjust. All segregation statutes are unjust because segregation distorts the soul and damages the personality. It gives the segregator a false sense of superiority and the segregated a false sense of inferiority. Segregation, to use the terminology of the Jewish philosopher Martin Buber, substitutes an "I-it" relationship for an "I-thou" relationship and ends up relegating persons to the status of things. Hence segregation is not only politically, economically and sociologically unsound, it is morally wrong and sinful. Paul Tillich has said that sin is separation. Is not segregation an existential expression of man's tragic separation, his awful estrangement, his terrible sinfulness? Thus it is that I can urge men to obey the 1954 decision of the Supreme Court, for it is morally right; and I can urge them to disobey segregation ordinances, for they are morally wrong.
*Why We Can't Wait* (New York, 1964), pp. 82–83.

30. *Shuttlesworth* v. *Birmingham,* 394 U.S. 147 (1969).

31. *Walker* v. *City of Birmingham,* 388 U.S. 307, 321 (1967).


CHAPTER 7

1. Michael Walzer, "The Obligation to Disobey," 7 *Ethics* 163, 173 (April 1967).

2. Ibid., pp. 170–171.

3. Nicholas W. Puner, "Civil Disobedience," *43 N.Y.U. Law Review* 651, 710 (1968).

4. *Annual Report of the Director of the Administrative Office of the United States Courts, 1969,* pp. II–37.

5. See Appendix A for complete statistics on draft opposition.

6. *Haywood* v. *United States,* 393 F.2d. 780, 781, 1 SSLR 3070 (5th Cir. 1968).

## CHAPTER 8

1. *Provost Marshal General Report,* (James Barnet Fry) 39th Cong. 1st Sess. (1967), House Exec. Doc. No. 1., vol. 2, p. 194.

2. Ibid., p. 193.

3. See Leon Friedman, "Conscription and the Constitution," 67 *Michigan Law Review* 1493, 1545 (1969).

4. Fred Shannon, *The Organization and Administration of the Union Army, 1861–1865* (Cleveland, 1928), vol II, p. 192.

5. *Second Report of the Provost Marshal General to the Secretary of War on the operation of the Selective Service System to December 20, 1918* (March 1919), p. 376.

6. *Enforcement of the Selective Service Law,* Special Monograph No. 14, Selective Service System (1951), p. 15.

7. *Final Report of the Provost Marshal General on the Operations of the Selective Service System to July 15, 1919,* p. 52.

8. Ibid., p. 12.

9. *Conscientious Objection,* Special Monograph No. 11, Selective Service System (1946), p. 17.

10. "The Conscientious Objector," *Columbia University Quarterly* (October 1919), p. 732.

11. See generally, John Womack Jr., "Oklahoma's Green Corn Rebellion" (Honors diss., Harvard University, 1959).

12. *Second Provost Marshal General Report,* loc. cit., p. 212.

13. H. C. Peterson and Gilbert C. Fite, *Opponents of War, 1917–1918* (Seattle, 1957), p. 22.

14. Melvyn Dubofsky, *We Shall Be All* (Chicago, 1969), p. 356.

15. Peterson and Fite, op. cit., p. 29.

16. Ibid., pp. 8–9.

17. Ibid., p. 26.

18. *Schenck* v. *United States,* 249 U.S. 47, 51 (1919).

19. *Debs* v. *United States,* 249 U.S. 211, 215 (1919).

20. Mark DeWolfe Howe, ed, *Holmes–Laski Letters* (Cambridge, 1953), p. 203.

21. Peterson and Fite, op. cit., p. 36 ff.

22. *Enforcement of Selective Service,* op. cit., p. 89.

23. Ibid., p. 93 ff.

24. Lawrence S. Wittner, *Rebels Against War* (New York, 1969), p. 73.

25. Ibid., p. 77.

26. *Enforcement of Selective Service,* op. cit., p. 95 ff.

27. *Selective Service and Victory,* Fourth Report of the Director of Selective Service (1947), p. 223.

CHAPTER 9

1. "Of Holy Disobedience" in Lillian Schlissel, ed., *Conscience in America* (New York, 1968), p. 251.

2. David Mitchell, "What is Criminal," in Alice Lynd, ed., *We Won't Go* (Boston, 1968), pp. 94–96.

3. "The Movement: A New Beginning," *Liberation* (May 1969).

4. *New York Times,* 30 July 1965, p. 2.

5. *House Armed Services Comm., Full Committee Consideration of H.R. 10306,* 89th Cong. 1st Sess., No. 23, at 3130 (1965); Dean Alfange, Jr., "Free Speech and Symbolic Conduct: The Draft Card Burning Case," in *1968 Supreme Court Review* (Chicago, 1968), pp. 5–6.

6. In Alice Lynd, ed., op. cit., p. 203.

7. *New York Times,* 22 December 1965, p. 3.

8. When Hershey testified before the House Armed Services Committee on the 1967 extension on the draft, Chairman Mendel Rivers introduced him by noting, "This morning we have our old and distinguished friend—'old' friend in terms of appreciation, regard, confidence, and affection . . ." Congressman Durward Hall of Missouri used his five minutes of questioning time to praise Hershey in the most outrageous rhetoric: "I was a little concerned that this might be one of his last trips before this committee—God forbid—for I have never known anybody that contributed more to our deliberations, and can do it with the logic of an artillery commander and Pericles, and with the voice of Demosthenes." The ranking Republican on the House Committee, William Bates of Massachusetts, apologized for not prefacing his remarks with the usual encomiums: "I am sure the general will forgive me if I dispense with accolades, with only five minutes. I was complimentary to him yesterday." *Extension of the Universal Military Training and Service Act, Hearings before the House Committee on Armed Services,* 90th Cong. 1st Sess. (May 1967), p. 2612 ff.

With such a secure relationship with Congress, Hershey did not hesitate to oppose administration proposals or policies he found objectionable. As noted below, in early 1967, a special Presidential Commission on the draft headed by Burke Marshall recommended sweeping changes in the law. In testimony before the House Armed Services Committee, Hershey objected to many of the Marshall proposals. He "completely disapprove[d]" of the elimination of state headquarters or of state quotas: "After all, we have States, they are a fact, and I think it is the strength of this country . . ." (Hershey may have been the only member of the federal government with the flags of all fifty states in his office.) He also disapproved of the *Seeger* decision: "I'm very disturbed, because I don't think it is practical to try to start letting people become conscientious objectors individually." A strong believer in universal military training, Hershey preferred retention of the pre-1967 system of taking the oldest first and skipping no one unless they were properly deferred or exempted. The rationale of the Marshall proposals was that a surplus of younger, draft-age men was becoming available, and it would be fairer to have draftees selected by chance, with those not picked being free to plan their careers unless a national emergency took place. Hershey's reluctant and lukewarm support of the administration's random selection system was due in part to his objection that some eligible, available men would slip through the system without serving. He said: ". . . if you have a theory that most everybody is going to go, then there is no question about what we are doing presently is the better, because it starts at the top and comes on down without sparing anybody, and you have pressure on everybody." However, since the calls were lower than the available manpower, he was willing to accept a random system: "That is one thing the Executive made a decision on, and I am a member of the Executive branch of the Government." Nevertheless he still took issue with the manner in which the Defense Department would arrange the random selection. Hershey would expose those receiving deferments to priority call once they became available while the Defense Department would simply place them into the grab-bag once again where they would have equal chance with others to avoid service.

9. Jessica Mitford, *The Trial of Dr. Spock* (New York, 1969), p. 22.

10. "Disruption and the Draft," *Liberation* (November 1967), p. 35.

11. Tom Bell, "Organizing Draft Resistance," in *We Won't Go,* p. 210, n. 2.

12. Staughton Lynd, loc. cit.

13. *WIN Magazine,* 28 April 1967, p. 7.

14. *In Pursuit of Equity: Who Serves When Not All Serve,* Report of the National Advisory Commission on Selective Service, p. 48–50.

15. The 1967 extension of the law narrowed the definition of conscientious objection and placed restrictions on any pre-induction review of a draft board order by a court. (See discussion at p. 170). In addition, the 1967 extension of the law included a new provision requiring the Justice Department to "proceed as expeditiously as possible with a prosecution under this section . . . upon the request of the Director of the Selective Service System or [to] advise the House of Representatives and the Senate in writing the reasons for its failure to do so." (Section 12(c).)

The background of this last provision was as follows. For some time Hershey had complained that local U.S. Attorneys refused to prosecute all draft violators. In 1967, he submitted to the House Armed Services Committee a series of letters relating to specific cases in which he said an unjustified refusal to seek indictments occurred. In one instance, a young man with conscientious objector status (1-O) was reclassified 1-A and ordered for induction when his draft board learned he was working for an electronics company making tape recorders for the Army. He refused to report and the Selective Service System requested prosecution. The U.S. Attorney wrote there was no "basis in fact" for the reclassification and did nothing. In another instance, a Jehovah's Witness had been convicted and sentenced to six months for failing to report for civilian work in lieu of induction. After release, his draft board again classified him 1-O and once more ordered him to report for civilian work. When he did not do so, the Justice Department was asked to prosecute a second time. This time the local attorney declined, saying the registrant was "a sincere and dedicated Jehovah's Witness, and a second prosecution would have no beneficial enforcement effect. To the contrary, it might well arouse the ire of the Court and thus in the long run harm the Government's enforcement policy."

In still other cases, Hershey's office asked for prosecution of young resident aliens who had not registered as required by the law. The Justice Department claimed there was no proof of willful failure to register, only inadvertence. When the Justice Department told Hershey that there was no point in bringing these cases since the courts would dismiss them anyhow, he answered that prosecution would have a helpful deterrent effect on other registrants. But Attorney General Ramsey Clark took the position that normal prosecutorial discretion would be applied in draft cases as in any other area. The government has a duty to the courts not to bring unnecessary, losing actions that clog the calendars and to the public not to harass them with actions that have no basis in the law. Predictably, Congress sided with Hershey in this dispute. The House Committee upbraided Fred Vinson, Jr., the head of the Criminal Division, when he told them Stokely Carmichael could not be prosecuted because of the First Amendment for saying "We ain't goin' in, hell no." Rep. Alton Lennon of North Carolina said: ". . . are you suggesting to me and the committee and to the American public that a man ought to be permitted to stand up and almost incite a riot and say to the student group 'Hell no, we ain't going in'?" He insisted that in such cases "prosecute it, and let the Court consider it and pass on it."

Since Section 12(c) has been in effect, there has been only one instance of a formal request to prosecute, followed by a flat refusal and a formal letter to Congress. A thirty-year-old philosophy teacher from George Mason College in northern Virginia, James M. Shea, turned in his draft card in the summer of 1967. He held a 3-A classification since he was married and the father of three small daughters. The draft board declared him a delinquent since he was not in possession of his card, classified him I-A, and ordered him to report for induction. He refused, but no indictment was brought against him. In its letter to Congress, the Justice Department wrote that prosecution was held in abeyance until the Supreme Court rendered a decision on *Oestereich* v. *SSS Local Board No. 11* (discussed on p. 171). The Supreme Court's decision in that case made it clear that no action could be taken against Shea.

CHAPTER 10

1. *The Resistance Newsletter* (October 1967), p. 3.
2. *New Left Notes,* 2 October 1967, p. 3.
3. See Staughton Lynd, op. cit., chap. 9.
4. Dennis Sweeney, "The Long March," *Resist* (April, 1968), p. 2.
5. *United States* v. *Harris* (N.D. Calif.) Transcript of Proceedings, p. 108, 122.
6. See Alice Lynd, ed., op. cit., p. 238 ff.
7. Paul Goodman, "We Won't Go," in *Like a Conquered Province* (New York, 1965), p. 399.
8. Staughton Lynd, op. cit.
9. See Denise Levertov, "The Intellectuals and the War Machine," *The North American Review* (January 1968), p. 14.
10. Norman Mailer, *Armies of the Night* (New York, 1968), p. 89.
11. Ibid., p. 88.
12. Ibid., p. 90.
13. The account is drawn from Jessica Mitford's *The Trial of Dr. Spock* (New York, 1969), from testimony at the Spock trial, and from personal interviews with some of the participants.
14. *Wolff* v. *Selective Board No. 15,* 372 F. 2d. 817, 822 (2d. Cir. 1967).
15. *New York Times,* 8 November 1967, p. 23.
16. *New York Times,* 10 December 1967, p. 1.
17. Jessica Mitford, op. cit., p. 56.
18. See Appendix A for statistics on draft resistance.


CHAPTER 11

1. *Report of the Director of the Administrative Office of the United States Courts* (July 1–September 30, 1968), p. 8.
2. *WIN* Magazine, 15 February 1968, p. 14.
3. During the Spock trial, Robert Talmanson (a resister) and William Chase (an army deserter) tried to establish sanctuary in the Arlington Street Church in Boston but were dragged out by the police. Ron Moyer and Anthony Ramos of Providence, R.I., sought refuge in the Church of the Mediator in the latter city at the invitation of the pastor, Rev. Albert Q. Perry. Don Baty was carted off by federal marshals after staying in Manhattan's Washington Square Methodist Church following his failure to appear in court. Federal agents seized David Hawk, later a Vietnam moratorium leader, in the chapel of the Union Theological Seminary.

4. One resister attacked the idea that white middle-class students must "insist on sharing the fate of those who are less privileged." He claimed that resisters must "remain free to work . . . [and] every man who successfully avoids estalishment-made alternatives *takes another man with him* by example . . . Middle-class men are not going to turn against the war because their classmates go to prison, but because they do not, thereby placing an undesirable burden on those who lose their deferments or do not go into exile or underground." *New York Review of Books,* 1 February 1968, p. 28.

5. *New Left Notes,* 1 September 1967, p. 4.

## CHAPTER 12

1. Jessica Mitford, op. cit., p. 247.

2. *New York Times,* 14 July 1968, section IV, p. 8.

3. Noam Chomsky, Paul Lauter, and Florence Howe, "Reflections on a Political Trial," in *Trials of the Resistance* (New York, 1970), p. 82.

4. Ibid.

5. *United States* v. *Spock,* 416 F. 2d. 165, 182, 2 SSLR 3090 (1st Cir. 1969).

6. *Oestereich* v. *Selective Service Board,* 393 U.S. 233, 237 (1969).

7. *Gutknecht* v. *United States,* 396 U.S. 295, 306–07 (1970).

8. *Breen* v. *Selective Service Local Board No. 16,* 396 U.S. 460 (1970).

9. Staughton Lynd, op. cit.

10. Jessica Mitford, op. cit., p. 67.

11. *The Presidents' Commission on an All-Volunteer Armed Force* (February, 1970), pp. 10, 32–33, 121.

12. Besides a wealth of historical material (prepared by Staughton Lynd), the lawyers cited two cases in support of this proposition: *Shuttlesworth* v. *Birmingham,* 394 U.S. 147 (1969) (discussed above at p. 97) and *Williams* v. *Wallace,* 240 F. Supp. 100 (M.D. Ala., 1965). In the second case, Negro demonstrators under Martin Luther King were allowed to march on a public highway from Selma to Montgomery to dramatize their fight for voting rights.

13. "Civil Disobedience," 21 *Rutgers Law Review,* 17, 23, 24 (1966).

14. *United States v. Sisson,* 297 F. Supp. 902, 905 (D. Mass. 1969). See also *United States* v. *Bowen,* 2 SSLR 3421 (N.D. Calif. December 24, 1969). The district judge held there that a Catholic draft resister opposed to the Vietnam War but not all wars was entitled to conscientious objector status.

15. "Guideline for the Free Exercise Clause," 83 *Harvard Law Review* 327, 347 (1969).

16. Ibid., 337.

17. "Individual Conscience and the Selective Conscientious Objector: The Right Not to Kill," 44 *N.Y.U. Law Review* 875, 888, 893 (1969).

18. *United States* v. *Moylan,* 2 SSLR 3363 (4th Cir. October 15, 1969).

19. Joseph L. Sax, "Civil Disobedience," *Saturday Review,* 28 September 1968, p. 56.

20. Lawrence R. Velvel, "Protecting Civil Disobedience under the First Amendment," 37 *George Washington Law Review* 464, 485 (1969).

21. H. L. Nieburg, *Political Violence* (New York, 1969), p. 54.


## APPENDIX FOOTNOTES

1. *The Selective Service System: Its Operations, Practices and Procedures,* Hearings before Subcommittee on Administrative Practice and Procedure of the Committee on the Judiciary, United States Senate (October–November 1969), pp. 372–73.

2. *Oestereich* v. *Selective Service Board,* 393 U.S. 233 (1968); *Mc Kart* v. *United States,* 395 U.S. 185 (1969); *Gutknecht* v. *United States,* 396 U.S. 295 (1970); *Breen* v. *Selective Service Board,* 396 U.S. 460 (1970); *Toussie* v. *United States,* 397 U.S. 875 (1970); *Welsh* v. *United States,* 398 U.S. 33 (1970); *Mulloy* v. *United States,* 398 U.S. 410 (1970); *United States* v. *Sisson,* 399 U.S.—(1970); *O'Brien* v. *United States,* 391 U.S. 367 (1968).

3. 5 *Columbia Journal of Law and Social Problems* 190.

4. *United States* v. *Feliciano-Grafals,* 2 SSLR 3475 (D.P.R. Jan. 23, 1970).

5. *Federal Prisoners Confined;* periodic reports of Federal Bureau of Prisons.

# Index